THE FIGHT FOR LOCAL CONTROL

American Institutions and Society

A volume in the series
edited by Brian Balogh and Jonathan Zimmerman

THE FIGHT FOR LOCAL CONTROL

Schools, Suburbs,
and American Democracy

Campbell F. Scribner

CORNELL UNIVERSITY PRESS **ITHACA AND LONDON**

First published 2016 by Cornell University Press

Printed in the United States of America

Library of Congress Cataloging-in-Publication Data

Names: Scribner, Campbell F., 1981– author.
Title: The fight for local control : schools, suburbs, and American democracy / Campbell F. Scribner.
Description: Ithaca : Cornell University Press, 2016. | Series: American institutions and society | Includes bibliographical references and index.
Identifiers: LCCN 2015038569 | ISBN 9781501700804 (cloth : alk. paper)
Subjects: LCSH: Education and state—United States—History—20th century. | Education—Political aspects—United States—History—20th century. | Democracy and education—United States—History—20th century. | Educational change—Political aspects—United States—History— 20th century. | Suburban schools—United States—History—20th century.
Classification: LCC LC89 .S38 2016 | DDC 379.73—dc23
LC record available at http://lccn.loc.gov/2015038569

Cloth printing   10 9 8 7 6 5 4 3 2 1

for Stephanie

Contents

Acknowledgments

My life went through some dramatic changes while working on this book. In quick succession I lost a parent, had a child, got a job, and moved several times. Research and writing amid these strains required the support of many people, all of whom deserve acknowledgment and thanks.

Most importantly, I would like to thank my wife, Stephanie, whose encouragement makes everything possible and to whom this book is dedicated. She has listened patiently to scattered thoughts and frustrations, and has given me lots of time to write and travel. I would also like to thank my mother, Carroll Scribner, for her interest in my work and a lifetime of loving support, and my parents-in-law, Gil and Mary Frank, for supporting our family and providing insight into school politics in Wisconsin.

Next, special recognition is due to friends and colleagues who helped refine the content of the book. Bill Reese was a thoughtful reader of early drafts and a helpful model in his own research and writing, which pushed the narrative further back than its original origins in the 1960s. Adam Nelson likewise offered exacting and insightful commentary; some of his offhand remarks about the border between suburban and rural school districts would eventually lead me to the book's central argument. Jennifer Ratner-Rosenhagen pushed me to think more seriously about the connections between different segments of the conservative movement. Bill Cronon encouraged me to write for as broad an audience as possible and to underscore the interplay between ideas and physical space in history, which I have here tried to apply to issues of educational policy. Diana Hess provided insights into educational law and academic freedom. Robbie Gross, Frank Honts, and Britt Tevis each helped with book recommendations, critical reading, and other aspects of the writing process. Their friendship has helped me persevere through personal difficulties and grow as a scholar and human being.

The production of this book is obviously a testament to the skill and professionalism of the staff at Cornell University Press, where everyone has been wonderful to work with. I would particularly like to thank the editors of the American Institutions and Society series, Brian Balogh, Michael McGandy, and Jonathan Zimmerman, who have been enthusiastic supporters of this project from the moment I sent them the proposal. They secured excellent readers for the manuscript, moved promptly through each stage of revision, and at all times have been thoughtful and reassuring about the book's scholarly contributions. I have received an unprecedented, invaluable level of criticism and encouragement in my communications with Cornell, and greatly appreciate the time of everyone involved.

In a similar vein, my work—like all historians' work—relies almost entirely on the unseen efforts of archivists and librarians. I am greatly indebted to the staff at the Wisconsin Historical Society, particularly Simone Munson, who answered many questions and paged many boxes for me, as well as the staff at the Iowa State University Archives, Illinois University Archives, and University of Vermont Archives. Jimmy Bryant, at the University of Central Arkansas Archives, was kind enough to photocopy and mail an entire file of records, and Vakil Smallen, the coordinator of the National Education Association records at George Washington University, helped coordinate my research there. Dan Golodner, the archivist of the American Federation of Teachers collection at Wayne State University, was an eager and involved guide to that collection, and afterward helped clarify several points about American labor law.

I would also like to recognize those who spoke to me about their own experiences in rural schools. In Twin Lakes, Wisconsin, Joyce Beula, Bernice Richter, and William Smeeth remain proud of their 1960s activism and all agreed to interviews. Mrs. Beula still has copies of the *McGuffey's Readers* that her husband introduced in the local elementary school. Jim Hoecker, who spoke out against censorship as a high school student in Eagle River, Wisconsin, would go on to chair the Federal Energy Regulatory Commission during the Clinton administration, and was probably surprised to receive a call about a letter he wrote as a teenager. Finally, Charles Stannard shared helpful information about a sociological study of school districts in New Hampshire that he completed in the 1970s.

Two conference panels with Jack Dougherty and Andy Anderson made me reconsider the use of maps in this project. Assembling those maps required the assistance of the staff at the Robinson Map Library at the University of Wisconsin, as well as my colleague, John Krygier, and Christian Gehrke, his student, from the Geography Department at Ohio Wesleyan University.

THE FIGHT FOR
LOCAL CONTROL

Government is not in this country, and cannot be, the educator of the people. In education . . . we must rely mainly on the voluntary system. If this be an evil, it is an evil inseparable from our form of government.

—Orestes Brownson, 1839

A PAST FOUND

In the early 1950s, the people of French Island, a small farming community on the Mississippi River, packed into their local elementary school for a contentious meeting about integration. The building was in shambles, with no indoor plumbing, and rats and stray dogs roaming through the hallways. It was even older and less well kempt than the island's other school, an isolated, one-room structure three miles to the north. The principal and a small group of liberal-minded newcomers argued that combining the two schools would ensure better opportunities for all the island's children, but community leaders rejected their recommendations. Fistfights had broken out at previous meetings, and now county sheriffs brandished shotguns at the schoolhouse door. A week later, the leader of the anti-integration faction would be convicted of assaulting a state official. In an increasingly common chain of events, calls for independence and local control of public education slipped into acts of hatred and violence. Yet, perhaps surprisingly, this scene did not play out in the bloody bayous of the Mississippi delta but near the river's headwaters, a thousand miles north, in western Wisconsin. Nor did the integration in question involve mixing students of different races. Rather, the word referred to the consolidation of French Island's two school districts and their state-ordered annexation to the city of La Crosse.[1]

Until 1950, French Island had served as the city dump. Many of its fifteen hundred residents lived in squalor, supporting themselves with odd jobs, fishing, or petty crime. Henry Jolivette, the town chairman and the island's largest landowner, presided over a painfully provincial political arrangement. Most of his official duties were conducted in consultation with other "old timers" at the local tavern, and political opponents claimed they had never met the man when he was sober. Open elections had not been held for years, and membership on the state highway committee ensured that the island's only paved road went from the access bridge straight to Jolivette's driveway.[2]

French Island's two elementary schools presented a difficult situation for Wisconsin's Department of Public Instruction (DPI), which for a decade had pushed to improve the quality and uniformity of public education through a program of district consolidation and new school construction. The larger of French Island's schools, known as Lower Island, had not been renovated since its erection in 1890. In addition to its vermin problem, the building lacked running water and central heating, and could not accommodate the dozens of children moving to the island from La Crosse. First graders had to meet in an adjacent cottage, while seventh and eighth graders were bused to an urban middle school, with the Lower Island school board paying out-of-district tuition. Secondary students attended city high schools on the same basis. Further complicating the problem, the district's rising enrollments corresponded with a sharply declining tax base. La Crosse had annexed most of the island's unincorporated land in the late 1940s to build a new power plant and airport, leaving the school board without enough tax revenue to pay teachers' salaries. Nevertheless, Jolivette and other farmers resisted calls for Lower Island's dissolution, as did residents of the tiny Upper Island school district. "We're sitting well up there and we'd like to be left alone," an Upper Island resident remarked, although he acknowledged that the state disapproved of his district's poverty and the fact that a single teacher supervised all eight grades. For their part, voters in La Crosse wanted to be left alone as well. They showed no interest in assuming the costs of busing French Island's students, renovating its schools, or retiring its bonded debt, and were content to leave the island to its own devices.[3]

Frustrated state officials contended that the persistence of outdated rural schools was unacceptable, and that any workable solution would require not only island- but area-wide reforms. Given French Island's implicit dependence on La Crosse, the county school commissioner demanded to know why its districts "should *not* be annexed to the city . . . for school purposes." A Lower Island resident pointed out that annexation would leave his community without a representative on the city school board. "Representation is fundamental to American government," he said, and "I don't believe that the generations to come will thank us for trading [it for financial security]." "The district needs outside help," the commissioner retorted. "It must relinquish something." He proposed merging the rural districts, subjecting them to city administration, and building a new elementary school near the center of the island, exactly where Henry Jolivette's farm was located. That proposal eventually succeeded with the votes of suburban commuters, who doubled the island's population between 1945 and 1950 and began to demand representation on the school board and town council, straining existing political arrangements. Even Jolivette's most vocal opponents acknowledged that, for all his corruption, he essentially wanted "to keep [his] farming enterprise, and he felt that if [French Island] was to be developed as a suburb his land would be taken over by residential development," which was precisely what happened.[4]

Yet as state officials subsumed French Island's schools into the La Crosse district and the area continued to grow, demands for home rule did not diminish. If anything, they grew more strident. Within a few years suburbanites had joined with older residents to reject the town's full annexation to the city. Several referendums on the subject failed, and homeowners filed lawsuits to stop the city's piecemeal annexation of town property. By the 1970s, French Island had spent hundreds of thousands of dollars fighting for its independence and vowed "to carry the banner statewide for suburban communities' right of survival." Suddenly, strangely, suburban residents had found a new target for their antagonism, vilifying urban planners rather than obstinate farmers, and they demonstrated a new commitment to local representation, that practice "so fundamental to American government." It is difficult to overstate the importance of that change, for what seemed like overdue reforms in an insignificant setting would in fact reshape the future of U.S. education.[5]

French Island's evolution from a rural backwater to a prosperous suburb reflected a more general shift in U.S. society in the decades after World War II. Across the country, the convergence of rural school consolidation and suburban growth generated conflicts over school board representation and building renovations. Yet these disagreements faded as rural and suburban residents discovered a common interest in the local control of schools. Faced with encroachment from growing cities and a growing regulatory state, outlying school districts offered conservatives what contemporaries on the Left might have called a "usable past": a language, symbolism, and authenticity—and most importantly a grounded legal basis—for renewed assertions of local government. As these districts became flash points in struggles against state oversight, they established precedents for the autonomy of all suburban communities. What began as opposition to district consolidation in the 1940s had by the 1970s transformed into broader campaigns against race-based busing, teacher unionization, equalized school funding, and objectionable curriculum, with suburbanites in each case invoking rural tradition to thwart the expansion of city, state, or federal bureaucracies. The result of their efforts was not a return to the "little red schoolhouse" of the past but a series of court rulings that reasserted local prerogative and halted the centralization of district administration and finance, sustaining elements of rural democracy while creating new safeguards for suburban privilege. This is the first of two historical arguments that *The Fight for Local Control* sets out to prove: that the significance of school district boundaries and local governance extended the legacy of the one-room schoolhouse far beyond rural communities and long past its historical moment, revitalizing American conservatism in the years after World War II and establishing a framework that constrains debates about public education to the present.

Complicating matters, however, is the fact that courts could not settle the issue of local control entirely. While conservatives achieved clear victories in matters of busing and equalized funding, judges were less willing to grant local autonomy in other domains. Particularly in cases involving personnel and curricular disputes, they tended to reaffirm the authority of local school boards in principle while in practice expanding civil rights protections for teachers and students. These rulings facilitated the growth of teachers' unions, which in turn transferred many aspects of educational administration from school boards to unelected officials. Influenced by professional interest groups and an increasingly active judiciary, by the 1980s the school governance debate had shifted from an argument over whether there should be *any* state or federal involvement in education to an implicit acceptance of those roles and a struggle to define them. Conservatives, determined to rein in taxes and secular textbooks as well as improve academic rigor, began to discard their defense of local school boards for a new, bifurcated rhetoric of individual choice and state discipline. Calls for vouchers, home schooling, and religious exemptions shifted authority from school boards to individual parents, while property tax limits and standardized testing regimes granted greater authority to the state. Thus, the book's second argument, contingent on the first, is that even as conservatives established protections for local control, they began to retreat from it, pursuing by other means the goals once secured by local governance.

The bipartisan struggle to capture or redirect state and federal policy represents a significant departure from most of the twentieth century, when local control underlay almost every educational debate and divided interest groups along starkly different conceptions of democratic participation. Liberals were never strong supporters of local school governance. They conceived of democracy in terms of national rather than local citizenship and usually hewed to the standard of equal educational opportunity across districts, measured in terms of racial balance, per pupil spending, modern facilities, and other "inputs." Liberals assumed that achieving these goals required larger districts and greater state and federal oversight. When they encountered resistance, they pursued their agenda through the courts, the branch of government least accountable to the electorate. Conservatives, meanwhile, tended to equate democracy with limited government. They celebrated the variation, freedom, and civic participation that local control allowed, and worried when decision makers, whether judges, administrators, or teachers, were unaccountable to local voters. Sometimes they framed this position in terms of individual rights and at other times in terms of majority rule, but conservatives' core educational principle was the protection of traditional values and community governance from outside interference.

Whichever of these perspectives one finds more compelling, the turn toward federal intervention in education marks a troubling change. One need not idealize the politics of the twentieth century in saying so—conservatives' defense of local school districts, in particular, could be profoundly cynical in its disregard for educational quality and its perpetuation of racial and socioeconomic segregation. But at least they understood that inequality was a sacrifice for small, participatory government. As conservative activists changed course, choosing to advance their agenda through court decisions and state and federal policy, they undermined almost every aspect of local school governance except the boundaries between districts, which remain insoluble. As a result, today's public school systems retain the worst aspects of local control even as they have lost its redeeming features. State and federal reforms have done little to remedy inequality between districts, as liberals once hoped, but they have sharply limited the ability of voters and school boards to shape their children's education, as conservatives once feared.

As with any major political shift, the new educational paradigm has met with some resistance. Indeed, its bipartisan support has mobilized an equally diverse group of critics. High-stakes testing has been a point of particular discontent, with liberals chafing at the standardized testing regime installed during the Bush administration, under No Child Left Behind, and conservatives grumbling about the Common Core standards supported by the Obama administration. Both sides have begun to invoke localism, albeit selectively, for political gain. Standardized tests are unlikely to vanish, of course, and a return to complete district autonomy seems quixotic; far too many corporate investments and political careers have been staked on state and federal reforms. Nevertheless, public discontent offers a chance to reevaluate our assumptions about school governance, and either side would be wise to take advantage of the opportunity.

The Fight for Local Control is a history of the United States' confounding relationship with its school districts, institutions that embody the nation's ideals of civic participation while at the same time reinforcing its most stubborn inequalities. Some readers may see the loss of community control as a blow to democratic governance, an attempt by state and federal bureaucrats to stifle local decision making. Others might conclude that local districts themselves were undemocratic because they thwarted equal educational opportunity, and that support for local control was little more than a pretense for exclusion. Between those positions lies a hard choice—and, we can only hope, a false one—between community and equality. The chapters that follow could support either position, but their even-handedness should not imply indecisiveness or apathy. The book simply advances a more fundamental claim: Namely, that voters have been denied opportunities to make either choice, to wrestle with the ultimate purposes of public education in this country. Whatever one thinks of its social outcomes, local school admin-istration was once the nation's most direct form of democracy, and it has been lost without being debated on its merits, subordinated to high-stakes politics and top-down intervention. Yet despite the efforts of judges, labor unions, think tanks, and corporate foundations to dictate school policy, among voters there remains a widespread commitment to localism, a diffuse yearning for civic par-ticipation and empowerment. They deserve an open discussion about the costs and benefits of community-based schooling—a choice and not an echo. The chap-ters that follow do not offer specific policy recommendations, but hopefully they can spark meaningful deliberation about the purpose of our schools, our duties to each other, and the meaning of community in the modern United States.

The Scope of the Book

There is an old adage that "all politics are local," which implies that voters care less about abstract principles of government than about daily experience and perceptions of their own well-being. The phrase ascribes to the electorate a level-headed pragmatism that Americans seem to find appealing. Since the 1960s, however, political polarization has spawned an opposite interpretation, which portrays voters as ideologically driven and sees local politics as little more than a stand-in for national debates. In either case, one must acknowledge the impor-tance of local politics, and especially of public education. As arbiters of moral and civic standards, guarantors of opportunity and merit, and catalysts of grass-roots activism, public schools are both the nation's most widespread social ser-vice agencies and the ones most responsive to public oversight. They are integral to the American experience. As a result, education used to figure prominently in discussions of the nation's history, especially in the grand scholarship of the 1950s and 1960s.[6] It receded in subsequent decades, but historians have begun to rediscover education as an important component of civil rights movements, for-eign and domestic politics, and even economic development, from the nine-teenth century to the present.[7]

The Fight for Local Control explains the origins and evolution of local school governance by examining interrelated changes in the United States' metropolitan landscape during the postwar era. In particular, it takes a new perspective on suburbanization, one of the most significant demographic shifts during that period. Although historians have begun to recognize the varieties of suburban development—adding working-class, ethnic, and high-tech neighborhoods to standard images of lily-white bedroom communities—most have ignored the continued salience of rural history in the suburbs. Rather than analyzing suburban growth entirely in relation to cities, as other scholars have, this book connects the hardening line between cities and suburbs to the blurrier boundary between suburbs and the countryside. Suburban communities defined themselves in the context of both rural and urban neighbors and created cultural, political, and legal connections between their borders that were shifting and interdependent. Although suburbanites could characterize themselves as either urban or rural based on their interests, they generally united with rural areas to thwart urban expansion and social policies. The convergence of rural and suburban interests appeared in many places, from popular music and television shows to congressional maps and presidential speeches. In the context of local governance, it was visible in the actions of town councils, zoning commissions, and most of all school boards, which are the focus of this book. Across all of these areas were a set of conflicts and compromises that historians have yet to incorporate in explanations of metropolitan growth.

Also underlying the discussion of local politics are particular interpretations of government and geography that should be made explicit. Critical readers might already have noticed some imprecision in the use of such terms as "local control" or "urban," "suburban," and "rural" areas. The following section tries to provide some working definitions before outlining the contents of subsequent chapters.

To appreciate the prolonged struggle for local control, one must first understand the meaning of the term itself. Many scholars and activists today refer to localism in vague or inconsistent ways, especially when discussing school governance. Some characterize as local any agency below the federal government, essentially conflating calls for local control with those for states' rights. Although both of those phrases suggest a commitment to small government—and thus became popular slogans for midcentury conservatives—their meanings are nevertheless quite distinct. Whereas states' rights imply the supremacy of state government and a rejection of federal intervention, local control implies the right of municipalities to operate independently of state *or* federal governments. To characterize state government as local is especially misleading when it comes to education, which over the past century has witnessed dramatic and contentious expansions of state power at the expense of localities. From another angle, some commentators have begun to characterize vouchers, charter schools, and other sorts of decentralized, market-based educational reform as manifestations of local control. They are not. One of the great selling points of school choice programs is that they allow families to obtain education outside of their neighborhood attendance zones while at the same time replacing the traditional, community-based governance of elected school boards with the power of individual decision making. If anything, market-based reform is best understood as extra- and sub-local, widening the selection of schools while atomizing their governance structures. Local control is a historically constructed phenomenon, with contested and ever-changing meanings. The idea that localism can be exercised at the state level or decoupled from community governance speaks both to mutability of the term and (as later chapters explain) to the shifting ideologies of its users. But neither of these interpretations accurately captures its meaning in the mid-twentieth century, and collapsing the distinction between the term's past and present obscures important changes. For the purposes of this book, then, local control will be defined in its historical context, referring to the funding and administration of community-based school districts by popularly elected boards.[8]

In its delineation of rural and suburban communities the book remains necessarily (and perhaps purposely) more vague. The United States Census Bureau has repeatedly changed the way it labels different-sized communities in an attempt to reflect new settlement patterns over the course of the twentieth century. In 1910, for instance, it first standardized the distinction between rural and urban areas, defining the latter as any incorporated territory with 2,500 or more residents. In 1950, as suburbs became a recognizable feature of the metropolitan landscape, the bureau further distinguished between "urbanized areas" (cities with 50,000 or more residents) and "urban clusters" (usually suburban areas with 2,500 to 50,000 residents), and continues to use those designations today.[9] Unfortunately, because these categories are simply numerical they cannot distinguish the character of a community and do not always capture areas in transition. The imprecise boundaries between rural and suburban areas have led some sociologists to apply fine gradations when discussing their overlap, distinctions between suburban, exurban, penurban, peri-urban, and so forth. Insofar as this project aims to describe a broader political shift and is not a social science study of a single type of community, it opts for a more inclusive definition. The only limiting criteria are that the towns in this study began the postwar period with 2,500 residents or fewer, experienced a burst of population growth or residential development, and had small, neighborhood- or town-based school districts. Many remained rural throughout the period of the study, despite their transformation from farmland into subdivisions, while others claimed to be rural even as they outgrew the formal definition of that term, a point that is central to the book's argument.

The significance of neighborhood- and town-based school districts raises a few final points about geography. First, it precludes analysis of many Southern states—which adopted county-wide districts at the turn of the century and, with the exception of a few regions in Appalachia, consolidated their one-room schools by the 1940s—as well as some states in the Mountain West.[10] That caveat shifts attention away from the Sunbelt, where the convergence of suburbanization and education has already been the subject of much scholarly discussion, and redirects it to a broader swath of the country, with examples drawn from Oregon and Southern California to New Hampshire and Maine.[11]

That shift is valuable not only because it is more inclusive but because of its effects on historical interpretation. One influential study of Sunbelt conservatism, Matthew Lassiter's *The Silent Majority* (2006), examines school politics in Virginia, North Carolina, and Georgia—all states with county-wide school districts—and underscores similarities and differences with the arguments made here. *The Silent Majority* opens with a description of "massive resistance" to school desegregation after *Brown v. Board of Education* (1954). In the rural South, county-wide districts and large African American populations meant that courts could actually achieve meaningful desegregation within districts. As a result, rural politicians—still vastly overrepresented in state legislatures—rejected *Brown* outright, going so far as to shut down public school systems. Lassiter points out that their radicalism did not play well in the suburbs, which were whiter, more middle class, and far more willing to compromise. Suburban areas offered a way forward, combining token desegregation with structural protections for white supremacy and suburban privilege. Lassiter contends that a new, "color blind" conservatism developed in the 1970s, built on housing segregation and other forms of structural racism rather than explicit exclusion of minority groups, a politically useful fiction that quickly spread nationwide and "played a crucial role in the fading of southern distinctiveness and the national collapse of the New Deal Order."[12] Thus, Lassiter's argument is premised on a *disjuncture* between rural and suburban school politics—with the latter offering conservatives a more palatable sort of racism—and also on the county-wide districts that enabled racial compromise. Yet focusing on the convergence of Southern and Northern suburbs downplays the ways in which the educational politics of the South remained distinct. Color-blind conservatism spread to suburbs nationwide, but it did not do so under the conditions that Lassiter describes. Rather than relying on housing segregation and the dispersal of minority students across an entire county, suburbs in the North and West grounded color blindness firmly in the rhetoric of local democracy, and they developed that ideology not in opposition to but in cooperation with rural communities. In fact, as noted in the conclusion of this book, local control has perhaps proven even more influential than color blindness, since it has made inroads into the very districts that Lassiter examines. Just as national politics converged around a new, Southern, suburban paradigm in the 1970s, today the South is becoming more like the North in its systems of racial exclusion, moving away from county-wide districts in favor of local school administration, and again making implicitly racist policies more palatable.

The Fight for Local Control tries to offer a representative sample of school district politics from across the country, encompassing sweeping changes in educational policy and aggregating the experiences of hundreds of disparate communities. Such an expansive study could potentially sacrifice depth of analysis for breadth. To include the detail associated with a local case study, each chapter of the book interweaves events in one state, Wisconsin, with a broader, national narrative of educational reform. No state is perfectly representative when it comes to school district politics: Demographics, traditions of localism, and different structures of government ensure that the extent and pace of school reform vary across the country. Nevertheless, Wisconsin has several qualities to recommend it. While it was more rural than the nation as a whole, the timing and methods of its school consolidation campaign were typical among Northern states. Its countryside attracted thousands of suburbanites, vacationers, and retirees from the Chicago–Milwaukee area, one of the nation's largest metropolitan corridors. Wisconsin was also politically variable: It usually voted Republican, but under that label could swing from the right-wing populism of Senator Joseph McCarthy to the small-town progressivism of "Fighting Bob" LaFollette. As in other Northern states, Democrats began making inroads during the late 1950s—winning the governorship, and holding both Senate seats from the 1960s to the 1980s—but met sharp resistance from suburban conservatives, who threw support behind the segregationist George Wallace in 1968 and 1972 and comprised the backbone of the right-wing John Birch Society, which moved its headquarters to Appleton in the 1980s. Finally, apropos of the subject at hand, Wisconsin had tangled commitments both to the local control of schools and education reform, with state universities and the Department of Public Instruction pushing for the latter. Thus, the Wisconsin Historical Society has probably the most comprehensive collection of records relating to rural school consolidation anywhere in the country, encompassing not only university and government reports but the personal papers of legislators, activists, and school board members, as well as the proceedings of an inordinate number of court cases.[13]

This book will be of use to historians, policymakers, and teachers, but also to a larger swath of Americans, who retain an attachment to public schools and grasp for an understanding of their past. Local inquiry and dialogue have long been a cornerstone of American education, and their exercise by school boards and other community groups will ensure that our schools continue to flourish in the future. In order to understand the policy debates surrounding public education, as well as their own rights and responsibilities in school governance, community members need to understand the historical context from which public schools emerged. *The Fight for Local Control* tries to provide that context in a rigorous but accessible way, with attention to long-term trends and the lived experience of small-town Americans.

Most importantly, it tries to do so without the romanticism and nostalgia that frequently attends discussions of the one-room schoolhouse. Christopher Lasch once observed that nostalgia devitalizes history, rendering it both one-dimensional and harmlessly distant from the present. Nostalgia does not "unambiguously assert the superiority of bygone days," he wrote, but rather "contains an admixture of self-congratulation," for by "exaggerating the naïve simplicity of earlier times it implicitly celebrates the worldly wisdom of later generations." The goal of this book is not to glorify small schools or local control, both of which suffered from serious shortcomings, but to remind readers about the values that those institutions embodied, the noble and ignoble reasons that Americans embraced them, and the process by which they were lost, often without the sort of public discussion that democracy demands. In short, the book hopes to raise century-old questions about education that remain relevant today, to advocate for "the persistence of the past [and] the manifold ways in which it penetrates our lives," to describe the sort of living history that nostalgia flatly precludes. It does so modestly, without offering specific answers or solutions, and with the recognition that others have already raised the issues at hand. Questions about local democracy persist not because they are philosophically intractable or merely of scholarly interest but because there are voters in many communities that keep asking them. *The Fight for Local Control* is an attempt to recognize and support their efforts.[14]

The Plan for the Book

As with its geographical scope, the structure of the book is important to its argument. *The Fight for Local Control* tells its story in two broad sections. First, it outlines the significance and politics of localism in the twentieth century. Chapter 1 explains local control in the context of suburbanization, conservative politics, and school reform, and demonstrates how the confluence of these issues changed practices of municipal government. Chapter 2 outlines in greater depth the history of rural school consolidation, which began in the 1890s but remained contested seventy-five years later, long enough for suburban newcomers— discussed in chapter 3—to clash and then cooperate on the issue with their rural neighbors. After documenting the impact of suburbanization on rural school districts, chapter 3 will also look at the invocation of local control to oppose court-ordered busing for racial desegregation. The central contention of the first three chapters is that the prolonged period of rural school consolidation provided conservative activists with a counterweight to liberal school reform in the 1970s.

Taking the busing issue as a template, subsequent chapters explore the legacies of rural-suburban cooperation across three other areas of educational policy. Chapter 4 analyzes the rise of teachers' unions outside of metropolitan boundaries. As teachers and administrators began to demand tenure protection, rights of collective bargaining, and professional control of curriculum and hiring, they usurped the responsibilities of rural school boards, which had previously handled almost all aspects of the academic program. The conflict between professional practice and local democracy resulted in scores of lawsuits in consolidated districts, which in turn gave otherwise marginal communities an outsized and understudied significance in public sector labor law. State and federal courts gradually changed in their handling of these cases. Wholesale deference to local control weakened by the mid-1970s, as judges liberalized public employees' right to strike and began to subject school boards to mandatory arbitration. Their rulings continued to affirm the primacy of elected representatives in school governance—and often kept unions on the defensive in outlying communities themselves—but overall they signaled a victory for fair labor practices and professional rights. Collective bargaining, in turn, reinforced state and federal calls for more educational spending, obliging school districts to raise significantly more revenue in absolute terms even as state and federal subsidies comprised a larger portion of district budgets.

Chapters 5 and 6 elaborate on the role of rural and suburban districts in school finance debates, from the equalized funding controversies of the late 1960s to the tax revolts of the late 1970s. Many historians have assumed a connection between these phenomena, arguing that suburban areas spearheaded resistance to redistributive tax policies and (in states where they failed) campaigned for constitutional limits on property taxation—especially in California, which passed Proposition 13 in 1978. These chapters challenge that assumption in two respects. First, while court cases limiting equalized funding are usually interpreted in the context of urban/suburban politics, they actually turned on courts' understanding of older, rural educational practices. Moreover, the connection between equalized funding and tax limitation is less clear than some historians make it seem: So-called tax revolts often predated redistributive funding and were as likely to occur in states that rejected equalization plans as those that adopted them. The real source of anti-tax sentiment in the 1970s was not so much the redistribution of property taxes as declining local control over their collection and expenditure, the result of professional land assessment and school administration, respectively. As with teacher unionization, these changes were most contentious in exurban areas, where the rising cost of public services fell disproportionately on farmers. There were initial attempts to restrain spending by rejecting school bond referendums and subjecting schools to market competition through open enrollment or voucher programs, but these met strident resistance from teachers' unions and other interest groups. It was the failure of local austerity measures that eventually forced activists to turn to statewide spending limits.

Chapters 7 and 8 conclude with a discussion of curricular debates and the conflicting rights of school boards, teachers, and parents to determine course content. Curriculum was often a means of reasserting community control in the wake of school consolidation and a point on which rural and suburban conservatives could unite. Censorship campaigns on the suburban fringe marked the beginning of a movement to reaffirm the power of parents and school boards to choose classroom materials. From a legal perspective, however, equating local democracy with parents' rights was short lived. School board decisions often contradicted the wishes of individual parents, and as courts promoted the rights of minority groups they became less willing to countenance the free rein of local majorities. By the mid-1980s, narrowing legal grounds pushed conservative Christians in particular to decouple parents' rights from community control and describe themselves as a victimized minority, petitioning courts for exemptions from objectionable classes or the right to leave public education altogether. Again, much of the relevant case law came out of rural communities and responded directly to the effects of school consolidation on compulsory attendance and parental authority.

The evidence underlying these arguments requires a final word of explanation. While many histories focus on a single person, incident, or institution, a fifty-year study of small communities and local governments across the country is naturally more extensive, gleaning small pieces of information from a broad range of sources. Most of the incidents included in this study entered the historical record only briefly and did not generate enough documents to appear in centralized repositories. Rather, they were the subject of newspaper articles and editorials, oral histories, state government publications, and occasionally surveys and unpublished dissertations from the period, mostly written by educational researchers or sociologists. Small-town disputes were most likely to appear in archives when they attracted the interest of state or national organizations, although even then they turned up less often than one might expect. Local conflicts over district consolidation, teachers' unions, school funding, and curricular reform appear in the archives of the National Education Association (NEA) and American Federation of Teachers (AFT), but only when committees investigated them. And while groups opposed to school consolidation existed in almost every region of the country during the postwar period, only a handful of universities and historical societies preserved their records.

The best information about small-town disputes often comes from court records. Attempts to curb the power of local school boards frequently resulted in lawsuits, which enabled state and federal courts to arbitrate significant shifts of power in local affairs. Historical arguments based on judicial decisions sometimes exaggerate the role of conflict in social change; in this case, reinforcing the notion of educational "culture wars" while obscuring more gradual or consensual reforms.[15] Conflict seemed especially likely during the shift from the liberal Warren court of the 1950s to the more conservative Burger and Rehnquist courts of the 1970s and 1980s, when the judiciary increasingly involved itself in contentious areas of race, religion, and voting rights. Yet while ideological differences certainly affected the judiciary's interpretation of local control, there was a significant degree of consistency across rulings. As with related questions of minority rights, when faced with disputes over unions, funding, or curriculum, both liberal and conservative judges acknowledged and thus codified the role of local democracy in education. But both struggled, as well, to balance traditions of local control with changing conceptions of educational adequacy—questioning, for instance, whether school boards could ban state-sanctioned textbooks or persist in unequal systems of school funding. Often, the determinative difference was simply that liberal rulings included stronger exceptions to local control than did conservative rulings, conceding the point in principle to constrain it in practice. In any event, the book uses court cases advisedly, and corroborates them whenever possible with other evidence of local reaction to school reform.

THE MEANING OF LOCAL CONTROL

Richard Hofstadter's *The Age of Reform* (1955) remains a touchstone in U.S. history, a book whose style and interpretive methods continue to influence our understanding of the twentieth century despite the fact that critics have largely discredited its thesis. Hofstadter's work drew from the modernization theory and liberal-democratic politics of his era, both of which suggested that efficient statecraft—and particularly government regulation of the economy—could produce sufficient prosperity to undermine the radical appeals of communism or fascism. Although described as a "consensus" position, this view was less widespread than its proponents let on. Anti-communist rhetoric legitimized a multitude of anti-Semitic, racist, and homophobic groups during the 1950s, all of which stoked the sort of hysteria and demagogy that liberals wanted to stifle. Hofstadter hoped to situate these groups in a historical context and, in doing so, to relegate them to the past. He found the precursors of his own time in the agrarian revolts of the late nineteenth century and the progressive reforms of the early twentieth. Invoking concepts of "status anxiety," "authoritarian personalities," and other emerging psychological theories, he argued that populist protest movements were animated not only by class conflict, as scholars had previously assumed, but also by strains of paranoia, intolerance, and anti-intellectualism, a hostility to elites and economic modernization that was misguided at its inception and dangerous in its persistence. For Hofstadter, the reforms of the 1890s and 1910s were neurotic attempts to re-empower a group that had never really existed—the economically independent yeoman—while at the same time reinforcing outdated assumptions about individual liberty and economic competition.

15

Turn-of-the-century protest movements were ultimately a conservative force, he argued, "concerned not with managing an economy to meet the problems of collapse but simply with democratizing an economy in sound working order"; they cherished tenets of individual striving and success, and attacked banks and monopolies as aberrations of the free market rather than its logical outcomes. These views were markedly different from the economic and political centralization that appeared with the New Deal in the 1930s. New Deal regulation not only weakened the basis for free-market capitalism, Hofstadter argued, but its bureaucratic structures usurped earlier, community-based systems of reform, replacing local granges and civic clubs with national planning commissions and development agencies. Although these changes encountered local resistance, Hofstadter interpreted them as signs of progress and national maturity, the sort of regulatory state befitting an industrial, urban society. Hofstadter summarized his entire argument with a single, pithy phrase: "America was born in the country," he wrote, "and has moved to the city."[1]

What Hofstadter did not realize was that even as he wrote, the nation was moving back to the country, with profound consequences for American politics. As suburban voters returned to small towns, they reversed many of the gains of New Deal liberalism, often acting through the same institutions and with the same people that Hofstadter had left for dead. Farm bureaus, bible studies, town councils, and school boards once again became sites of national protest, as farmers and small-town elites joined with suburban newcomers in campaigns for public morality and the authority of the white middle class. Rural and suburban areas resounded calls for individual freedom and the end of economic planning or government oversight. Their rallying cry was local government, which they perceived as a fundamental right under threat from overreaching bureaucrats.

It is important to point out that like Hofstadter's independent yeoman, the right to local government was a myth. But it was a myth in multiple senses of the word. For most of U.S. history, a community's right to control its own affairs was mythical because it was legally baseless. State constitutions assigned localities few responsibilities and construed those narrowly, with legislatures retaining the right to reorganize or dissolve local agencies at will. Yet because the idea of local government evokes such deep-seated American values as egalitarianism, self-determination, and civic participation, it has also functioned as a sort of creation myth, an integral part of Americans' self-conception. The meaning of local control became the subject of national debates during the early twentieth century, when traditions of local government seemed particularly imperiled, and those debates have persisted in various forms to the present, often in terms similar to Hofstadter's in *The Age of Reform*.[2]

For middle-class whites in the early 1900s, urbanization, immigration, mass media, and other modernizing forces portended the breakdown of local custom and their own civil and religious authority. The sheer scale of new social problems seemed to overmatch the institutions that existed to control them: Town councils struggled to manage crime, sanitation, and residential growth, for instance, while churches could no longer guarantee social welfare or ensure moral conformity. Surveying the cities of the East Coast during the 1910s, journalist Walter Lippmann observed, "We are not used to a complicated civilization. We don't know how to behave when personal contact and eternal authority have disappeared. . . . We have changed our environment more quickly than we know how to change ourselves." Like Hofstadter, Lippmann argued that when social problems transcended municipal boundaries or strained the capacity of local institutions, Americans had no choice but to cede power to higher levels of government and qualified experts. "Take the City of New York," he wrote. "As a health problem, a transportation problem, a housing problem, a food problem, a police problem, the city which sprawls across three states ought to be treated as one unit," as a metropolitan health district, for instance, or a regional transportation authority, run by civil servants and non-elected officials.[3] Many philosophers and social critics agreed with Lippman's diagnosis, if not necessarily with his solutions. John Dewey, Lewis Mumford, Randolph Bourne, Robert and Helen Lynd, and others struggled to discern whether deliberative democracy could function in the absence of local participation, and worried that the rise of cities had perhaps rendered institutions like the town meeting and the local school board ineffective, anachronistic, or redundant. It may seem strange that local control acquired legal status in the midst of their hand-wringing, but the same fears impelled states to develop legal protections for "home rule" during the period.[4]

The codification of home rule was a contested process, and expansive enough to include multiple interpretations, from the installation of Lippmann's technocratic elite to a re-empowerment of small-town voters, but in either case it fell short of its democratic rhetoric. Supporters of home rule usually came from dominant social groups and tended to pursue self-interest rather than the general good. While they never secured complete municipal autonomy, their efforts to protect local participation slowed the rise of government regulation and erected barriers against social planning or wealth redistribution. Thus, as states codified the right to local government—as the second myth of localism began to overtake the first—the preservation of decentralized democracy created a patchwork of profound inequality across the American landscape. And, predictably, as inequalities grew more pronounced, it was their beneficiaries who most stridently defended the right to local government.[5]

Calls for home rule influenced many aspects of social policy during the twentieth century, but they tended to cohere tightly around issues of suburbanization, conservative politics, and school reform, with a powerful constellation of interests voicing support for the local control of education. The remainder of this chapter will examine local control in the context of these three issues, with attention, first, to the ways in which law and politics solidified municipal boundaries, and also to the ways in which historians have interpreted local control. It would be difficult to do either without referencing Hofstadter's *Age of Reform*, not as an accurate exposition of midcentury politics, since it fundamentally misinterpreted the trends of its own era, but neither as the straw man that many historians have begun to reference simply to toss aside. Several of Hofstadter's concepts remain important to our understanding of local government, as do his broader questions about the contested meaning of American democracy. The task at hand is to extend that analysis in a way that is not dismissive of conservative activists or of Hofstadter himself, and thus to understand the persistent legacy of small-town institutions in fights for local self-determination.

Urbanization and the Origins of Home Rule

For most of the nineteenth century, municipalities had no explicit right to self-government. Chartered by and subordinate to state legislatures, they were merely convenient instruments through which the state could discharge its duties.[6] Although in practice states lacked the capacity to regulate their towns and cities closely, legislators still controlled the purse strings for infrastructure, sanitation, and other municipal services. During the 1890s, as city budgets increased and political machines expanded the influence of nonwhite immigrant groups in statehouses, this entanglement of state and local politics stoked new fears of political corruption and tax hikes. As legal scholar David Barron argues, "Each new piece of special legislation seemed to reveal that a state-centered legal structure facilitated . . . the spending, taxing, and regulatory powers of local governments more than it checked local governmental overreaching. The premise that cities were mere creatures of the state . . . seemed only to encourage state legislators to think of local power as an extension of their own power."[7] Two broad reforms at the turn of the century invoked localism to limit this sort of corruption and to preserve the power of white, native-born Americans: one was legislative and conservative, favoring small towns, the other administrative and liberal, favoring cities. As these reforms vied for supremacy in state governments they set the stage for metropolitan conflicts in the era after World War II.

The first reform sought to counterbalance the growth of urban political machines by preserving the political power of the countryside, accomplished largely through the manipulation of voting districts. Most states stopped reapportioning districts around 1900, or began to base them on area rather than population. When the federal census of 1920 found more Americans living in urban than rural communities, Congress flatly rejected the constitutional mandate to reapportion its seats. Representatives from rural states denounced the census as "viciously inaccurate, unreliable, and unfair," insisting that urban migration was a temporary phenomenon and that the nation would soon see "a remigration to the farm." After a decade of debate they finally ceded power to more populous states, but only with the understanding that future population gains would be accommodated with the existing number of representatives—435 voting members, as of 1929—and that redrawn districts would continue to favor voters in the countryside.[8] Those compromises resulted in staggering levels of rural overrepresentation. By midcentury, less than twelve percent of the population of Vermont, Connecticut, and Florida could elect the majority of those states' lower houses, while in ten other states, less than a third of the voters could elect majorities in both houses and for federal offices. Not a single state counted urban votes at their full weight, and in some areas a single farmer could outvote hundreds of his fellow citizens. This "rule of the rustics" not only ensured the success of farm bills and conservative social causes but prompted state legislators to embrace limited government and a general deference to local opinion. Essentially, the preservation of democracy in small towns came to justify its miscarriage in metropolitan areas.[9]

As the historian Robert Wiebe argues, a rising urban middle class advanced a second, markedly different vision of local control during the 1890s. Its members responded to urbanization with bureaucratic rather than political solutions and did not want to limit cities' representation in statehouses so much as protect them from democratic interference altogether.[10] Like Walter Lippmann, they believed that by devolving power to city managers and exempting urban areas from special legislation, expertise and systemization could ensure better government than the electoral process.[11] They particularly advocated constitutional provisions for home rule, which granted cities the right to manage their internal affairs and limited legislatures to matters of statewide concern. Eleven states adopted such provisions between 1890 and 1925.[12]

Like many Progressive Era reforms, the administrative approach to home rule resists characterization as an entirely "liberal" or "conservative" policy. David Barron points out that the reform appealed to many laissez-faire conservatives because it restored "the idealized small-scale, low-tax, low-debt, highly privatized" vision of municipal government. Local control was "far less flexible" than state oversight, he argues, "and that was precisely its virtue. Its very rigidity would promote an old conservative vision of the city," governed responsibly and frugally by administrative leaders.[13] To be viable, however, urban self-determination also required an expansive, increasingly liberal interpretation of government power, one that allowed cities to exercise eminent domain, annex surrounding territory, and regulate environmental, transportation, and commercial development beyond their borders. Indeed, from the 1930s to the 1960s, urban administrative regimes and state regulatory agencies grew in tandem. Both advanced goals of professional management and regional planning, and extolled expertise, centralization, and efficiency as prerequisites of political and economic modernization. In public education, economic development, and many other areas of government they sought to replace chaos with consolidation, to concentrate and (strange as it may sound) depoliticize municipal politics.[14]

The conservative/legislative and liberal/administrative visions of home rule coexisted for several decades, but demographic changes during the 1950s gradually tipped the balance in favor of the latter. City and state planners increasingly influenced rural affairs and threatened to dissolve some local governments altogether. Rural conservatives tried to protect local prerogative through grassroots protest—by flouting new zoning and environmental regulations, for example, or propagating conspiracy theories about the fluoridation of local water supplies—but they were losing ground. In 1955, the sociologist Daniel Bell, one of Richard Hofstadter's collaborators, dismissed their actions as the last stand of a "dispossessed" class of old-stock Americans, resentful of an increasingly cosmopolitan nation and seeking in vain "to defend [their] fading dominance . . . through the institutions of small-town America." If they were unable to adapt to modern life, he argued, this group would soon fade into obscurity.[15]

Bell's prediction was to some extent correct. The survival of small-town government depended on rural overrepresentation, and that arrangement was becoming more difficult to defend. In *Baker v. Carr* (1962) the U.S. Supreme Court held that disputes over federal voting districts were judicable and that due process required adherence to the principle of "one man, one vote," weakening rural voters' electoral advantage. In *Reynolds v. Sims* (1964) the court extended its logic further, ordering states to reapportion both their upper and lower houses on the basis of proportional representation.[16] While the partisan implications of these rulings were initially unclear, redrawing districts in favor of cities seemed sure to empower liberals in both parties and to marginalize rural conservatives. Political scientists assumed that reapportionment would open the door to a wave of "slum clearance, labor and welfare legislation, civil rights laws, and other items high on the liberal agenda."[17]

Yet those policies failed to materialize. Overlooked in discussions of rural-dominated legislatures was the fact that cities already controlled a nearly proportionate number of votes in most states by midcentury. The areas that stood to gain the most from reapportionment were those stymied by rural overrepresentation *and* marginalized by city governments. With the fastest growing populations and interests falling somewhere between urban and rural agendas, it was suburbs that would determine the course of twentieth-century politics.[18]

Although suburbanization and municipal autonomy would become inextricably bound by midcentury, there was little connection between the two in the 1890s, when the passage of constitutional amendments for home rule coincided with the creation of the first "streetcar suburbs." Most suburbanites welcomed annexation to adjacent cities, which brought them inexpensive infrastructure and municipal services. City councils, in turn, were eager to widen their tax bases and find space for new residential and commercial development. Thus, at least through the 1910s, most cities could expand their borders unimpeded by suburban resistance. Only as suburbs grew larger, and paving and sewer technologies more affordable, did they begin to agitate for local autonomy. Identifying a pattern that holds true today, Richardson Dilworth writes that "large infrastructure projects in cities [in the early twentieth century] were often accompanied by well-publicized political scandals," and insofar as suburbanites "did not want to be taxed at exorbitant levels [by] what they viewed as venal political organizations," they increasingly chose to fund and administer their own services. During the 1920s, many suburbs incorporated as independent entities, adopting home rule as a means of defending local prerogative and, in their view, good government.[19] By the 1940s, dozens of autonomous suburbs ringed cities such as Newark, Chicago, and Detroit, blocking further growth and igniting a new competition for residents and revenue. In the ensuing land grab, local governments raced to annex and develop as much territory as possible, lest their neighbors encircle them or leave them without a viable tax base.[20]

An additional fourteen states adopted home rule amendments after 1945, and by then the trend was clearly linked to suburbanization. Historian David Freund points out that over a thousand new municipal governments appeared during the 1950s, and that by the end of that decade, almost fifteen percent of all metropolitan municipalities were less than ten years old. "Communities jumping on the home-rule bandwagon were both younger and smaller than their prewar predecessors," he writes; ninety percent of cities created between 1940 and 1965 had fewer than ten thousand people, while a third of all metropolitan cities comprised less than a square mile of area, many of them previously unincorporated rural areas.[21]

Incorporation invested these new municipalities not only with annexation but zoning power, another Progressive Era reform intended to professionalize and rationalize urban development. Zoning sought to put land to its "best use" by separating manufacturing from residential areas and by imposing lot sizes, health codes, and scores of other regulations on builders. Reformers argued that these measures would improve public health and aesthetics while replacing a chaotic housing market with the predictability of managed growth and decline.[22] By the postwar period, however, municipal fragmentation seemed to apportion suburbs all the growth and cities all the decline. Zoning allowed suburban governments to mandate the construction of single-family homes, for instance, and (through restrictive covenants) to exclude occupancy by racial or religious minorities, creating an attractive investment for white, middle-class homeowners while trapping the poor in blighted urban neighborhoods.[23] Freund writes that zoning became so entwined with local prosperity that "suburban officials and homeowners learned to see political autonomy and land-use control as practically synonymous."[24]

Urban historians have long recognized the impact of suburbanization on racial and class stratification, as well as its corresponding influence on twentieth-century politics.[25] In doing so, however, they have analyzed suburbs almost wholly in relation to city centers, where the ravages of white flight have been most visible and structural injustices most acute. Few have examined the border between suburbs and rural areas.[26] Meanwhile, similar sensibilities have pushed rural historians in the opposite direction. While they now study mining, fishing, and other sorts of nonfarm labor, as well as the experiences of women and ethnic minorities, declining rural populations and living standards have made rural history more insular, focused on the memory of vanishing communities and lifestyles. The field rarely examines communities that have outgrown traditional conceptions of rural life: once a town becomes a bedroom community, it ceases to generate interest.[27] Only in the past decade, as a new suburban history has diversified understandings of metropolitan boundaries, have historians recognized that they can no longer "[underemphasize] social, cultural, and political connections between the suburbs and rural hinterlands" by portraying the latter as empty land awaiting development, rather than a rich cultural space that continues to influence new residents.[28]

That argument is directly applicable to the politics of home rule. In a study of legislative reapportionment, for example, Douglas Smith notes that redrawn voting districts "freed suburbanites across the country from urban control just as effectively as [they] ended rural and small-town domination," and that "suburbanites, most of whom were white, often discovered that they had more in common with rural and small-town residents than with their disproportionately nonwhite urban neighbors."[29] The shift not only united suburban and rural areas against social welfare programs and urban renewal, as Smith suggests, but allowed rural residents to expand the definition of home rule itself. Most states had originally limited home rule to cities with 2,500 residents or more, reasoning that municipal services in smaller towns would require the support of state government rather than protection from it. In the process, however, they also left small towns vulnerable to annexation by larger neighbors. As elite suburbs extended further into the countryside—or carved out ever-smaller enclaves near the city—they joined the fight for rural self-government in order to ensure their own survival, demanding rights of autonomy for small communities as well as large ones.

Wisconsin serves as a case in point. In 1946, twenty years after the state adopted a home rule amendment for villages and cities, activists in Shawano formed the Wisconsin Towns Association to extend the same protections to rural areas. (The state defined a town as any contiguous, unincorporated land within a county.) In 1967 the director of the Towns Association complained, "The idea of government economic planning [still] appeals to many intellectuals and politicians today. What they forget is that . . . millions of individual plans are coordinated through the marvelous mechanism of competition and the free market. The question is whether each of us should be *free* to make his own plans, or whether all of us should be *forced* to work or consume according to some Master Plan drawn up for us by some supposed group of supermen." "Why," he demanded, "does the present law allow a town to be pulled apart by annexation, consolidation or incorporation when a village or city cannot be touched? This, too, is discrimination!"[30] That question, with its celebration of the free market and intimations of reverse discrimination, put a particularly rural spin on broader conservative talking points. Yet by the time the Wisconsin legislature finally granted home rule to small towns in 1974, it was less concerned with rural autonomy per se than with the threat of "forced busing" and tax equalization in wealthy suburbs, issues of educational policy that had come to unite rural and suburban interests. Similar trends elsewhere remind us that a full explanation of local control cannot simply cover the structure of municipal governance but must understand its interrelationship with conservative politics and education as well.

Local Government and the Rise of the "New Right"

Midcentury conservatives were the most strident champions of local control, which they associated with small government and individual choice. Yet the near-unanimity of their support also raises interesting questions about the coherence

of the term and of the conservative movement itself. What exactly did local control mean to conservatives, and how did it help unite and mobilize a political
movement?

During the 1950s, many liberal commentators drew a sharp distinction between
populist and truly conservative politics in America. None disputed the prevalence of
"people's" movements in the nation's history: a commitment to egalitarianism and
economic opportunity for the middle class had driven numerous waves of reform
during the nineteenth century, they observed, often accompanied by the same hostility to minorities, intellectuals, and elites that animated anti-communist crusades
during their own time. But they argued that that phenomenon had nothing to do
with conservatism, a political philosophy built on Old World traditions of social
order, class distinctions, and intellectual elitism. In 1950 Lionel Trilling quipped,
"there are no conservative or reactionary ideas currently in circulation," only "irri-
table mental gestures which seek to resemble ideas." Hofstadter's *Age of Reform* appeared five years later, dismissing the "pseudo-conservatism" and status anxiety of
the American Right, whose real impulses, he argued, were either crassly economic
(in the case of business interests) or borderline psychotic (in the case of conspiracy
theorists like Joseph McCarthy or, later, the John Birch Society), but in either case
were unworthy of the intellectual tradition of Edmund Burke.[31]

Since the 1980s it has become almost obligatory for historians to measure the
meteoric rise of conservative thought in America against the condescension of
Trilling, Hofstadter, and other midcentury liberals. The latter have become so
discredited that historian Leo Ribuffo has advised colleagues to discard them
once and for all.[32] All the same, it seems worthwhile to acknowledge two areas in
which these writers were right: namely, the conservative movement often *did*
resemble a series of "mental gestures" rather than a coherent ideology, and in
many ways the influence of capitalists and radical populists *did* strain its connections to traditional conservative thought.[33] Liberals were naive to assume that
those tensions would halt the movement's rise, of course—and more naïve to
miss the weaknesses of their own ideologies—but the contradictions of conservatism remain central to its history.[34]

Early histories of the Right often struggled to explain the relationship between conservative and populist politics. In the field's foundational text, *The
Conservative Intellectual Movement in America* (1976), George Nash refused "to
equate conservatism with McCarthyism," since "whatever the 'grass-roots' of
American conservatism may have been . . . its intellectual leadership was not xenophobic."[35] To the contrary, he emphasized that conservative traditions of
libertarianism and traditionalism derived almost exclusively from Europe.[36]
Before 1945, their adherents were insular and fractious, propounding ideas in
small magazines and debating societies. Gradually, however, they exchanged phil-

osophical purity for a more pragmatic politics of old-time religion, patriotism, family, and private property. Nash argued that libertarians could hold to the former tenets, and traditionalists to the latter, only with "the cement of anti-Communism." For him, anti-communism was the siren song of mass politics, the first issue on which "conservatives sensed that *they* were on the popular side" and on which majoritarian democracy could advance a conservative agenda. Unfortunately, because it also encompassed the populist demagogy that he disdained, Nash never clearly defined anti-communism or explained how it united such diverse philosophies. Essentially, his narrative legitimized the Right by cataloguing its full spectrum of ideas; but by stripping those ideas of social context it could not explain their coalescence.[37]

Local government was an institution that appealed to both populist and conservative sensibilities, and thus offers helpful insights into their coalition. Localism became a means to defend both morals and liberties against an overweening, bureaucratic state. It promised lower taxes, fewer regulations, and more modest policy goals. It ensured a free market in housing, allowing families to choose their neighbors and their children's schools rather than forcing them to accept racial integration or other sorts of "social engineering." Most of all, it provided the opportunity for democratic deliberation, ensuring responsive representation for citizens and preventing the rise of a strong central state. Thus, local government served the same role that Nash ascribes to anti-communism: it allowed a movement of intellectual elites to accept majority rule, and helped religious and libertarian voters arrive at a tenuous truce.[38]

Conservatives found compromise easier after Earl Warren was appointed chief justice of the Supreme Court, in 1953. Almost immediately, Warren, the former governor of California, shepherded his fellow justices to some of the most liberal rulings in the history of the court, initiating two decades of judicial (and more generally, federal) intervention in local affairs. In addition to legislative reapportionment, the justices expanded protections for accused criminals and established new rights to privacy, diminishing the power of local lawmakers, courts, and police, which until then had often acted with impunity from judicial oversight. Even more divisive were the court's rulings on public education. *Brown v. Board of Education* (1954) outlawed racially segregated schools, though it took a passel of subsequent rulings—and increasingly coercive mandates—to achieve even minimal compliance. Meanwhile, *Engel v. Vitale* (1962) and *Abington v. Schempp* (1963) prohibited state-sponsored religious exercises in schools. Both initiatives generated widespread resistance, with parents complaining that judges "put the Negro into the schools, and took God out."[39]

Needless to say, conservatives resisted these developments, which to them represented an intrusion into community decision making and individual rights.

When business magnate Robert Welsh founded the John Birch Society, in 1958, "Impeach Earl Warren!" became the organization's unofficial slogan. Using a monthly newsletter and public advertisements, Welsh called for local resistance against federal dictates. Birch Society members began to run for town councils and school boards, where they passed symbolic denunciations of communism and the United Nations, or disrupted meetings with organized heckling and grandstanding. The Birch Society attracted media attention as a new type of extremist organization, but in fact its infrastructure and methods were not new at all. At least since World War I, the American Legion, the Sons and Daughters of the American Revolution, and other groups of self-styled patriots had promoted conservative causes across the country. The strength of these organizations was not merely that they generated local enthusiasm (which could easily splinter, overreach, or lose focus) but that they disseminated uniform talking points to their members while concentrating power around the national leadership. Thus, ironically, while the John Birch Society and other groups agitated for local control they also represented an increasingly coordinated conservative movement, willing to pursue their goals through the same national institutions that they criticized.[40]

By the late 1960s, the success of the grassroots right was no longer measured by school board victories but by its influence on national elections, epitomized by politicians like Richard Nixon, and the appointment of conservative judges to undo the damage of the Warren court. Although that strategy was somewhat effective—Richard Nixon replaced three members of the court with more conservative successors and nominated four conservatives in all between 1969 and 1971—the right wing was mistaken to put its faith in the Burger court, which several scholars have labeled an "incomplete counterrevolution." As later chapters explain, ostensibly conservative members of the court actually reinforced many of the earlier civil rights rulings, and in areas of gender equality and individual privacy went even further than the Warren court had, most famously with *Roe v. Wade* (1973). Although the justices supported local control in some instances, the commitment to individual rights tended to undermine their support in practice.[41]

The tenuous status of localism in the courts eventually led conservatives to adopt new tactics. In *Age of Fracture* (2012), historian Daniel Rodgers argues that right-wing activists resisted the "centralizing ambitions" of midcentury liberalism by borrowing the Left's language of rights, participation, and community, which they harnessed to "the anti-statist anger of those who had felt betrayed by the social projects of the 1960s and early 1970s." Rodgers specifically mentions campaigns against court-ordered busing, property taxes, and the secularization of school curriculum, suggesting that public education was central to conservative reformulations of community and rights discourse.[42] Yet one should note that demands for participatory democracy did not merely reinstate older notions of community governance. Rather, they entwined with newer, liberal beliefs about state and federal power. As Rodgers notes, court rulings in favor of minority groups and rights of conscience began to shift conservative populists and intellectuals away from the rule of local majorities to the narrower rhetoric of individual rights, with corresponding emphasis (in education) on parental choice, market competition, and religious exemptions. At the same time, many conservatives also came to recognize the benefits of stronger state and federal oversight, which promised greater academic quality and accountability and greater discipline on school spending. By the end of the 1980s, these trends led to the paradoxical alignment of market-based reforms and federal accountability standards that would produce No Child Left Behind (2001) and undercut the conservative commitment to localism. Moralists and libertarians would hang together, but at strata above and below local government.

School Reform and the Threat to Local Control

In an educational context, the dichotomy between individual choice and federal governance is not a new development. Quite the contrary: the two positions correlate to a longstanding philosophical argument about whether parents or states reserve the right to educate children. Parents have traditionally claimed sovereignty on the basis of natural rights. Because families are bound biologically, emotionally, and spiritually, parents seem the best protectors of their children's interests, which are taken to be an extension of their own. Moreover, since they bear the expense of childrearing, parents can assert a proprietary interest in their offspring. For most of the eighteenth century these beliefs led families to teach their own children or participate in an unregulated educational market, with parental prerogative both standing in for and stifling the growth of state-controlled education. At the turn of the nineteenth century, however, when the nation's leaders sought school systems appropriate to new forms of republican government, reformers like Thomas Jefferson proposed a national school system based on Plato's *Republic*, a treatise that recognized schools' centrality to social improvement and effective citizenship. Plato saw the family as an antisocial institution that undermined the rule of reason by propagating baseless folk wisdom and undermined the public good by favoring some children over others. He hoped to ensure equal opportunities for all children, regardless of the circumstances of their birth, by dissolving nuclear families and allowing the state to monopolize education. Rather than relying on the individual decisions of parents, a republican school system would operate as an all-encompassing machine to advance talent and instill patriotism, ensuring both fair outcomes and social stability.[43]

Over the course of the nineteenth century, Americans came to doubt the free market in education as a sufficient guarantor of the public good—rising immigration and urban poverty seemed to demand some sort of government intervention—but neither did they endorse proposals for fully centralized school systems. Local control became an inelegant compromise between the two positions. Schools benefited from public funding and oversight but still comprised the smallest, most intensely local stratum of government, with multiple districts operating *within* a single municipality. Districts were required to offer some provision for tax-supported education, but parents retained significant control over its duration and content. That compromise did not solve all disputes over parental or state responsibility; it merely established a minimal standard of uniformity while allowing communities a degree of self-determination. Between 1800 and 1915, hundreds of thousands of small, one-room schoolhouses appeared across the country, built and administered by local parents.

It is important to remember, however, that constitutionally, education remained a state responsibility, and that school districts were no freer from oversight than towns had been. Indeed, beginning in the 1920s and certainly by the 1940s, school district consolidation became a glaring exception in the trend toward home rule. Thousands of small communities maintained political independence at the same time that they *lost* control of their schools. Preparation for the growing number of white-collar jobs in the decades after World War II required massive expansions in secondary education, with broader course offerings and more modern school buildings than small districts could provide. Lobbying from business and professional groups impelled state governments to raise school funding thresholds and strengthen standards for attendance, curriculum, and facilities, issues that had previously been left to local authorities but were in principle state interests and therefore excluded from home rule charters. As a result, even as new municipalities and special districts used home rule legislation to fragment the suburban landscape, the number of school districts declined steadily through the 1970s (see figure 1).[44]

School district consolidation was accompanied by a growing state and federal role in education during the postwar era. By the late 1940s, the financial deprivations of depression and war had delayed school renovations and construction for nearly twenty years. School districts faced a profound shortage of classroom

Local government agencies, 1945–80

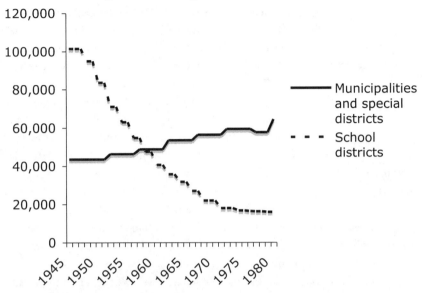

FIGURE 1. Even as suburbs multiplied and established rights to home rule, school district autonomy diminished until the 1970s.

space, soon to be compounded by the demographic pressures of the baby boom. The persistence of outdated buildings accounted for the thousands of one-room schools still in use, but it also put them squarely at odds with growing calls for school construction funds from the federal government, so-called general aid to education. Federal funding proposals foundered through the 1950s, hung up over questions about whether money would be available for racially segregated schools or parochial schools, as well as whether the federal government had the right to get involved in education in the first place. The launch of Sputnik in 1957 and the "discovery" of American poverty in the early 1960s allowed compromise on those issues and finally provided a rationale for state and federal aid to schools, altering the educational landscape with astonishing speed. State support for schools rose from $1 trillion to $31.8 trillion nationwide between 1945 and 1975, while the passage of the National Defense Education Act (1958) and the Elementary and Secondary Education Act (1965) boosted federal contributions from $41 million to $6.3 billion. Although consolidated districts and wider tax bases raised the amount of local spending as well, property tax revenues fell as a proportion of overall expenditures—from 64 percent to 46.5 percent—lessening the tax burden on landowners while opening the door to new systems of top-down, bureaucratic oversight. Soon, courts and regulatory agencies were using subsidies from the Elementary and Secondary Education Act as an incentive to implement district-wide desegregation programs. By 1979, the Carter administration made the Department of Education a cabinet-level post, cementing the federal government's role in educational policymaking.[45]

But paradoxically, and to the frustration of many reformers, the same factors that had increased state and federal involvement in education also redoubled the importance of local school boards. One reason was that the growing importance of education tightened connections between public schools and municipal growth. Suburbs enticed homebuyers with promises of good schools at low tax rates, but they could only sustain those conditions with a wealthy property base. Communities that attracted too many newcomers (or those of too modest means) faced costly, contentious school expansions, while those that achieved affluent, low-density growth could maintain better schools with less effort, solidifying their elite status and strengthening their hand in future development. As one might expect, then, local control of education became sacrosanct anytime that it gave one town a competitive advantage over its neighbors.

Another source of conflict was the high level of civic participation in the suburbs. In 1957, sociologist James Coleman observed that suburban parents were "taking part more and more in school-community organizations," a trend he attributed to their own educational levels and the accessibility of political offices. Schools were an ideal site for grassroots activism. They received the lion's share of tax revenues and remained most communities' largest public forums, open to any adult who wanted to speak or serve on the board. Moreover, schools imbued almost any political cause with the aura of children's welfare, leading board members to hold forth on issues well outside their purview—from street crime to international communism—and requiring principals to add classes addressing their concerns. Thus, while suburban parents supported the efforts of state or professional groups to improve the quality of education in general, many saw attempts to take school administration out of local hands as a threat to democracy, particularly when coming from unelected officials.[46]

The argument here is not that suburbanites reversed trends toward centralization or a robust state and federal role in education, but rather that they manipulated these trends in ways that preserved their interests and established legal protections for local control within the new regime, even without constitutional provisions for home rule of education. It is no coincidence that support for school district consolidation waned during the mid-1970s, just as the process began to affect the suburbs. Although suburban districts were by that time larger and more bureaucratic than their rural predecessors, they were not as large as reformers had hoped. They were too small to overcome the effects of housing segregation, for instance, which installed racial and class segregation as firmly between districts as it had once been within them. They were also too small to equalize per pupil spending: despite increases in state and federal aid during the 1960s, most districts continued to rely on local property taxes for a significant portion of their funding, ensuring that property-rich suburbs would not have to share resources with their needier neighbors. Finally, while consolidated districts allowed for more qualified teachers and administrators, they were often not large enough to shift curriculum, hiring, or spending decisions from school boards to superintendents. In each of these areas, school governance remained closely aligned with issues of municipal independence, and in each of them legacies of rural education played a decisive role.

Unfortunately, existing histories of education do not explain the interaction of rural and suburban schools very well. For nearly forty years, historians of education have operated within the paradigm of David Tyack's *The One Best System* (1974), with the preponderance of scholarship focusing on the rise of urban school systems during the Progressive Era, and their subsequent decline.[47] Surprisingly little has been written about schools outside of cities during the same period. Suburbs have appeared peripherally in discussions of racial desegregation—usually in the undifferentiated context of "white flight"—but there are almost no scholarly histories on the character or development of suburban schools themselves.[48] Meanwhile, most studies of rural education focus on the nineteenth century and end with the onset of district consolidation in the early twentieth. Few have followed the process to its conclusion or explored its aftereffects.[49]

Suburban schools and the legacies of rural education have only recently attracted some scholarly attention. Tracy Steffes, in a book about state regulation of schools during the Progressive Era, devotes an entire chapter to district consolidation. Echoing a point that Tyack and others first made decades ago, she argues that nonurban areas and "the 'primeval forest' of state government and law . . . [still remain] largely uncharted territory" for educational historians, and calls for new research to expand beyond the traditional urban sites.[50] Economist William Fischel likewise devotes several chapters to rural schools in his book about educational funding, while Jonathan Zimmerman's book traces the cultural legacy of the one-room schoolhouse into the twentieth century.[51] Historians Jack Dougherty, Karen Benjamin, and Ainsley Erickson have published articles on the connections between suburban schools, real estate markets, and segregation.[52] Finally, John Rury, in studies of metropolitan Kansas City, has illustrated some of the connections between rural and suburban resistance to school district consolidation.[53] While the remainder of this book is indebted to the work of all of these scholars, it also offers a different, more detailed view of the relationship between educational modernization, conservative activism, and the structures of suburban inequality.

Conclusion

It is difficult to overstate the significance of local government in twentieth-century politics. As state and federal officials asserted new forms of regulatory power, school boards, town councils, and other municipal agencies emerged as a counterweight, becoming sites of public protest and ultimately obstructing many aspects of social and economic reform. Their advocates developed effective, commonsense slogans equating localism with democracy, equality, and freedom, giving the impression that home rule and local control meant something clear and unchanging in U.S. politics. They did not. Like any political position, the defense of local government was a product of changing times and selective interpretations. Its meaning shifted as Americans confronted new spatial and demographic arrangements, and its legal success depended largely on its capacious meanings.

Local autonomy had almost no legal basis before the 1890s, when a handful of states added home rule amendments to their constitutions, and even then it was primarily used to empower cities at the expense of suburban and rural areas. It was the rise of mass suburbanization between the 1910s and the 1950s that prompted calls to protect small-town government, with attendant rights of zoning, tax collection, and geographical integrity. Conceived in opposition to political machines and profligate spending, the notion of local control became popular with a variety of interest groups, especially rural and suburban conservatives, for whom localism preserved existing systems of political power and smoothed over potential areas of division. Local control accorded well with ideas of small government and the free market while sanctioning communities' racial, linguistic, and religious norms, satisfying libertarians as well as traditionalists, and rural elites as well as suburban homeowners. As Suleiman Osman notes, between the 1950s and the 1970s, the defense of localism became "a crusade against 'planners' and 'big developers'—all epithets for the New Deal coalition of realtors, planners, business leaders, politicians, civic groups, and nonprofit institutional directors who since World War II had spearheaded a program of urban redevelopment in cities around the country."[54]

Despite pressure from central planners and scrutiny from state and federal courts, Americans' commitment to local control has proven remarkably durable. Legal challenges to school segregation, discriminatory housing, environmental policy, or any other area of local concern continue to provoke widespread backlash and grassroots political activism. Richard Hofstadter attributed such reactions to small-town Americans' reflexive, neurotic defense of their social privilege. That interpretation was perhaps understandable during the anti-communist hysteria of the 1950s, but one wonders, in hindsight, what was so psychotic about defending one's self-interest amid major redistributions of wealth and power, a reaction that in any other context would simply be described as democratic? Moreover, who could now claim that liberalism actually produced the benefits that Hofstadter considered self-evident, that the celebration of "large institutions, comprehensive planning, social science, and cooperation between big government and big business" was inherently superior to the "smallness, intimacy, voluntarism, subjectivity, and privacy" that it replaced? Ultimately, the shortcomings of Hofstadter's argument stem less from his conflation of populism and paranoia than from his conclusions about their legitimacy, which he dismissed outright. Conservative populism was neither a contradiction in terms, as Hofstadter assumed, nor was it a relic of a premodern society. The democratic institutions and traditions that he described were integral to the practice of local government, and thus inseparable from the long arc of American democracy. Inveighing against them merely encouraged conservative groups to compromise on local issues, craft new forms of political rhetoric, and mobilize voters around seemingly longstanding rights that were suddenly under threat.[55]

It is important to explain the lasting appeal of localism—and small-town conservatism in general—because many commentators continue to misinterpret its basis and pathologize its adherents. Just as Hofstadter tried to explain why Progressive groups were committed to ostensibly backward notions of economic progress, books like Thomas Frank's *What's the Matter with Kansas* (2004) cannot understand why today's working- and middle-class voters support economic policies that benefit the wealthy. Both authors frame their answers in terms of psychological maladjustment. There is a conservative type, they assume—irrational, morally rigid, unable to accept change—whose misplaced fervor impedes any attempt at social reform. From communism to abortion, cultural issues whip conservative voters into a frenzy while distracting them from their economic interests, making them pawns of shadowy corporations. These claims are as specious as they are condescending. Several historians have pointed out that conservative economic policies have promised real benefits to consumers, small-business owners, and rural Americans since the 1970s, and done so in culturally sensitive ways. Others have questioned why economic issues are intrinsically more important than voters' moral and religious values. It often seems that liberals have discounted the voices of working-class Americans, seeking to uplift or educate them instead of acknowledging their legitimate hopes and insecurities.[56] Rather than assuming that they are dupes of corporate interests, or nostalgists who, "unable to face the future, [have] sought refuge in the past," it is helpful to understand defenders of local government on their own terms.[57] To its supporters, local government ensures self-determination, egalitarianism, diversity, and efficiency, all counterpoints to the failures of centralized government.

Its detractors, meanwhile, see exclusion, corruption, and redundancy, the very features that made centralization appealing in the first place. Weighing the merits of these positions requires a fair assessment of both sides as well as a long-term understanding of their history. The best venue for that analysis, and the site of the most fervent and sustained debates about the meaning of local control, is the local school district.

THE LONG HISTORY OF SCHOOL DISTRICT CONSOLIDATION

Few stories in U.S. history seem as straightforward as the disappearance of the one-room schoolhouse over the course of the twentieth century. State-ordered consolidation followed a dramatic, inexorable course. Of the two hundred thousand one-room schools in operation across the country in 1915, only twelve hundred remained open in 1975 (see figure 2).[1] In their place rose larger, age-graded schools with certified teachers and professional administrators, supervised by centralized school boards and state departments of education—a more modern, efficient, and urban system, proponents argued, albeit one increasingly abstracted from parents and local taxpayers. Many historians have described this process, but they have done so almost wholly in the context of the Progressive Era, when consolidation began, and have rarely explored its conclusion. That is, in part, because historians use turning points to punctuate larger trends of cultural ascent or decline, a structure which heightens contrasts and offers clear explanations of cause and effect but also tends to foreshorten events at the beginning and end of the story, ascribing them meaning only in terms of the change at its center. In this case, by focusing on the onset of school consolidation in the early twentieth century, historians reduce the thousands of one-room schools operating in subsequent decades to a sort of denouement or epilogue.[2]

Taking a longer view reveals a more complex story. Almost half of the United States' one-room schools closed in the years after World War II, and there were significant variations in the pace and extent of consolidation even then.[3] Rates of annual decline in the upper Midwest, for example, correlate closely with the national average. Yet Illinois, which had the most school districts in the nation at

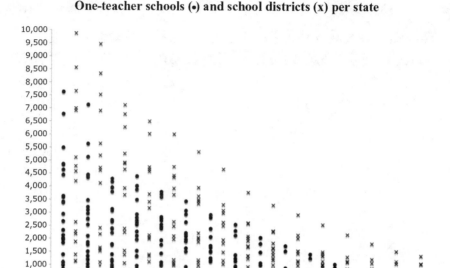

One-teacher schools (•) and school districts (x) per state

FIGURE 2. Often seen as a vestige of the nineteenth century, more than fifty thousand one-room schools continued operating through the middle of the twentieth century.

the end of the war, passed a reorganization plan in 1945 and closed its smallest schools in the space of only a few years. Wisconsin and Iowa also closed theirs very quickly—Wisconsin fell from several thousand one-room schools to eight in just five years—but did not do so for another decade. Michigan followed suit shortly after that, but by preserving many of its small high schools it retained twice as many districts, proportionally, as either Wisconsin or Iowa. Minnesota, meanwhile, passed a reorganization plan in 1948 but gave school districts until 1970 to comply with it, resulting in a more even rate of decline and more complete consolidation of districts than in any of the other states (see figures 3 and 4). These variations, which can be found in every region of the country, should remind us that consolidation played out in diverse local contexts and was neither uniform nor inevitable. Like any transfer of power, its timing, methods, and extent were politically contested and often lurched their way through state legislatures.

In each of these states and across the country, consolidation's degree of success depended on concessions to local control. When state governments respected local prerogative, as in Minnesota, the process proceeded slowly but smoothly. When they did not, faster change generated friction and long-lasting resistance

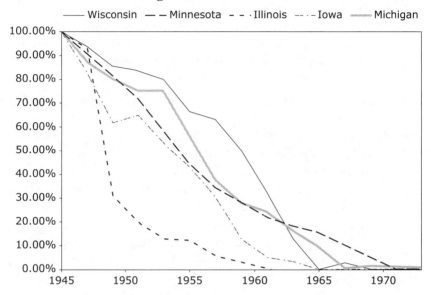

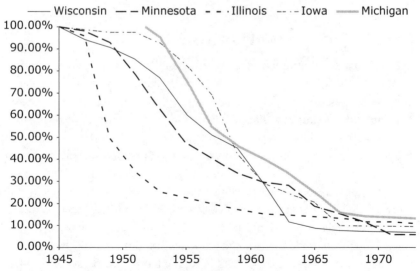

FIGURES 3 AND 4. The pace and methods of school consolidation differed between states.

to state encroachment. One-room schools had almost entirely disappeared by the 1970s, but their prolonged period of closure both reflected and caused ongoing debates about the centralization of school governance—that is, while consolidation stood as one of the most successful reforms of midcentury liberalism, it remained unresolved long enough to contribute to liberalism's decline.

Although every state differed in its educational policies and every community in its reaction to them, the history of rural school consolidation can be divided into three general periods. During the first, from 1890 to 1945, school closures followed a divisive but generally democratic process initiated at the local level and buoyed by increased state funds for school construction and the transportation of students. These incentives increased during the second period, from 1945 to 1965, but so too did penalties for districts that refused to consolidate. State departments of education began to raise requirements for school size, funding, and curriculum, forcing many rural districts to combine regardless of local preference. It was during this period that opposition groups formed, hoping to end what they regarded as the overreach of unelected officials. Their efforts were only marginally successful, and the vast majority of one-room schools closed by the mid-1960s. Nevertheless, residual opposition continued during the third period, from 1965 to 1985, when resistance to consolidation merged with broader critiques of the financial and moral costs of modern education.

Origins of Consolidation

Before the twentieth century, most Americans attended small schools administered under the "district system." Predating and often transgressing town boundaries, neighborhood school districts operated with significant independence from municipal boards, much less state legislatures. A group of farmers or townspeople would elect a school board and petition their state to recognize the new district. After granting recognition, the state's tiny, typically under-funded department of education yielded almost all of its authority to local board members.[4] Without the leverage of supplementary funding, state officials could only advise or gently reprove school boards, ensuring that communities administered schools according to local needs and standards. District voters levied their own property taxes, erected their own modest, one-room schoolhouses, and decided which teachers to hire, what textbooks to assign, and how long terms should last between harvest and sowing seasons. Ungraded classrooms, in which pupils of various ages intermingled and learned at their own pace, combined virtues of social cooperation and individual merit. The study of basic reading, writing, and arithmetic constituted a clear standard of what schools were to teach, just as oral recitation confirmed that students had learned it. Single-year contracts and the practice of "boarding out" in local homes kept teachers accessible and accountable to the community. The schoolhouse itself bolstered civic engagement by serving as a site for voting, recreation, and public meetings. Thus, supporters regarded the one-room school as a symbol of American democracy and common-sense education.[5]

While rural communities took pride in this system, critics claimed that it perpetuated gross disparities in educational quality. In many communities, local custom marginalized racial and religious minorities, disenfranchised tenant farmers, and allowed the same sort of nepotism, graft, and neglect associated with machine politics in the city.[6] Some districts, out of parsimony or simple poverty, chose "to get along with an old dilapidated [schoolhouse], with a six-month school, and the cheapest teacher money could buy."[7] Even under ideal circumstances, opponents noted, a single teacher could not master the breadth of material that a larger faculty could, and students lacked opportunities for age-based competition and camaraderie. By the turn of the twentieth century, high school and college credentials had become increasingly important for employment and even the best rural schools lacked the necessary laboratories, gymnasiums, shops, and equipment for students to pursue specialized, college-preparatory education. In most states only a fraction of rural students attended high school, and at rates five times lower than those in cities.[8] These disparities threatened to put rural students at a disadvantage compared to their urban counterparts. Rather than clinging to quaint traditions of local control, critics argued that true democracy required the consolidation of rural school districts. Parents would have to yield authority to professional administrators and centralized school boards, but their children would accrue the benefits of efficiency already evident in urban systems.[9]

Most states lacked the political will to close one-room schools outright, but by enlarging the districts in which they operated, officials felt that they could undermine residents' willingness to subsidize schools outside of their own neighborhood. They also argued that the increased tax valuation of a consolidated district would create economies of scale, lower the cost of transportation, and allow each school to provide a wider range of academic and social services.

Reorganization began in the late nineteenth century, when states first passed legislation allowing districts to merge their assets and debts. In the 1890s, several New England states forcibly expanded neighborhood districts to correspond with town boundaries, while elsewhere in the country states created or expanded structures of county administration. The county system found fullest expression in the South, a comparatively poor region with a short tradition of public education and the self-imposed financial burden of supporting racially separate school systems. There, the creation of county districts provided enough valuation to sustain high schools—at least for whites—as well as large enough populations of

white and black students to protect racial segregation. Some western states created county districts as well, but in most of the country, county superintendents
merely advised local school boards, leaving traditions of community control intact. With agricultural mechanization, population growth, and the increased
cultivation of farmland, thousands of new one-room schoolhouses continued to
appear every year.[10]

In 1908, when President Theodore Roosevelt commissioned the Country Life
Commission to study standards of living in rural areas, one of the group's primary
recommendations was the consolidation of one-room schools to promote better
teaching and more comprehensive social services. Warnings of a "rural school
problem" gained further traction during World War I, when military induction
found rural youths far less healthy than their urban counterparts—victims of poor
diet, farmwork injuries, lack of adequate medical care, and alarmingly high rates of
illiteracy. These shortcomings threatened to undermine military preparedness and
perhaps U.S. society as a whole, for although urban manufacturing was becoming
more technically sophisticated, much of the workforce still came from the hinter
lands. Smooth production demanded that rural-born workers be able to read, follow orders, and handle the machinery of a twentieth-century factory. To many
reformers, the inadequacies of rural schools seemed a potential source of unem-
ployment and urban blight. Moreover, growing cities required new efficiencies in
food production, so even children who stayed on the farm had to become adept
with machinery and familiar with scientific agriculture, neither of which were
likely to be taught in one-room schools.[11]

By the 1910s, then, the same coalition of education associations, social welfare reformers, labor unions, businessmen, and academics that imposed professional supervision over city school systems also worked to eliminate one-room
schoolhouses in the countryside. In 1914, the Carnegie Corporation published a
pioneering study of reorganization in Vermont, calling for stronger state oversight and a drastic reduction in the number of school districts.[12] The Brookings
Institution produced a similar report for Iowa, noting that "localism has apparently run riot . . . in the case of one-room schools. The consequences are [the]
exceedingly wasteful use of buildings and teaching positions."[13] In California,
Stanford University professor Ellwood Cubberley castigated rural teachers as "almost entirely ignorant of . . . science" and "those qualities of leadership so essential in rural progress," while the National Education Association (NEA) issued
dozens of papers condemning the low pay and lack of professional development
available to them nationally.[14]

Despite a growing consensus on the issue, consolidation proceeded slowly. In
1920, Massachusetts, a perpetual leader in education reform, still had 801 one-
room schools and only 333 consolidated schools. Across the border, less than

two percent of New Hampshire's students attended school in a consolidated district.[15] Nor did combining districts necessarily mean drastic changes to school facilities, especially in the tiny, independent townships of the Northeast and Midwest. Many towns responded to district consolidation by opening larger one- or two-room schools or dividing the newly formed grades between existing schools, so that first through fourth grades would meet in a one-room schoolhouse on one side of town, and fifth through eighth in another.

Some states passed legislation for supervisory unions, which allowed districts to maintain their one-room schools but to pool resources for their joint administration. Yet most districts ignored the reform and those that took advantage of it did not, as reformers had hoped, follow the path to voluntary consolidation. Vermont, for example, responded to the Carnegie study by making supervisory unions mandatory in 1915. Four years later, the state still had over twelve hundred one-room schools and a cohort of frazzled superintendents, each splitting time between dozens of schools and local boards. Under pressure from rural townships, the legislature rescinded the law in 1923. Similar reverses occurred in many other states, underscoring the fact that consolidation was rarely a smooth process.[16]

Neither a unified urban system imposed on resistant rural communities nor a consensual reform that they initiated and welcomed, school district consolidation was a shifting combination of the two, reflecting changes and variability in rural Americans' commitment to local education.[17] Most rural residents supported the construction of high schools, for instance, but at a smaller scale than reformers preferred and with as much provision for local control as possible. Beginning in the 1890s, the most popular methods for providing secondary education were to transport pupils to neighboring towns and pay tuition for their enrollment, or to join union high school districts, which maintained separate boards for component elementary schools.[18] Both arrangements drew complaints from educators. Tuition-based enrollment, they pointed out, offered parents some degree of choice but then denied them a voice in school governance—an argument strikingly similar to present-day critiques of vouchers and charter schools. Moreover, out-of-district placements left the receiving schools susceptible to huge fluctuations in attendance. In Minnesota, for example, where rural districts made enrollment decisions only weeks before the term began, a high school student in the 1930s remembered when "sixty-nine freshmen showed up [unexpectedly] and they didn't even have a place to sit down or enough books." The staff at union high schools could better predict the size of incoming classes but not their students' abilities. Because elementary districts had no way of coordinating their curriculum, high school teachers received students with varying levels of preparation. Meanwhile, the preservation of multiple school boards led to obvious redundancies in equipment, personnel, and maintenance costs.[19]

As long as representation skewed in favor of rural voters, state legislators were unlikely to push too hard on consolidation. As early as the 1920s, however, rural opinion had begun to fracture, resulting in conflicts between rural residents themselves as often as with state officials. Some parents wanted their children exposed to more courses and extracurricular activities in consolidated districts, while others worried that bigger schools would leave children alienated or unable to participate. Some resisted consolidation out of loyalty to local sports teams, while others welcomed it in hopes of fielding more competitive teams. Verbal and physical altercations broke out when school boards discussed the subject, and close votes were common. Consolidated schools, once built, frequently became targets of arson and vandalism. In probably the most extreme example, a disgruntled school board member in Bath, Michigan, believing that the cost of a new consolidated school had caused the foreclosure of his farm, dynamited the building, killing thirty-eight children.[20]

The biggest points of contention in most communities were the potential savings of and distance from the new school buildings. Between the 1920s and the 1940s, state legislatures provided extra funds for school construction and student transportation, essentially transferring money from urban to rural taxpayers in order to encourage consolidation. They tied these funds to nominal standards for curriculum and facilities, set low enough that even most one-room schools qualified, but with clear premiums for those willing to combine. For many farmers, especially those without school-aged children, the decision was coldly economic. It was already common for boards to suspend a school they found too costly, dumping students on neighboring school systems at the last minute on a tuition basis. The same strategy could help shield valuable farmland from taxation by poorer or more populated neighbors: Thousands of districts flouted calls for centralization by maintaining school boards but no schools. By the same logic, however, many abandoned their commitment to local control the moment that state support promised to lower their taxes.

For other rural residents the choice was not so simple. Local schools were a point of pride and gave many communities a reason to exist. Some districts were willing to tax themselves at significantly higher rates than their neighbors to maintain their own schools, worried that consolidation would depress property values and population in outlying areas while accruing more prestige and business for larger towns. Others were simply unconvinced about the promised efficiencies, state subsidies notwithstanding.[21] The financial strains of the Great Depression and World War II brought funding issues to a head but did not offer any clear resolution. Whereas states such as West Virginia used plummeting property values to establish county districts and close one-room schools, others, like Iowa, gave up on consolidation when collapsing farm prices rendered centralized high schools too expensive to build.[22]

Similar divisions appeared over the transportation of pupils. In the 1910s, improved state and county highways lessened the isolation of rural areas, prompting more farm families to invest in automobiles and take advantage of urban shopping and recreational opportunities. Reformers hoped that a mobile population would be willing to transport their children to higher quality schools as well, and to some extent they were. Nevertheless, studies of consolidation votes repeatedly found that distance from a new school inversely correlated with a family's support for its construction. Long rides on a school bus were inconvenient and dangerous in inclement weather, to say nothing about the costs of gas, maintenance, insurance, and drivers. Worse, busing left children unsupervised for long stretches of the day—exposed, parents worried, to the gossip and vices of town life—and prevented them from participating in after-school activities.

To overcome reservations about the cost and distance of consolidation, local, county, and state officials frequently offered concessions to rural areas, including the retention of rural teachers and school buildings, overrepresentation on new school boards, and generous formulas for state aid. These compromises made consolidation politically palatable but undermined many of the efficiencies that it was supposed to achieve, ensuring that the move toward a modern system of public education was gradual, uneven, and, at least through the 1940s, carried out largely on rural terms.[23]

Overreach and Opposition

Consolidation began during the Progressive Era but peaked in the years after World War II. In absolute numbers, the greatest decline in one-teacher schools took place from 1942 to 1952, while the steepest annual percentage losses occurred between 1956 and 1968. Most closures still resulted from local initiative and state incentives, but they also reflected a shift to more coercive policies. Whereas state departments of education grumbled about rural intransigence in the 1920s, legislative apportionment ensured that consolidation decisions remained largely in the hands of rural voters. That political balance began to shift by the 1950s, as cities and suburbs increased their representation in statehouses, educational interest groups expanded their lobbying efforts, and, crucially, rural districts that had already consolidated felt less obliged to support those that had not. Thus, even before court-ordered reapportionment undermined rural political power in the 1960s, liberal coalitions had already begun to dictate many states' educational policies, establishing the sort of formal, bureaucratic oversight that favored larger school districts.

Supporters of consolidation continued to emphasize the importance of local initiative, but more as a nicety than a necessity. Just as rivers and mountains impeded school reorganization "due not so much to their being natural obstacles as to the fact that modern highway improvements had not [yet] . . . overcome them," the once-formidable barrier of local control could now be leveled with a mixture of rhetorical deference and political steamrolling. In a typical remark, an NEA commissioner apologized that "the importance of community values is [often] overlooked in efforts to develop [larger] administrative units," even as he concluded that "people in many rural and small communities have a totally inadequate conception of the scope and quality of education needed for present-day living." The American Association of School Boards likewise encouraged its members to "distinguish between petty localism and the state-wide view" of school governance. Of one-room schools, the American Association of School Administrators said flatly: "They are outdated and outmoded. They have outlived their usefulness. They can no longer do the job that needs to be done."[24]

Nor did reformers any longer confine themselves to criticisms of the one-room schoolhouse alone. Union and small-town high school districts, once considered the goal of successful consolidation programs, were soon deemed too small to meet rising educational standards. Some policymakers began to speak openly about shifting all states to county-wide districts, claiming that ten thousand administrative units—the number operating in Illinois alone in 1945—would suffice for the entire nation. In a widely read report, Harvard University president James Conant argued that high schools with fewer than three hundred pupils could not offer the comprehensive curriculum required for Cold War preparedness, and that enlarged districts represented the most important reform in U.S. education. On the basis of these recommendations, states that had already consolidated their one-room schools underwent another round of painful district closures in the early 1960s.[25]

As the push for larger districts met predictable pockets of resistance, some state officials began to employ methods that violated traditional practices of local control and that many rural residents found undemocratic. The simplest way for states to promote consolidation was to deny subsidies to districts without a requisite number of teachers or students, or to those that lacked adequate facilities, curriculum, or means of local tax support. These standards, ostensibly set by legislatures, could be rapidly reinterpreted or selectively enforced by state superintendents, who tended to blur the lines between legislative mandates and their departments' internal policies. Thus, departments of education could tighten funding to small school districts or make it contingent on higher standards of compliance. Whereas states had once offered extra subsidies to K–8 or union high school districts willing to adopt a K–12 structure, many now denied funds to those districts altogether, essentially forcing their reorganization. Rural areas tended to overlook the preferential funding they had received in the past when they protested that these measures denied them a meaningful vote or a fair return on their tax revenues. Unfortunately, even those willing to forgo state funds often found their credit ratings damaged; unable to borrow money for improvements, their closure became a self-fulfilling prophecy. Opponents also objected to states' increasingly common practice of requiring a simple majority vote across areas slated for consolidation rather than majorities in each affected district, which allowed larger towns to outvote and annex their neighbors in the countryside. Finally, opponents complained that teachers' unions, textbook publishers, and other special interests exercised undue influence over state administrators, who misled local leaders by extolling the virtues of consolidation without addressing its shortcomings.[26]

Statewide opposition groups began to form by the mid-1940s. These were small organizations, usually with no more than a thousand members, but they compounded their influence by coordinating lobbying and letter-writing campaigns with a wider network of farm bureaus, civic associations, and right-wing pamphleteers. Most based their rhetoric on the preservation of local democracy and on the quality of schools rather than their size. As one writer put it, "the general public knows little of what goes on in their schools . . . [and] the bigger the school unit the less the public is going to take part." By publicizing what they considered the unjust actions of state bureaucrats, these groups hoped to stop the ongoing centralization of educational policy. They failed, but in many places they did manage to slow the pace of consolidation and retain some degree of local control.[27]

Wisconsin was at the center of the anticonsolidation movement. In 1939, only fifty-two percent of the state's sixteen- and seventeen-year-old farm children were enrolled in high school—nearly ninety percent of the state's area was not even located in a high school district—and although its urban schools ranked first in the nation in that category, its rural schools ranked forty-second. That year, the state legislature made a tentative move to close the smallest rural districts by shifting the basis of state funding from the number of teachers in a school to the number of students, denying any aid to schools with fewer than ten pupils. It also empowered the state superintendent to dissolve and reorganize districts with less than $100,000 in assessed property valuation. The new regulations closed hundreds of schools but also sparked a backlash among rural voters, who mounted statutory challenges to them in 1941, 1943, and 1945. Their campaigns eventually forced legislators to transfer reorganization authority from the state superintendent to voluntary county committees. The committees then refused to convene, stalling any further reform. From a peak of 7,777 school districts in 1938—ninety-seven percent of which employed fewer than three teachers—Wisconsin still had 5,445 in 1950.[28]

Advocates of consolidation recognized that further progress was impossible without compromise. In the late 1940s, the Wisconsin legislature approved busing subsidies for rural schools while at the same time denying state aid to suspended districts (those which taxed residents but did not operate a school) and raising the charges for out-of-district high school tuition.[29] Rather than dictating new district boundaries themselves, legislators devolved responsibility to county committees, now required to meet and equally comprised of rural and village residents. These committees, heralded as a compromise between state-ordered consolidation and local initiative, were meant to convince rural residents that consolidation could provide better education without jeopardizing the democratic governance of schools. As the state superintendent G. E. Watson said, "[We must] reorganize school districts to overcome local district inadequacies and to create a local district structure that can justify state equalization aid support as well as strong leadership and strong local control. It was the belief of the legislature that reorganization of school districts would go a long way to enable communities to solve their own local school problems. . . . Each county situation requires a plan of its own, designed specifically to meet its needs and meriting the support of the people to be served."[30] Despite Watson's assurances, the county committees continued to generate criticism. One woman in Polk County complained, "Any legislation that groups the powers of the masses into the hands of the few isn't good, and [is] absolutely contradictory to the principles that founded our country and our educational system and our democratic way of life." Her sentiments were widely shared, and in 1949 the legislature instituted a referendum system to let majorities in the affected districts decide whether or not to consolidate.[31] Preserving rural schools was widely popular and their closure was hardly inevitable. The historian William F. Thompson argues that even as Wisconsin's legislature worked to modernize the educational system, it "tailored the process of reorganization to meet the demand of local communities [so] that basic decisions about local schools remained in local hands. This was a major victory for those people who opposed forced consolidation by the state."[32]

Even so, by coupling state support and regulation with safeguards for local governance, the Wisconsin legislature eventually won rural residents over to the logic of consolidation. Melvin Sprecher, a school committeeman near Sauk City, acknowledged that while his town gave up a "valuable asset" in its one-room school, he recognized that the "rural area and urban area [should come] together equally to share responsibility for financing the school system. Our country kids [needed] equal opportunity to urban kids to get ahead." Alfred Ludvigsen, an assemblyman from rural Waukesha County, overcame his opposition as well, conceding "that school consolidation, if accomplished under proper procedures, was a means by which small and financially hard-pressed school districts could consolidate their resources and thus preserve local control." Satisfied that consolidation did not mean the imposition of state regulation, an additional fifty-six percent of Wisconsin's districts closed voluntarily by 1960.[33]

Not everyone was convinced. As compromise made school consolidation more tenable it marginalized groups such as the Wisconsin Rural Schools Association (WRSA). Founded in 1944, the WRSA was the state's largest advocate for one-room schools. Its directors claimed to represent farmers who were "bitter and rebellious over the fact that legislation affecting hundreds of school districts . . . was being slipped through the Legislature by the State Educational Department without any public discussion."[34] Activists tried to mobilize pockets of resistance through litigation and mass protest, but most rural districts closed willingly, ensuring legitimacy for the reorganization plans and irrelevance for the WRSA.[35]

By the middle of the 1950s, the association's cause had grown desperate and headlines in its *Messenger* newsletter became increasingly shrill. Invoking the anti-communist language of the McCarthy era, they denounced the Department of Public Instruction's (DPI) "Dictatorship by Bureaucracy," labeled the state superintendent "A Dictator in Action," and questioned the "betrayal" of certain state legislators. In vain, writers pleaded that "the evils of 1947–1949–1951– 1953 may be undone and the people of Wisconsin may again lift their heads to the former proud reputation as leaders in education and not dogs of some foreign 'ism.'" By the end of the decade the WRSA's directors were forced to restructure the organization due to declining membership.[36]

As the 1950s drew to a close, one-room schoolhouses seemed to be on their last legs in Wisconsin. Yet they continued to generate controversy because of the state's abrupt and unpopular endgame. After two decades of slow progress, administrators at the DPI grew impatient and decided to replace popular referendums with more efficient methods of reorganization. In 1959, the legislature approved a law that all rural schools had to integrate into high school districts by 1962 or lose state funding. The ruling forced over a thousand districts to close in a single year, effectively killing the one-room schoolhouse in Wisconsin. After falling from 5,445 in 1950 to 2,371 in 1960, the number of districts in the state fell to 572 in 1965. The number of students in small rural schools fell as precipitously. In 1960 there were 28,443 students in single-school districts. There were only 1,695 in 1965. Wisconsin's newly elected state superintendent, Angus Rothwell, pronounced rural schooling the most pressing inequality facing Wisconsin students, and consolidation the most necessary reform. His public statements continued to stress local control in the matter, but they gave it significantly less credence than his predecessor had a decade before (see figures 5 and 6).[37]

While rural residents had anticipated these changes, many were angry about the way in which they were implemented. Putting high school boundary lines in the hands of the state superintendent meant that rural boards no longer administered their own schools and that they had only limited choices about where to send their children. Some board members, applying to join an adjacent district, made gloomy speeches "that they would integrate with a high school district only because state laws . . . require it, and not because they prefer to integrate. They do not wish to give up their independence." Meanwhile, city and town boards lobbied the DPI to cede them portions of the closed districts, hoping to increase their own tax bases. From one farmer's perspective, "it was like a land grab . . . and that is how our town got divided. Some of the people in these villages would try to get as much territory as they could." An assemblyman from Green Bay agreed, "This is an annexation bill as well as an education bill." Finally, the state's rush to complete consolidation ensured that the process was

FIGURE 5. Halfway Prairie School, a small, wooden structure in Mazomanie, Wisconsin, operated from 1844 until statewide consolidation in 1962. (Author's collection)

FIGURE 6.   Wisconsin Heights High School, in Mazomanie, Wisconsin, is typical of the large brick and cinderblock buildings erected after consolidation. (Author's collection)

poorly managed. Even parents who supported consolidation in principle complained about overcrowding and inexperienced teachers at the new schools, lack of representation on consolidated boards, and the wastefulness of one-room schoolhouses standing idle.[38]

Discontent revived accusations of Soviet-style dictatorship. Melvin Sprecher, the committeeman from Sauk City, remembered being accused of being "communistic or socialistic" and getting threatening telephone calls after visiting farming communities. "We were the most hated men in the world," he sighed. Voicing the era's populist paranoia, an angry father warned that "school administrators have put their faith in the power of psychology to overwhelm the minds of the unskilled members of the boards of the state. . . . Indoctrination is already extensive and many minds are conditioned for the 'New World.'" Another declared, "I would rather my boy and girl never learn to read, in preference to existing under the seemingly unavoidable socialistic police state of the future." Although such rhetoric was neither new nor unanimous in farming communities, its resurgence in the early 1960s was a direct response to the state's expedited consolidation policies. In various forms, it continued to simmer for decades.[39]

Other states experienced similar types of backlash. In 1945, the Iowa state superintendent proposed a system of county supervisors, increased transportation aid, and forced closure for schools that did not meet minimum standards for size and curriculum. The measure passed in 1947 and was revised in 1953 to give the state superintendent even more power to close schools. Because of these provisions, the president of the Iowa Association of School Boards proclaimed,

"the period of bitter hate and animosities developed over school district reorganization attempts is approaching an end in Iowa." Nothing could have been less
prophetic. In 1957, citizens from the state's smallest counties formed the Iowa
Schools Organization (ISO), a group intended to preserve local control of education. In 1959, the organization campaigned to make the state superintendent
an elected office and attempted to dissolve the newly formed state board of education. Neither entity represented public opinion, they argued: The superintendent was beholden to special interests like the Iowa State Education Association,
and voting for the state board had, at that organization's behest, been conducted
only in county seats, denying small districts any voice in the election.[40]

The legislature rejected the ISO's petitions on a sixty-to-forty vote and instead, like Wisconsin, passed a measure requiring all schools to join a high school
district by 1962. Undaunted, the ISO sued the state superintendent for abusing
his authority to close substandard districts. They pointed out that the number of
districts denied state funds had risen substantially over previous years, despite
no change in the standards or in the districts themselves (see table 1). Indeed,
whether on the basis of size, curriculum, or per pupil spending, there seemed to
be no way of knowing which districts would be disapproved in any given year. If
not outright favoritism, they argued, this was certainly not democracy. The Iowa
Supreme Court sustained the ISO's objections in 1964, ruling that the superintendent's actions were arbitrary and violated the state constitution. The following year, the state senate ignored the superintendent's recommendations and
required fewer vocational classes in high schools, making it easier for rural districts to adhere to curricular standards. The senate also rejected a proposal to
raise minimum enrollment from 300 to 1,500 students per district. In the meantime, campaigns to remove the state board of education continued, loudly if un-
successfully, through the 1970s.[41]

TABLE 1.   Iowa's spike in involuntary closures suggests both state coercion
and community resistance during the final years of district consolidation.

	IOWA SCHOOL DISTRICTS, 1958–62		
	DISTRICTS	ONE-TEACHER SCHOOLS	INVOLUNTARY DISTRICT CLOSURES
1958	3,303	2,067	2
1959			44
1960	2,022	863	73
1961			7
1962	1,164	224	1

Underlying all of these changes was a rhetorical commitment to participatory democracy rather than state bureaucracy. "Over the last 20 years," wrote an Iowa state senator, "our state department of public instruction has grown from an agency of less than a dozen employees to more than 350 full- and part-time employees, more than half of them being paid all or partly from federal funds and therefore under no control by Iowa electors." Whether or not they supported one-room schools or rural districts in particular, many Iowans believed in local control of education and resisted what they perceived as the high-handedness of unelected officials on the matter.[42]

The same sort of political back-and-forth played out in almost every state undergoing the rapid, final stages of school consolidation. The Kansas Supreme Court declared a district reorganization law unconstitutional in 1945 after a challenge from the Kansas Rural School Association, and school closures there continued at a dramatically slower pace through the 1950s.[43] In 1962, the Pennsylvania Association of Township Supervisors opposed that state's reorganization plan, arguing that "the democratic method, having failed to achieve the central concentration of educational powers desired by the professional educators, is to be replaced by an autocratic method, and reorganization is to be made compulsory with no provision for the participation of the people in the process." The group raised enough public support for the Pennsylvania House of Representatives to repeal the measure, though the Senate kept it in place on a party-line vote.[44] Vermont reinstituted supervisory unions in 1945, but the Committee for Home Rule in Vermont Towns—formed to address alleged abuses by the state department of education—remained a critic of their administration throughout the 1960s and ultimately secured means for their dissolution in the 1970s, when several districts seceded from their unions.[45]

None of these groups preserved one-room schools at any significant scale, and none halted state involvement in public education. One might therefore characterize their victories as narrow or temporary. But they were not fruitless. In many states advocates of local control fought off attempts to close rural districts in the 1960s, while both state and federal courts curbed the power of unelected officials over local school boards. In doing so, these groups restored a greater degree of democracy to school consolidation and, significantly, managed to preserve many districts until political appetite for the process had abated.[46]

Resistance by Another Name

Even where it was ostensibly complete, school consolidation could generate conflict for decades. Rural residents who were unable to prevent the centralization of school governance continued to resist those aspects of it that they deemed undemocratic, especially the rising power of teachers' unions, the growing divide between school costs and local tax bases, and professional rather than parental control of the curriculum. In 1974, the NEA complained that rural parents continued "[to] resist efforts to initiate curriculum innovations and new teaching techniques . . . [or to] turn their schools over to professional educators," and that "the rural school principal frequently resists . . . allowing teachers and students academic freedom . . . [in order] to placate his generally conservative school board."[47] In Vermont, controversies over district consolidation led to the firing or resignation of entire school faculties as late as 1980, while a Wisconsin farmer predicted that "the effects of school consolidation . . . will live on for another generation yet."[48]

Lingering resentment over consolidation often converged with new anxieties about academic and moral decline in the classroom. The educational researcher Alan Peshkin documented community conflicts in Crandall, Illinois, thirty years after the consolidation of surrounding school districts. Although Crandall was a hamlet of only two thousand people, residents of smaller, neighboring towns regarded it as a new Gomorrah, "a hotbed of immorality engendered by a population of transient, trailer camp, and divorced persons." Concerns about "smoking, drinking, and sex" and the propriety of sending middle school girls and teenage boys to the same campus led the district to reject centralized junior high schools in 1967, despite the wishes of its administrators. One school board member complained, "We've operated from one crisis to the next ever since I've been on the board. . . . Citizens throw monkey wrenches in our plans so they can't work." Several had begun to threaten lawsuits, and attempts to secede from the district recurred throughout the 1970s.[49]

The same sort of divisions appeared around issues of cost and representation. In 1946, New York's department of education encouraged the towns of Truxton and Preble to consolidate with the city of Homer, a small commercial center in the state's dairy region. While the county commissioner promised that the merger would lower costs, a group of farmers calling themselves the "Preble rebels" objected. By refusing to let them attach themselves to an even cheaper district to the north, they contended, the state was in fact imposing a tax hike. The commissioner, under pressure from rural assemblymen, granted the farmers' transfer and backed away from other objectionable aspects of the reorganization plan: he assured outlying towns that they would maintain a permanent majority on the Homer school board and that Truxton would be allowed to maintain its own high school within the reorganized district. When the district reneged on those promises in the late 1960s, it created a deep division within the community. An observer noted that "even the supporters of the merger [of the Truxton and

Homer high schools]" felt that they were "forced into the decision by the State Department of Education," which would no longer approve aid for the outdated Truxton building. And while property taxes had fallen in the first year after consolidation, they rose steadily thereafter. By the 1970s, rural parents were again voicing their dissatisfaction by complaining that the larger high school encouraged "juvenile delinquency, tobacco smoking, sex, and drug abuse" as well as the promulgation of "liberal ideas."[50]

While many contemporaries regarded these protests as expressions of rural backwardness, they are better understood as ongoing attempts to assert local democracy in public education and, often, to air legitimate grievances about supposed benefits of consolidation that had failed to materialize. While larger administrative units were more efficient in theory, projected cost savings seldom accounted for rising salaries and budgets. Consolidated districts had to staff central offices and distribute materials to distant schools and agencies, an arrangement that could be more expensive than the local systems it replaced.[51] Likewise, although rural residents were prone to see corruption in every action of urban school boards, consolidation did create new opportunities for exploitation and mismanagement, and it seems unlikely that embezzlement, kickbacks, or preferential contracts were any less prevalent than they had been when the stakes were lower.

Transportation was also more costly than reformers expected. Outlying districts understandably asked why busing thirty children to a consolidated school was more efficient than sending a single teacher in the opposite direction, especially when children had to wait for school buses along busy roads in bad weather, and railroad operators repeatedly complained about nearly missing buses at track crossings.[52] Abrupt consolidation orders and the demographic pressures of the baby boom meant that children usually arrived at overcrowded facilities, to the point that many towns actually reopened one-room schools (or their equivalents) to accommodate extra students, continuing an older pattern of operating schools as population dictated.[53] Finally, whereas rural schools had saved money through poor attendance and attrition—allowing them to teach upwards of sixty students in a thirty-student classroom—parental involvement also obscured their rates of dropouts and delinquency. Large high schools, opponents argued, wasted thousands of dollars trying to keep every student in school but had little to show for it.[54] Whether any of these shortcomings outweighed the benefits of consolidation was, of course, a subjective judgment, but renewed criticism in the 1970s suggests that many voters felt misled in their initial support for consolidation, and that larger schools had not fulfilled their promise to rural parents.

A new generation of educational researchers voiced many of the same criticisms. Alan DeYoung, Craig Howley, Jonathan Sher, Faith Dunne, Timothy Weaver, and others questioned their predecessors' equation of size with school quality and worked to reestablish the importance of the local community in educational policy.[55] Several participated in the Experimental Schools project, a federal initiative to revitalize small rural schools, and coordinated their research with family farm activists and groups such as People United for Rural Education.[56] Like many of their contemporaries in urban settings, these scholars criticized the efficacy and accessibility of large institutions, particularly for children from poor families and marginalized populations. They challenged the notion that consolidated schools produced better academic achievement or socialization for rural children, or that they did so more affordably. "One is led to conclude," wrote Weaver, "that some schools simply produce better results than others, but the factors which explain those differences have virtually nothing to do with school size." Since rural students had lower rates of extracurricular participation, advanced coursework, and parental involvement at consolidated schools, he continued, it "simply does not make sense to argue that a retreat from consolidation would harm students."[57]

These arguments won some converts among rural teachers and administrators. Looking back on his career, in 1975, the state superintendent of Vermont wrote: "In the light of trends of recent years I sometimes wonder if I shouldn't have been more vociferous on the human side of education, urgent in warning of the perils of bigness. . . . Probably the most visible effect of my work as commissioner is the crop of union high schools spread over the state. Sometimes I wonder if they have brought us what we wanted. Could they? . . . I must say, I have a great deal of sympathy for some of the expressions of longing for 'the good old days.'"[58] Nostalgia was common, but in most areas it was too weak to stop ongoing trends toward consolidation. Even in Nebraska, whose five hundred one-room schools comprised nearly half of the nation's total in the mid-1970s, exasperated rural activists could not understand why so many residents ignored the latest research, why "the question of whether children receive a good education in consolidated school districts never seems to arise." The primary reason was the depopulation and increasing poverty of rural areas. Academics could tout the benefits of small elementary and high schools, but ultimately communities had to exist to support them. As corporate agriculture forced ever more families off the land—aided by the boom and bust of commodity prices in the late 1970s—it left even some consolidated schools unviable and smaller units numerically impossible. Depleted districts were pushed to their physical limits, with some students busing hours each day to learn with even a small group of peers. Families that remained faced economic hardships, further reducing the community participation and financial commitments necessary to operate small schools. Deprived of the political and social structures that had sustained the one-room schoolhouse, rural communities were left with little more than memories and bitterness, too little to nourish its revival.[59]

Nevertheless, the consolidation campaigns that began in the 1890s are far from settled. Even today, many rural communities are still at odds over the management of local schools. To take one example, Ohio Public Radio conducted an investigative report on rural school districts that did not approve tax levies from the 1970s through the 2010s. Asked why they would not pay for building renovations or increased salaries, local voters complained that their teachers were already overpaid and that the schools were run by "elitist bureaucrats." "The trust is broken," one of them observed, and "it goes back to when several local districts were consolidated." A teacher agreed, saying, "People hold grudges for something that happened sixty years ago and they're going to bring it up to the end."[60] It is far too simple to attribute the persistence of these feelings to stubbornness or personal animosity alone. Just as rural residents supported one-room schools for a variety of reasons, opposition to the current education system draws from numerous sources, including religious faith, anti-tax sentiment, and cultural politics. Ultimately, however, these justifications spring from, and stand in for, a longstanding commitment to community empowerment and the place of local convention in public education.

Conclusion

Rural school consolidation is probably not the first thing that jumps to mind when one thinks about educational reform. The one-room schoolhouse has become sufficiently remote that most Americans have either forgotten about it or relegated it to times long past, with little connection to contemporary educational debates. That oversight is understandable but unfortunate. The closure of rural schools was arguably the most profound change in U.S. education in the last hundred years. The creation of large, modern school systems required massive transfers of wealth and power—a process negotiated and contested at every level of government— and it marked a sharp break with traditional notions of the rights of families and communities. Working together, lawmakers, professional organizations, and state departments of education began to assert control over public education, claiming responsibilities that had previously belonged to school boards and cementing their authority with a glut of new rules and requirements. As state funds flowed to local districts, political authority moved in the other direction: from neighborhoods and towns to legislatures and departments of education.

These changes, divisive enough in themselves, became a crucial test for school reform more broadly. The legal and political success of consolidation campaigns enabled states to assert a new role in education, one that was in no way confined to rural areas. Bureaucratic supervision, judicial arbitration, and rising expectations for school funding and administration would become central to later debates about educational opportunity in cities and suburbs. Indeed, the successful consolidation of rural school districts implied that states had both the right and the responsibility to mitigate inequalities between other districts. Liberal policymakers increasingly demanded uniformity in public education, often at the expense of community. To end invidious local distinctions, they insisted, all school districts would eventually have to succumb to the fate of the smallest.

Rural conservatives rejected the state role in education as overweening and coercive but they struggled to defend themselves against its demands. Most outlying communities lost their local schools. Yet others would take up their decades-long fight against consolidation. Paradoxically, support for small school districts found great success among people with few memories of the one-room schoolhouse and in areas that defied patterns of rural decline. Many towns would preserve their local schools even as they outgrew their rural identity. As suburban families moved into outlying districts, they too discovered the value of small schools and community participation, and many joined rural neighbors in their defense. Their efforts not only initiated a cultural renaissance for the one-room schoolhouse—already an object of popular nostalgia—but reinvigorated debates about the size and administration of school districts themselves. Public anxieties about the control, cost, and content of modern education encouraged activists to reassert traditions of community control, and those traditions proved portable. As consolidation crept from the countryside to the city, the rhetoric of resistance followed. Rural districts were symbols of a simpler past, to be sure, but more than that they became a means to change educational law and politics in the present.

THE EXURBAN EXCHANGE

In the television comedy *Green Acres*, a Manhattan lawyer named Oliver Douglass moves to the fictional town of Hooterville for its "fresh air" and "farm living" only to find himself enmeshed in a series of silly misunderstandings with the locals. An episode from 1970 opens with a pig named Arnold (a stock character) sitting at an elementary school desk, a peashooter in his mouth. When the principal expels Arnold for disrupting class, his owner, a semiliterate farmer, ascribes the action to "prejudice" and the other students go on strike. Douglass tries to arbitrate but is quickly confronted by a suspicious, Bull Connor-style sheriff, setting up a string of punch lines about busing and "outside agitators," references to the school desegregation controversies then wracking the nation. Whereas earlier episodes had avoided mention of current events, these jokes began, gently but overtly, to reference them.[1]

If the shift in tone was meant to attract younger viewers, it was too little too late. *Green Acres* fell victim to CBS's "rural purge" that year, in which the network replaced all of its small-town sitcoms with edgier, urban comedies like *All in the Family* and *Mary Tyler Moore*. Many of the canceled shows still enjoyed strong ratings, but network executives concluded that for a rising generation of Americans, their hayseed humor had become contrived and stale.[2] *Green Acres* obviously relied on rural stereotypes, but it also reflected real demographic changes. Thousands of New Yorkers did move to rural New England, New Jersey, and Pennsylvania during the 1960s, hoping to restore old farmhouses and adopt country ways. And just as Hooterville's goofier characters were set off by nondescript, almost suburban set pieces—including a modern high school, houses with well-kept lawns, and well-dressed, accent-less townspeople—rural towns across the country were rapidly transforming into caricatures of themselves, with agricultural and folk traditions lingering on as local color or tourist attractions in an increasingly sanitized, suburban landscape.

A pig's expulsion might have gotten laughs as a rustic retelling of contemporary educational conflicts, but it should not obscure the changes that suburban growth actually wrought in rural schools, nor the broader connections between school politics in the city and the country. Newcomers to consolidated districts frequently found themselves in the middle of power struggles between administrators and resentful farmers. Their arrival required costly expansions to school facilities and changes in school board representation, points of contention with old-time residents. On the other hand, lingering campaigns against district consolidation also yielded alliances between the two groups, both of whom found reasons to resist the increasing power of teachers, principals, and other non-elected officials in public education. What became clear, first, was that enough residents overcame their differences to slow or stop consolidation on the rural-suburban fringe by the 1970s; and second, that their defense of democratic localism and small school districts played a determinative role in corresponding conflicts between suburbs and cities. That is, just as rural areas suburbanized, suburban areas increasingly identified as rural, invoking the legacy of the one-room schoolhouse to thwart attempts at racial or economic integration with their urban neighbors.

By juxtaposing community conflict with presumptions of rural innocence, then, the *Green Acres* writers were doubly mistaken. At the local level, towns like Hooterville offered residents no escape from divisive school politics; many divided bitterly over issues of funding and curriculum. Meanwhile, at the metropolitan level, rural traditions of community control seeped into suburban politics as a means of challenging liberal paradigms of integration, professionalization, and centralized governance.

The Rural-Suburban Fringe

The suburbanization of the rural United States was an eddy in the larger tide of metropolitan growth after World War II. Whereas forty-five percent of rural communities lost population between the 1940s and the 1960s, twenty-five percent grew faster than the nation as a whole. By the 1970s, these areas had twice the rate of home construction as their urban counterparts and encompassed as much as a third of the United States' rural population. Growth on the rural-suburban fringe was sporadic. It did not radiate in concentric circles from cities and did not occur uniformly across all rural areas. But it was pervasive enough for commentators to coin a new term for such communities, "exurbs," and to generate an extensive sociological literature about them.[3]

Three factors determined the contours of exurban development during this period. The first and most important was access to transportation infrastructure, particularly the interstate highway system. In 1956, the Eisenhower administration secured federal support for highway construction, primarily for national defense but also as an economic stimulus.[4] Popular images from the period associated highways with increased mobility (at least for middle-class whites) and the luxury of commuting to work or shopping centers from spacious suburban housing tracts. But highways had a significant impact on communities outside the suburbs as well. Over the next twenty years, studies found that rural counties with a federal highway in them either suffered less depopulation than those without, or, in many cases, actually gained population. Highways allowed factories to relocate to rural areas, where wages were lower and residents less likely to unionize, and encouraged rural wholesalers like Wal-Mart to build supply chains around long-haul trucking, sidestepping the costly regulation of traditional distribution networks. These shifts blighted many small towns, forcing the closure of main-street businesses and reducing employment opportunities to minimum-wage jobs, but they revitalized others as bedroom communities for increasingly distant cities.[5]

A second factor driving the growth of exurbs was their aesthetic appeal. Rural electrification projects of the 1930s and 1940s not only allowed for more household amenities but (with hydroelectric dams plugging huge reservoirs) created thousands of new lakefront properties.[6] Improved roads sparked a rise in tourism, generating seasonal jobs at parks and resorts and enticing some visitors to make their vacations permanent. By the 1970s, rural communities undergoing the most rapid growth tended to be in the scenic forests of the Great Lakes, New England, and the Rocky, Appalachian, and Ozark mountains. These areas promised newcomers natural beauty, low costs of living, and an opportunity to increase their acreage. Some of the migrants were wealthy jetsetters. The historian Annie Gilbert Coleman cites old-time Coloradans complaining about growth in mountain towns like Aspen and Telluride, which were "sacrificing their singularity to become plush look-alike playgrounds for urbanites."[7] Others were middle- or working-class parents seeking a more wholesome atmosphere for child-drearing. "More people are wanting to live in rural areas," observed a farmer in Trempealeau County, Wisconsin. "They don't like Chicago. They come here without any security and probably leave a good-paying job in Chicago or its suburbs . . . [to raise] a family."[8] The promise of independence, land, and a slower pace of life appealed to an older generation as well. With the expansion of government pensions, many retirees chose to relocate in "places that [offered] beautiful scenery or recreational attractions, from lakes to ski slopes and golf courses," and either bought homes in new retirement communities or farms and cabins with sizable parcels of land around them. In 1978, a Department of Agriculture survey found that while farmers remained the largest class of landowners in the United States, with thirty-eight percent of privately held acreage, the next largest group was retirees, who held 190 million acres, fourteen percent of all private land.[9]

The price of that land was the final determinant of residential growth. Scholars often associate suburbanization with bulldozers inexorably burying natural or agricultural landscapes—with Levittown, for instance, replacing rows of Long Island potatoes with a harvest of ranch houses. But that image holds most true for developments immediately adjacent to cities, where the comparative value of residential land could apply sudden, overwhelming pressure on farmers to subdivide. Beyond metropolitan boundaries, the sheer amount of available land ensured that development remained contingent on agronomic factors. High commodity prices increased the value of commercial farmland eightfold between 1950 and 1980, largely inhibiting residential growth in regions like Iowa's corn belt and the fruit valleys of central California. In the countryside, developers stood to profit the most from agriculturally marginal land, so subdivisions frequently appeared on hillsides, in deserts, or in swamps. Economists in New Hampshire and Minnesota during the 1970s were surprised to note that the soaring price of cropland was actually being outpaced by speculation in northern forests, whose value had increased tenfold over the previous decade on the sale of vacation properties. The Appalachians and the Ozarks also experienced what the author Thomas Wolfe had described in Asheville, North Carolina, twenty years earlier: "sleepy little mountain [villages]" beset by real estate agents "unfolding blueprints and prospectuses as they shouted enticements of sudden wealth into the ears of deaf old women" and "feverishly created [new streets] in the surrounding wilderness."[10]

By the 1950s, the encroachment of suburbs on rural communities had begun to generate interest among sociologists studying rural folkways or the decline of agricultural and extractive industries.[11] When examining the effects of residential growth on local politics, researchers usually pointed to a "culture clash" between old-timers and newcomers, with the latter demanding either more development (of schools, roads, and sewers) or less (of parks and green space) than rural residents were willing to subsidize with their property taxes. One sociologist characterized suburbanization in revolutionary terms. "Dry communities become wet," he intoned. "Churches lose their influence. . . . The new citizens have a haughty attitude toward local citizens and local businesses, [while] local citizens look upon these invaders as foreign intruders." Another warned that wherever "residential developments thin out and mix with rural villages and agricultural interests . . . cleavages are rife, community conflict . . . is likely, and the feeling of community is low." Most agreed that conflict was less pronounced in developments created entirely from scratch than in areas that remained quasi-rural and were therefore "divided between the pushy, progressive, and plastic world of the newcomers on the one hand, and the accustomed world of the old-timers . . . on the other." For several decades, the scholarly consensus assumed that dislocation and conflict were inevitable byproducts of exurban growth.[12]

The first book to bring the subject to popular attention, A. C. Spectorsky's *The Exurbanites* (1955), relied heavily on the culture clash model. Spectorsky, a journalist and future editor of *Playboy* magazine, offered a caustic look at Madison Avenue executives who moved beyond the reach of commuter rail lines to Scarsdale, New York; Fairfield, Connecticut; or Bucks County, Pennsylvania. Echoing the period's preoccupation with lonely crowds and organization men, he presented these transplants as conformist, exclusive, and superficial. In their search for a rustic escape, they blithely drove up real estate prices and, unable to understand "how an ancient village has been able to struggle along" without modern municipal services, turned "their particular public-spirited efforts to rid the river of the rats that [infested] it, or to solve whatever [else] the problem may be." By modernizing their adoptive communities, they marginalized older residents and stripped the towns of all but a façade of rural character.[13]

Growing Pains in Rural Schools

Much of Spectorsky's analysis dealt with school boards, which together with municipal boards and zoning commissions emerged as a primary site of conflict over growth. In Chappaqua, New York, he noted, the student population had risen from 829 to over 1,500 between 1940 and 1952, requiring the construction of new elementary and high schools and a steep rise in the town's property taxes. The bulk of the new students had moved from the city and its inner suburbs, and it was their parents who expressed the strongest support for the new schools. Faced with opposition from local farmers, the newcomers did what came naturally: They launched an advertising campaign. An editor from *Fortune* magazine chaired the parents' committee and an artist from *Collier's* supplied glossy brochures. Bonds soon passed and the schools were built. When the rural residents of neighboring Pleasantville, New York, grumbled that their taxes would not support "such scholastic fripperies as [the] full-time psychologist" demanded by exurban housewives, a similar campaign there succeeded in hiring a school counselor.[14] These examples are somewhat stylized, particularly since Spectorsky limited his attention to upper-class enclaves and did not examine middle- or working-class towns. Nevertheless, the same sort of growing pains affected all communities undergoing exurban development. Any influx of migrants could exceed the capacity of rural schoolhouses and, as in Chappaqua, force towns to issue bonds and raise taxes for school renovations and construction. New subdivisions also required bus transportation, the costs of which could exceed their total tax receipts.[15]

These financial strains were not unique to exurban areas. The spiraling costs of busing and school construction drove a nationwide campaign for federal aid to education during the 1950s. One could argue, however, that the most contentious situations appeared on the suburban fringe, where a few farmers usually bore the heaviest tax burden and retained de facto control of the school board. These landowners resented subsidizing new facilities for outsiders' children, especially when the survival of their own farms remained in question. Suburban parents, on the other hand, chafed at overcrowded conditions and ramshackle buildings. Many had hopes of high school or college for their children and ascribed local obstruction to selfishness or ignorance. As in Spectorsky's examples, they worked to gain control of the school board as soon as possible. Thus, warned an NEA report in 1956, the "rapid suburban concentration of people [could create] a strain upon political machinery designed to serve rural conditions which no longer exist."[16]

Within the schools, differences over the content of instruction were often as divisive as its costs. Whereas many farm families preferred "basic skills taught by a dedicated but maidenly teacher in a plain school building," one researcher noted, suburbanites were not only "irrepressible spenders" but "cult-like in their dedication to the cause of modern education," clamoring for kindergartens, guidance counselors, language labs, and other hallmarks of the progressive education movement. Most were less interested in the Future Farmers of America or 4-H clubs, the pride of many rural high schools, and these programs tended to decline as communities grew. A tragic example of the clash over costs and school culture occurred in Ruthton, Minnesota, in the early 1980s, when a farmer shot dead the owner of the local bank—a Philadelphia transplant—both because the man had threatened to foreclose on his farm and because he had tried to ban corporal punishment in the town's high school. From the perspective of rural residents, improving school facilities or broadening the curriculum not only seemed extravagant and unnecessary but threatened to undermine community mores and, by attracting more developers, to compound population growth and hasten their own obsolescence.[17]

A degree of class conflict underlay many of these incidents, but to portray them merely as clashes between poor farmers and affluent suburbanites is to oversimplify the issue. Even prosperous farmers tended to reinvest their wealth in land, leaving them vulnerable to changing property values and limiting the disposable income with which they could pay their taxes. Thus, their economic interests were fundamentally different from those of newcomers, who had other sources of income and, with a significant investment in their homes, often benefitted from rising land values and better schools. Residents could overlook significant differences of wealth when they divided into rural and suburban camps; whatever their personal assets, they recognized in school policy debates a choice between very different systems of education, taxation, and government. On one side was a traditional system, in which families depended on the land and schools reflected that dependence, reproducing local values while matching their budgets to the economic capacity of surrounding farms, mines, or forests. On the other side was a new system that subordinated production to consumption, commodifying communities themselves and offering families their choice of lifestyle at many different price points. Because suburban homes were marketed with promises of quality education, under the new system local schools became places of growth, competition, and, in multiple senses of the word, enrichment. One can appreciate why both groups might have felt threatened by their neighbors' worldview.

Rural New England offers numerous examples of this sort of conflict. When a researcher explained to the Raymond, New Hampshire, school board that he had arrived to study rural education, a board member glumly informed him that the town was no longer *really* rural since a new housing development had appeared at its edge. Events bore out her pessimism: Raymond was located in the fastest-growing region of the fastest-growing state east of the Mississippi, and the town soon attracted hundreds of new families from across the Massachusetts border. While school board members were "increasingly drawn from a more liberal, forward-looking segment of the community," the town's selectmen remained "conservative 'birth-right natives,'" setting up annual conflicts over land assessment and school budgets.[18] The essayist Noel Perrin complained about Bostonians who moved to New Hampshire for the scenery only to discover "that only about 40 percent of the kids who graduate from [the local] high school go on to any form of college." With little regard for local custom, he found, their remedy was inevitably "a new school building—and also modern playground equipment, new school buses, more and better art instruction at the high school, [and] a different principal."[19]

Observers in Vermont noted similar trends. "Having lost the backbone of their economy—the hill farms, the dairy and sheep industries, and the resort businesses—to out-of-staters," one found, locals seemed even more intent on preserving the "independence [of] local schools and town government."[20] With school budgets doubling every decade and more newcomers seeking a voice in town politics, board meetings devolved into predictable confrontations. One district in central Vermont deadlocked over school consolidation, with the superintendency alternating between nonnatives who supported the process and locals who opposed it. Finding the mixture of farmers and "artisan urban expatriates" too difficult to accommodate, the district ultimately split in two. The Committee for Home Rule in Vermont Towns blamed the entire push for school consolidation on "former residents of metropolitan suburbs," as well as "some misguided lifelong residents who are flattered by the attention paid them by 'important' out-of-staters." At a school board meeting outside Burlington in 1974, a farmer chastised a newcomer: "Stop trying to turn our land into another New York City. If you don't like it as it is, then leave!" Asked where he would be without the dollars that New Yorkers were injecting into the community, he snorted, "I'd be home right now, instead of talking to some darn fool about a [new school] building we can't afford to build.'"[21]

Such sentiments were widespread, but historians and sociologists have begun to question the universality of the culture clash thesis, citing incremental stages between agricultural and residential land use and several issues on which old and new residents could adopt complementary positions. For example, while rising land values made the cultivation of grain and livestock impractical, some farmers could produce perishable, high-value goods such as milk and orchard fruits very close to metropolitan boundaries, supplementing their income with farmers' markets or agritourism, in which suburban families paid a premium to pick their own apples or pumpkins.[22]

Seemingly intractable conflicts over public services and property taxes could also yield common ground. By the 1970s, land trusts, agricultural zoning, and differential assessment of farmland not only eased the tax burden for commercial farmers but also facilitated the growth of hobby farms and large estates. These, in turn, afforded suburbanites the sort of rustic charm that drove up home values. Economists who worried that exempting farmland would hurt local tax receipts frequently found that gentrification offset lost revenue.[23] The result was hardly an even compromise between rural and suburban interests—the word "preservation" suggested that only a few farms would be saved—but conservation measures nonetheless benefited both groups, creating a bulwark of small-scale agriculture and small-scale development that slowed further in-migration. In many communities, agricultural festivals remained points of civic pride, providing legacies of rural identity even as the industries they represented slowly disappeared.[24] In resort towns, too, newcomers came to recognize that unregulated growth could hurt both their view and their investment, and many began to join environmental protection or rural heritage groups.[25]

A similar phenomenon occurred around rural education. Some suburbanites expressed nostalgia for the one-room schoolhouse, which they saw "as a vanished idyll, destroyed by ravaging urbanization" and a source of innovative techniques such as open classrooms, peer-tutoring, and individualized instruction. A teacher in Barnard, Vermont, found that while some students attended her school only during September and October—"probably to afford their parents an opportunity to enjoy our foliage season"—there were enough permanent immigrants to support a private school whose ungraded classrooms were "similar to . . . one room schoolhouses in Barnard in years past." Another teacher who had moved to Vermont from New Jersey bemoaned "the chic couple in the Volvo . . . whizzing past your farm on the way to some writers' conference or antique shop" but appreciated that the same forces of development had given him the opportunity to work in a close-knit rural school. The children's author E. B. White, an immigrant to rural Maine, lamented that since "the State Board of Education withholds its blessing from high schools that enroll fewer than three hundred students," his town had to close its local schools and organize a larger "school administrative district, usually referred to as SAD." "Sad," he wrote, "is the word for it."[26]

But if White was sad, many of his neighbors were mad. "The schools are a mess," he continued, and some residents were so "violently opposed" to the state's consolidation decision that the town had "split wide open."[27] That cleavage suggests a culture clash not just between rural and suburban residents but between liberal and conservative segments within each of those groups. For just as rural parents could disagree over high property taxes, which sustained the village school but threatened the family farm, newcomers brought with them all the educational debates present in urban and suburban districts. "Modern education" could perhaps unify them when it came to replacing dilapidated school buildings, but on questions of school prayer, sex education, evolution, or phonics instruction, it became a catchword for controversy. On many of these issues, suburban conservatives' sympathies lay closer to those of their rural neighbors than to local teachers or superintendents, and, like farmers, they came to appreciate small districts as a means of curbing state and professional power in education. For their part, many rural residents recognized suburban growth as a means of preserving hometown schools. One state administrator complained that rural districts resisted consolidation "on the assumption that no matter how small and inadequate they are at the moment, they soon may be districts with large enrollment." "Expectancy and hope," he wrote, "stand in the way of reorganization."[28]

The course of school consolidation in Arkansas illustrates the point. In 1948, the state narrowly passed a consolidation law requiring that all school districts maintain public high schools. At the time, the Arkansas Education Association

(AEA), the state's largest teacher organization, garnered support for the reform as a means of ensuring equal opportunity for rural students, many of whom would otherwise have been confined to an eighth grade education.[29] As in other states, however, the AEA soon revised its definition of equality upward. It claimed that rural students needed access not merely to a high school but to the comprehensive programs of a *large* high school, preferably one with several hundred students. In 1966, the AEA proposed a bill to consolidate by force any school district with fewer than four hundred pupils. The measure prompted the defection of most of the organization's rural chapters, who re-formed as the Arkansas Rural Education Association (AREA). Rural teachers and administrators objected that the AEA was "interested only in making large administrational units which are easy to control because of their lack of contact with the people involved," and that "control and not educational improvement is their ultimate aim." One of the group's leaders, a graduate of conservative Harding College, called the consolidation bill "a brazen bid for centralized government control and outright dictatorship." Conversely, the AREA promised to promote "the principles of democratic rule" and ensure that "on an issue [like school consolidation] that would destroy a community, the people within that community . . . help decide their own fate."[30]

Strongest support for the AREA came from the communities around Hot Springs, Searcy, and farther north in the Ozarks, areas where small school districts had survived largely as a result of stagnant populations and systematic underinvestment from the state.[31] It seemed silly to finally consolidate these districts in the 1960s, argued local legislators, when the region was rapidly developing as a recreational and retirement destination. "If we can maintain these schools for another decade then it will solve a big problem," they insisted. "The buildings will already be there. If we don't do it, the people [exurbanites] will be looking for classrooms outside town, right where these are." Cutting the ribbon on a bridge in Calico Rock, the outgoing governor, Orville Faubus, noted that the improved roads that had once depopulated rural areas would now allow communities in northern Arkansas to grow, and he promised to support rural schools. Newcomers to the region seemed to follow Faubus's cue. Although Hot Springs representative Ode Maddox was initially apprehensive about campaigning on the school consolidation issue in a district reapportioned to include more suburban constituents, he was surprised to find strong backing for rural schools. In fact, studies showed that most of the signatures opposing the consolidation act came from urban and suburban districts that would not have been affected by its mandates. The rural school bill's defeat signaled a sharp rejection of the AEA's agenda and helped elect the state's first Republican governor since the 1870s.[32]

A similar turn against school consolidation took place in almost every state with growing rural areas and small districts to defend. The publishing magnate Meldrim Thomson moved to Orford, New Hampshire, in 1955 and served quietly on the school board until 1965, when the state threatened to close the town's high school. Successfully enjoining voters to oppose the "educational establishment" and keep the school open, he sparked a three-year controversy in which the board censored teachers, threatened the principal, withheld funds from the supervisory union, and rejected federal money for reading remediation. Thomson was soon elected governor of New Hampshire for his efforts. Attempts to merge districts in northern Michigan likewise met opposition from thousands of white, working-class families who had moved to the region after Detroit's 1967 race riots, winterizing hunting cabins for year-round occupancy. Upset with civil unrest and government regulation, they easily adopted local distrust of "the superordinate powers of persons like . . . the school superintendent." Soon, old and new residents alike came to see "corruption" in any attempt to wrest control of the schools from locals. Newcomers also fought against district consolidation in rural Tennessee, in the villages around Cedar Rapids, Iowa, and in northern California, where the Potter Valley schools successfully seceded from their supervisory union and, led by a retired rancher and a pair of wealthy advertising executives, reestablished a small, autonomous district. As exurbanites moved farther into the countryside, they reinvigorated their adopted communities with money and political voice, helping them resist consolidation even more effectively than purely rural areas.[33]

From School Consolidation to "Forced Busing"

Significantly, the distinction between suburbs and the countryside began to dissolve not only outward but inward. Although one-room schoolhouses had largely disappeared by the 1960s, state campaigns to raise school enrollments and efficiency started to affect in-lying, suburban communities as well as rural ones. In 1955, the nation's 174 metropolitan regions were still honeycombed with 7,031 school districts, half of them enrolling fewer than three hundred students and a third of them less than fifty.[34] These districts were either remnants of rural settlements overtaken by annexation, exclusive suburban enclaves, or some combination of the two. Many suburbs, for example, maintained separate elementary and high school districts—vestiges of rural union systems—and those with high property values were loath to assume the debt and expenses of their poorer neighbors. A contemporary pointed out that when it came to the defense of local control, "the problems usually accompanying [district] reorganization in rural areas tend to arise in exaggerated form when reorganization is attempted in suburban localities."[35] Resistance to school consolidation was sharp in suburban Los Angeles, where town boards described it as "one of the most serious threats ever presented to our education [system] in California," and in Pennsylvania, where opposition came not only from "rural areas that feel the compulsory feature of the new program is an infringement of home rule" but from "wealthy suburban residential areas where people feel their academic program is superior and wish to preserve their single identity as a school district." Districts east of Kansas City, Missouri, successfully defeated a regional consolidation plan in the late 1960s, while on the Kansas side it took a special act of the legislature to reorganize suburban districts; the affluent subdivisions of Mission Hills were the last in the state to submit, in 1971.[36] In Texas, too, the head of the Small Schools Association promised that "any type of reorganization [would] be hard to accomplish" statewide, despite legislative reapportionment: Conflicts over racial integration and school funding ensured that "an urban legislature . . . [would be] no more anxious to reorganize all of the school districts than the past rural legislatures."[37]

Local control of education was hardly a new concept for urban or suburban residents. Neighborhood schools, racially segregated by custom if not by law, had been a third rail in city politics throughout the twentieth century. Protecting a school's "integrity" ensured white residents stable home values and a degree of racial privilege at the expense of African Americans, Hispanics, and other minority groups, who were generally consigned to overcrowded and underfunded facilities. Urban school boards reinforced the effects of housing discrimination with gerrymandered attendance zones and schools built in the center of racially homogenous communities, so that even in cities without de jure segregation most children attended segregated schools. To threaten the sanctity of the neighborhood was to invite white flight and perhaps race riots.[38]

Yet these tactics could not always keep up with shifting housing patterns and growing numbers of minority students, especially as civil rights groups drew attention to the "ghetto school" phenomenon, and state and federal authorities applied more scrutiny to districts' administrative policies. Urban districts had to adopt new methods of subterfuge, which quietly (and tellingly) altered their conception of local control. A common way to cope with racial turnover was to allow white students to transfer out of a district, usually by sending them to nearby suburban or rural schools. The practice first gained visibility in the South during the 1950s. After the integration of Little Rock's Central High School, for instance, Governor Orville Faubus closed all the city's high schools for a year, forcing students to attend private schools or, more often, to enroll in rural districts at the city's edge, which were not obliged to desegregate. School closures proved unpopular in most areas, but transfers, vouchers, and "freedom of choice" plans persisted in the South through the 1970s. Indeed, it soon came to light that Northern districts had been using similar transfer policies for years. Milwaukee's North Division High School, for example, had become ninety-nine percent black by 1963, despite the fact that many white families lived in its catchment area. "Most whites transfer out of the district," said the principal. "They transfer for a lot of reasons. . . . Some even say it's because of the Negroes, but most aren't that frank."[39] Whatever reasons they gave, it is clear that for many white families in Milwaukee, Detroit, Boston, and other cities, the commitment to neighborhood schools applied only as long as those schools were segregated. When existing methods of exclusion failed, they consistently demanded that school boards move white pupils across district lines, a privilege that they denied students of color.[40]

Interdistrict transfers weakened ties between white families and urban school districts, but they still relied on the principle of local control. As courts undermined segregationist policies in urban schools, the promise of escape depended on the continued autonomy of rural and suburban districts. Transfers were merely a tactical retreat, a way to buy time while white flight established new lines of racial and economic stratification. It would be on district (rather than neighborhood) boundaries that local control made its final stand.

By the late 1960s, liberal policymakers and civil rights activists had begun to propose metropolitan solutions to racially segregated school districts. They argued that state policies had caused segregation and—since school districts were subordinate to the state—that remedies such as paired attendance zones, the transfer of minority students, and cross-town busing were both necessary and appropriate to fix it. Frustrated by a decade of failed desegregation programs, federal courts came to agree. In *Swann v. Charlotte-Mecklenburg* (1971), the U.S. Supreme Court enjoined districts under desegregation orders to take more drastic steps toward racial balance, including cross-town busing.[41] The justices acknowledged that transporting pupils beyond their neighborhoods might be unpopular and logistically difficult, but they insisted that constitutional demands had to be met. Interestingly, the court offered rural schools as a model of how quickly voters could adjust to busing programs. If rural areas had been "accustomed for half a century to the consolidated school systems implemented by bus transportation," the majority argued, surely cities could come to accept it too. The claim was dubious both in its chronology and its assumption of rural acquiescence, but it echoed liberal notions of educational progress: Modern democracy, and in this case racial integration, seemed to require the shift from local control to centralized administration, and the movement of schoolchildren between neighborhoods.[42]

Although the *Swann* decision overlooked the history of anticonsolidation movements in rural areas, that issue reappeared the following year when a district court judge named Stephen Roth followed the metropolitan approach to its logical endpoint. Whereas *Swann* mandated the desegregation of schools within a single district—albeit a countywide district, encompassing both Charlotte and its suburbs—in 1972 Roth ordered fifty-three districts in suburban Michigan to begin a two-way busing program with the city of Detroit. "School district lines are simply matters of political convenience," he noted, "and may not be used to deny constitutional rights." The ruling met immediate resistance. Thousands of suburban parents held their children out of school rather than submit to forced busing, and the state appealed to the U.S. Supreme Court. Roth's decision had all the makings of a landmark case, and because it turned on vexing questions of school district autonomy, both plaintiffs and defendants found themselves reexamining relevant case law—specifically, the litigation of rural school consolidation.[43]

As several historians have pointed out, the busing decision was a high-water mark for Detroit's liberal coalition, and civil rights and labor groups understandably felt that they had history on their side. Jeffrey Mirel notes that expanding population and political power between 1950 and 1965 had allowed urban lawmakers to reduce the number of Michigan school districts from 4,841 to 993, ending "what they believed was the ongoing subsidy of inadequate and inefficient rural school districts by urban taxpayers" and securing more resources for city schools. It stood to reason that Detroit could compel outlying communities to accept their share of the state's racial problems as well.[44] Moreover, as a legal matter, civil rights groups argued that the state's educational authority was beyond dispute. From the 1910s to the 1960s, state and federal courts had repeatedly affirmed Michigan's right to redraw, dissolve, or consolidate its rural school districts at will, regardless of local preference, and it was exactly these precedents that plaintiffs cited in support of the metropolitan desegregation plan. Legally, local control of schools seemed indefensible.[45]

As suburban parents held their children out of school, and state and federal legislators frantically cast about for a means of resistance, they too seized on the history of rural school consolidation, which from their perspective was far from settled.[46] Many of the towns affected by the busing order had suburbanized just a decade before and retained elements of their rural past. For example, residents of Warren, Michigan, said that their town's six school districts, holdovers from the era of one-room schoolhouses, remained "important community boundaries" and that most old-timers still identified with their school district rather than the municipality. Having moved to Warren specifically for the rural charm—one mother mentioned the working farm behind her children's elementary school—these parents refused to be pulled back into the city.[47] In public remarks, President Nixon perfectly captured their rationale. "Some people oppose income redistribution and busing for the wrong reasons," he said, "but they are by no means the majority of Americans, who oppose them for the right reasons."[48]

Underlying that evasive, euphemistic statement is an important point about shifting justifications for suburban autonomy. Antibusing activists could tell both reporters and themselves that their position did not stem from racism or class bias. To the contrary, it reflected a noble commitment to neighborhood schools and local democracy, institutions to which they had a historical right, and perhaps even a legal one. Suburbanites' commitment to community-based education was suspect at the time and has become even more so in hindsight. Historians have dismissed the notion that children in Detroit's suburbs were used to walking to school, as proponents claimed; most already rode buses. One could likewise argue that the sudden significance of one-room school districts was nothing more than a cover for racism. After all, the same communities had raised no objection when white students were transferred between districts to perpetuate segregation, and most residents had not lived in their districts long enough to form any deep ties anyway. But even the most opportunistic political stance requires some basis in reality, some appeal to virtue, and to write off local control as prevarication or self-deception is to misunderstand its power. While the Detroit suburbs were rife with fear and prejudice, the fact is that the "right reasons" to oppose interdistrict busing were there, lying unused and nearly forgotten, but right nevertheless. One only needed to take them up.[49]

The U.S. Supreme Court, pushed to the right by four Nixon appointees, did just that. Overturning nearly a century of precedent, the justices accepted the historical significance of local school districts. In *Milliken v. Bradley* (1974), the court disallowed the Detroit busing plan and narrowed the responsibility for desegregation almost exclusively to individual districts. Unless plaintiffs could demonstrate that suburbs were complicit in segregationist policies, busing would stop at district lines. "Boundary lines may be bridged in circumstances where there has been a constitutional violation calling for inter-district relief," wrote Chief Justice Warren Burger, but "school district lines may not be casually ignored or treated as a mere administrative convenience; substantial local control of public education in this country is a deeply rooted tradition." The effects of the ruling were swift and predictable. Across the country, thousands of white families fled to rural and suburban areas, leaving ever more students of color to shuttle around crumbling city school systems. A few affluent suburbs agreed to voluntary transfer programs, but most communities preserved local autonomy and racial imbalance.[50]

Conclusion

Michigan was hardly the only place where conservatives invoked traditions of rural localism to oppose busing.[51] The syndicated columnist Jeffrey St. John drew on his wife's childhood experiences at a consolidated school in Washington to characterize long bus rides as child abuse. Congressman Albert Quie, chairman of the House Education Committee, referenced twenty-mile routes in his section of rural Minnesota to propose national restrictions on interdistrict busing. Iowa Republican Charles Grassley was first elected to Congress in 1974 amid charges that he made implicitly racist statements against busing. He denied the charges, claiming that he had opposed the practice since the 1950s, when it was "more applicable in [rural] Butler County than it is in Waterloo" and was not associated with any "subtle appeal to prejudice" (see figure 7).[52]

The history of metropolitan busing in Wisconsin offers a particularly clear example of conservatives' conflation of rural and suburban school policy. Al-

FIGURE 7. Students board a school bus in Rock County, Wisconsin, circa 1950. Many rural residents resisted busing their children to centralized schools, raising objections that suburbs would later use to challenge racial desegregation plans. (Courtesy of the Wisconsin Historical Society)

though the Wisconsin (Rural) Schools Association failed to stop the consolidation of rural districts during the 1950s, a decade later it gained popularity among suburbanites in Oshkosh, Green Bay, and Milwaukee with its pledge "to oppose the relentless disruption of our present school system."[53] In 1969, a little-known candidate from the tiny town of Elmwood, campaigning on a platform of "more discipline, limited school spending, and more local control," almost unseated the state superintendent, winning majorities in suburban Waukesha and Racine as well as the state's rural counties.[54] When Milwaukee tried to install a race-based busing program in 1975, the Brookfield city council insisted that if "suburban home rule" were not preserved villages and school districts in adjacent counties would be "consolidated, attached, dismembered, or reduced" at the whim of urban politicians. Other writers denounced the "bigness of school districts," "proliferation of inefficient bureaucracy," "forced transportation of students," and annexations of territory without public referendums. Several specifically referred to their own experiences in rural schools, either to oppose busing outright or—in a presage of the city's later voucher program—to propose that Milwaukee students attend high schools of their choice on a tuition basis, as rural students had.[55] One Brookfield assemblyman, warning that the "boundaries between cities and suburbs . . . are crumbling," proceeded to collapse the rhetorical boundaries between suburbs and the countryside. "When this transplanted country boy is replaced . . . by a city bred legislator," he asked his constituents, "who will you have to [vote] for equal aids to Union Free Schools, against County assessors, against Unilateral annexation, against abolishing town government?" Those issues had previously been rural concerns but were becoming increasingly relevant to suburban voters.[56]

Suburban leaders not only adopted rural rhetoric for their own sake but took up an ideological defense of rural interests as well, working to stop the ongoing process of school consolidation in the countryside. The same Milwaukee-area representatives who denounced forced busing in the 1970s visited one-room Amish schoolhouses and appeared at small-town rallies to criticize sex education. They also received appreciative letters from rural parents and administrators who thanked them for their "continued and effective efforts to maintain the ability of school boards to act . . . without too much in the way of state control." Parents from little towns like Clear Lake and Thiensville wrote to solicit support for their union high schools, which were under pressure from the DPI to consolidate, while others opposed the creation of a state board of education, which would have further limited school boards' influence over curriculum and funding. Both bills went to defeat on the strength of suburban conservative votes.[57]

Like a broken clock, the process of school consolidation begun in the 1890s lagged so far behind the times that by the 1970s it had regained relevance.

Traditions of local control provided a basis for suburban autonomy, while residential development and revived political power offered rural school districts reprieve from closure. These overlapping interests undermined key elements of the liberal educational agenda, halting the consolidation of urban and suburban districts outright while slowing the process in the countryside. The convergence of rural and suburban activism was neither inevitable nor coincidental; it was the product of a grassroots campaign to reclaim local control of schools. That campaign was intentional but also decentralized, unplanned, and (at least at first) quite unlikely. In exurban areas, rural and suburban groups frequently clashed over educational policy, expressing sharply different views about child-rearing, school quality, and the fundamental character of their communities. Creating a way forward required them to unearth some elements of the past and to bury others, putting aside economic and cultural differences in their common fight against state oversight. It was that compromise, together with the mutability of local control as a political slogan, that made small-town schools a site of political compromise and experimentation, a crucible for new forms of conservatism and new approaches to educational policy. The same forces that stifled race-based busing would also redirect national debates about teachers' unions, property taxes, and curricular reform, making schools a central issue in the politics of the postwar Right.

THE STRUGGLE FOR STATUS

Over the past fifty years, the expansion of teachers' unions has become one of the most vexing issues in U.S. education. At the heart of the matter is whether public oversight is compatible with professional autonomy. Critics have long characterized public employee unions as the most parasitic of political interest groups. Through collective bargaining and the threat of strikes, they allege, public unions inflate tax rates, shield members from voter scrutiny, and undermine the power of elected representatives. In short, they impede not only the operation of the free market but the function of democracy itself. Supporters counter that public workers have often been exploited in the name of low taxes and, by counterbalancing conservative groups that would gut government regulation and funding for services like education, that unions actually safeguard the public good. Moreover, they insist that unionized teachers are professionals whose training entitles them to make curricular and pedagogical decisions without political interference, a claim that opponents vigorously dispute. To understand debates about teacher unionization, one must first understand underlying, contradictory conceptions of democracy.

These arguments have changed very little over the past seventy-five years, but their context has undergone a tectonic shift. Unions were the backbone of the New Deal coalition and enjoyed steady expansion once the National Labor Relations Act (1935) established rights to collective bargaining and fair labor practices. Yet public employees were initially excluded from the act's provisions. It took another twenty-five years of organizing and lobbying to extend, in 1962, the right of union membership to federal workers and subsequent campaigns for the recognition of state and local employees, which gave teachers access to collective bargaining. By the time most public employees organized, declines in private sector unionization had transformed them from the labor movement's latest addition to its last redoubt, raising the stakes further in arguments about their legitimacy.

As the single largest group of government workers, public school teachers have been central to the course of public unionization as a whole. Traditional histories of teachers' unions move from the formation of professional education organizations during the Progressive Era to desperation, radicalism, and isolated strikes during the Depression and war years, and from the political repression of the 1950s to the rise of teacher militancy in the 1960s.[1] A few incidents anchor the back end of this story: the era's first major strike, in New York City in 1962; a second in New York's Ocean Hill-Brownsville neighborhood in 1968 over issues of minority employment and community control; and similar confrontations in Newark, Chicago, and Detroit, all of which have allowed historians to discuss unions' impact on class, gender, and race in urban politics.[2]

Although it makes sense to study unions in the context of major cities, where the size and political power of the teaching force ascribes them self-evident significance, scholars have neglected the history of teacher unionization outside of metropolitan areas, a topic crucial to understanding the balance between professional and democratic control of public education. As teachers fought for professional status, pay, and protection, and as voters defended their right to dictate school policy, small districts became a site of profound ideological conflict. Indeed, the very features that have led scholars to overlook small districts—their lack of numbers or power, the conservatism and winner-take-all structure of small-town politics—often put the same districts at the forefront of antiunion activism, leading to bitter litigation and overrepresentation in public sector case law.[3]

Lawsuits yielded mixed outcomes. Courts generally preserved the power of locally elected representatives over hiring, firing, and contract negotiation, while at the same time liberalizing the right to strike and holding school boards accountable to established protocols for dealing with their employees. In several states, courts decided cases in favor of local boards (who continued to intimidate their teachers) even as the acrimony of small-town disputes impelled legislators to liberalize restrictions on collective bargaining and strikes at the state level. Thus, while teacher unionization achieved uneven gains on the metropolitan fringe, in their legal precedents, small districts were crucial to the expansion of public unionization as a whole. Moreover, the expansion of teacher organizations reinforced trends toward professional control and increased school funding, infringing on the tenets of low cost and community control that had long been pillars of U.S. public education.

Unionization Outside the Metropolis

For most of U.S. history, teachers in rural and suburban districts differed markedly in their professional status from those in the city. By the late nineteenth century, reformers had forcibly consolidated urban districts to forge a system of age-graded schools, replacing corporal punishment and curricular chaos with emulative competition and hierarchical organization. The segregation of young children facilitated the transition to a largely female workforce that was not only less expensive but also more willing to pursue specialized training. Urban (and increasingly, state-level) reforms turned teaching into a profession, with strict licensing requirements based on claims to specialized knowledge and practice. Despite low pay and limited autonomy, local teacher organizations defended their professional gains through self-segregation, based on race, gender, and instructional level, and strict abstention from strikes. A growing number of them also affiliated with the National Education Association (NEA) or American Federation of Teachers (AFT) to lobby for training, tenure rights, and increased school funding. Together, the two groups comprised a vocal education lobby.[4]

These changes took longer to reach the countryside, where through the early 1900s teaching remained a part-time job suited to farmers, transients, or young women biding their time until marriage. Opportunities for professional development increased as states raised certification requirements—and as university extensions and normal schools began to offer rural residents access to postsecondary education—but the commitment to local control and single-teacher schools impeded curricular reform or meaningful organization among rural teachers.[5] School boards grudgingly hired better-trained teachers in response to rising standards but resisted consolidation until the 1950s and 1960s, when loopholes closed and curricular requirements became too difficult to fulfill in single-school districts. By that time, it was easy for critics to cast teachers' unions as the instigators and primary beneficiaries of rural school consolidation. Many argued that NEA affiliates wanted to close small schools merely "so they can unionize them," and that "control of teachers [depended] on large, urban-type schools" and weakening ties to the local community.[6] For their part, union leaders charged that "small districts are shot through with cronyism and paternalism and employee fear and distrust." Even after these districts consolidated, the NEA encountered aggressive assertions of community control, which put local union leaders at risk of dismissal and blacklisting under almost any pretext, with predictably cooling effects on local organizing.[7]

The story of unionization in Wisconsin illustrates these changes, which were underway nationwide during the postwar period. The Wisconsin Education Association (later changed to the Wisconsin Education Association Council, or WEAC) was founded in 1853 as the state's primary professional organization, followed in 1919 by the much smaller Wisconsin Federation of Teachers (WFT), which became the first statewide federation of the AFT. Before the 1960s both organizations had the majority of their affiliates in urban areas. WEAC offered some resources for rural teachers but organized few locals outside the state's largest cities. The WFT tried to organize outlying districts in the 1930s but faltered in 1939, when the Wisconsin legislature stripped tenure rights from the sixty-five hundred teachers in rural schools, a concession to school boards as the state took its first steps toward district consolidation. Through the 1940s and 1950s it was difficult for unions to reestablish a foothold in small districts. Common were experiences like those of eighteen teachers at Spooner High School in 1946, all of whom were threatened with dismissal after affiliating with the WFT. The school board only ended up firing six of them, but pointedly included the two union officers.[8]

With the final round of school consolidation and the state's recognition of collective bargaining, in 1959, the number of WEAC locals doubled, with most growth coming in small towns and rural areas. A quick glance at the number of local associations bearing regional names (such as the Wisconsin Heights Association of Teachers, in Mazomanie) or hyphenated names (like the Rosendale-Brandon or Delavan-Darien Education Associations) underscores how many of these organizations were appearing in consolidated districts, many with less than 50 full-time employees. Membership grew rapidly as well, from 21,000 members in the state association and only 2,756 in the national in 1945 to over 46,000 members in each by 1975. Over the same period, WEAC expanded to 269 affiliates across the state, while the WFT had 38 (see figure 8).[9]

Unionized teachers were often the first representatives of organized labor in rural and suburban communities, where opponents of school consolidation saw their growth as a threat to local democracy. To resist them, residents tapped into the stream of antiunion literature propagated by the John Birch Society and conservative business interests. As early as 1963, farm bureau book clubs were reading anticonsolidation pamphlets in conjunction with Ayn Rand's *Objectivist Newsletter* (1961) and materials from the Foundation for Economic Education.[10] Their opposition to organized labor registered with local teachers. One union member replied warily when asked why his chapter had refused to support a

WEAC affiliates 1945

WEAC affiliates 1955

WEAC affiliates 1965

WEAC affiliates 1975

FIGURE 8.   Teacher unionization followed closely on the heels of school district consolidation in rural areas, where both trends were rapid and contentious.

strike in a nearby district. "I come from an association with only seventy people," he said, "and there is a lot of insecurity when you only have seventy people. When we saw that Milwaukee wasn't going to go out [in support], we didn't want to stick our neck out." The union also refused to "stick its neck out" when angry parents used the incident to intimidate the district's English and sex education teachers: Controversial materials were dropped without debate. Another teacher remarked that he remained "very much an outsider" in his town despite working there for fifteen years; others said it was "very difficult [negotiating] at a small school," where teachers "were working from weakness."[11]

Although expressions of antiunion sentiment varied from place to place, they tended to recur around issues of school spending and curricular control. Tax hikes (discussed in chapter 6) were a primary concern for rural residents, not only because unionized teachers would demand better salaries and benefits, but because they would lobby for new facilities that many voters were unwilling to finance. Control of the curriculum (discussed in chapter 7) also generated friction, for as unions secured guarantees for tenure and academic freedom they enabled teachers to include controversial material over the objections of parents or community members. Issues of cost and academic content were not always distinct. For example, in western Michigan in 1967, the Imlay City Federation of Teachers—describing itself as "the real, and only, labor movement we have in outstate Michigan"—negotiated a contract clause requiring the school board to "take advantage of federal funds available for special and remedial programs at all levels." Conservative board members ignored the clause when they canceled a local Head Start program, objecting to the principle of federal involvement in education and to the district's responsibility for funding the program as subsidies tapered off. The union sued to continue the program but a state court found in the board's favor, invalidating any contractual provision that impermissibly "controls or restricts . . . the free exercise of discretion for the public good vested in a public officer or board." The Imlay City ruling chastened union leaders, who had hoped to achieve other workplace goals through contractual guarantees, and checked the bargaining power of teachers across the state.[12]

Antiunion activism was pervasive in small districts, but it was hardly confined to resentful farmers. In areas experiencing suburban growth, conservative newcomers often echoed rural resentment of unionized teachers, whom they feared would implement controversial curriculum or the sort of watered-down vocational classes then in vogue with progressive educators, or who might demand higher salaries and new facilities. Again, complaints varied from place to place—some activists supported new buildings, for instance, and opposed vocational courses because of their nonacademic content rather than their cost—but many newcomers worried that unions would shield teachers from the democratic control that made small school districts appealing in the first place. Thus, amid community change, population growth, and the modernization of curriculum and facilities, both rural and suburban conservatives sought to preserve local control by limiting teachers' salaries and their influence over school policies.

The confluence of suburbanization and the assertion of local control was evident on the outskirts of Keene, New Hampshire, where in 1972 the school board revoked the principal's right to hire faculty, reprimanded teachers because of parent complaints, and fired the head of the teacher's association before breaking off all negotiations with the union.[13] Menominee, Michigan, struggling to accommodate rising enrollments, similarly rejected union negotiations until the press and public were allowed to observe them, claiming that community oversight was integral to the town's traditions of open government. Union representatives, accustomed to closed negotiations, refused to cooperate.[14] Between 1960 and 1970, the town of Millard, Nebraska—a farming village that had just consolidated its one-room schoolhouses—grew from 1,012 to 7,460 residents and was targeted for annexation by the city of Omaha. The school board, still dominated by rural representatives, denounced annexation as an attempt "to dissolve local government and to force the residents of the several school districts affected to join the Omaha System against their will, merely for the sake of creating a larger district." Voicing an argument increasingly common in suburban communities, board members declared that "the school system should be locally controlled by residents of the area, and that local money should be expended on a local level rather than from a central headquarters." Although Omaha annexed the town of Millard in 1971, it failed to consolidate the school district, which continued to operate as a separate, suburban entity. Thus, rather than joining the state's largest public employees union, local teachers had to maintain their own smaller association. One member saw the very existence of a union as proof of the town's "evolution from a small, rural, German community to a suburban area," but nonetheless remembered "agricultural board members" who felt otherwise. "One simply did not question the decisions of the Board," she recalled, and while the community generally approved building projects and pay raises, it maintained strict control over the curriculum and personnel decisions.[15]

Rural and suburban interests were not predestined to align against teachers' unions: Issues of professionalism and academic freedom could cause friction both between and among the two groups. Particularly in districts where rural overrepresentation thwarted the wishes of suburban parents, unions could occasionally exploit divisions between voters and the school board, claiming the mantles of both professional freedom and popular support.[16] Yet even when voters supported teachers against overreaching board members, they did so in the name of local democracy. In Bennington, Vermont, for instance, parents clashed with their union over keeping seventh graders in one-room elementary schools (which were not required to hire certified middle-school teachers) but rallied to its defense when the superintendent and rural board members arbitrarily fired teachers and staff. Worried that such meddling might hurt instruction, they demanded the expansion of the school board from three to five members to ensure better representation.[17] A similar situation unfolded in Jefferson County, Idaho, where conservative board members used population growth to split a recently consolidated district in two, allowing them to void the union's contract and fire teachers at will. Voters ousted the board's leaders, whom they considered too

antagonistic, but also passed a measure reaffirming that the local superintendent, a member of the Idaho Education Association, had no right to "[question]
the actions of the local board." The school board in Keokuk, Iowa, had union
leaders jailed for violating a strike injunction, then conceded to their release
when a majority of the townspeople took the union's side. Thus, small-town voters were not inherently opposed to teachers' organizations. In districts adjusting
to population growth and rapid educational reform, any threat to democratic
control invited public backlash. Nevertheless, teachers were more likely than
school boards to run afoul of local opinion, especially when statewide unions
seemed to use coercive tactics against elected officials.[18]

From the teachers' perspective, coercion was necessary for dealing with intransigent school boards; extra-local intervention was the only way to establish
meaningful professional authority. In addition to courting the support of union
lawyers, negotiators, and canvassers, teachers in small districts invited greater
supervision from state departments of education and labor relations boards,
which they hoped would curb contract violations and arbitrary dismissals. While
teachers' interests did not always align with those of regulators, either, the simple
recognition of state authority in public labor disputes marked an important shift
away from unfettered local control. It was for this reason that the president of
the Michigan Federation of Teachers cheered the state's inquiry into local bargaining impasses. She reasoned that any decisions would necessarily come at the
expense of local school authorities, since the state mediation board "was anxious
to establish its power" in education disputes.[19]

State oversight of labor practices established a firmer basis for judicial scrutiny
of school boards, as well as new mechanisms for resolving contract disputes. The
most significant (and to school boards, the most intrusive) of these mechanisms
was binding arbitration, in which courts or labor boards appointed a neutral
party to investigate the cause of a contract dispute and craft an equitable solution, to which both parties would be legally bound. Advocates of local control
complained that this arrangement bypassed the decisions of elected representatives in favor of bureaucratic appointees, leaving school governance twice removed from the voters. The prospect of outside arbitration also encouraged new
negotiating tactics, which, from the teachers' side, were bound to shift toward
direct confrontation and mass action.

Sanctions, Strikes, and Democracy

Before the 1970s, the NEA sought to preserve its professional reputation by avoiding trade union tactics and decertifying local associations that broke its no-strike

pledge. When the smaller AFT and some rogue locals struck during the 1940s, their militancy unleashed a wave of right-wing attacks and, in many states, legislation prescribing prison time for public employees who walked off the job. While teachers' unions won collective bargaining rights in the 1960s, striking remained illegal and salaries and benefits low. Instead of pursuing direct action against school boards, the NEA conducted surveys of state school systems and lobbied for broad-based increases in school funding. Framing educational quality as a statewide issue positioned teachers' unions as a civic watchdog rather than a narrow interest group. When legislatures did not cooperate, the NEA would impose sanctions, threatening mass resignations among its members and discouraging new teachers from taking jobs in the state. Although sanctions had to be applied selectively, the threat of bad publicity proved effective during the early 1960s, when legislators in Utah and Oklahoma agreed to increase academic standards and school funding following NEA pressure campaigns.[20]

The NEA used the same tactics against local districts that it considered particularly retrograde in their labor practices. In a local context, however, statewide unions were not regarded as civic watchdogs; they looked like outside bullies and met with stiff resistance. A typical situation occurred on the island of Nantucket, a popular vacation spot off the Massachusetts coast, where residential growth doubled student enrollment between 1945 and 1955, forcing classes to meet in the post office, private garages, and even an idle tugboat.[21] The school board, in Massachusetts called a "committee," invited a team of Harvard University researchers to survey the island's educational system and recommend strategies to manage growth. The team's final report reflected the era's assumptions about school quality. It recommended more vocational courses and, despite sharp resistance from local residents, the closure of two nineteenth-century elementary schools on the windward side of the island.[22] A new superintendent, Charles Minnich, tried to implement these recommendations in 1962. In response, the high school principal—a Nantucket native who had long kept her teachers untenured and cowed—threatened to resign, and large crowds began attending school committee meetings in her support.[23] Teachers soon complained that students were tape-recording their lectures, and John Birch Society literature appeared in the high school library. A local women's club called for the resignation of Minnich and several high school teachers. By the end of the year conservatives won a plurality on the school committee and fired him.[24]

Minnich became a martyr for organized labor and delivered the keynote address at the NEA's national convention that year.[25] The Massachusetts Teachers Association (MTA) responded to the Nantucket situation with a boycott, which prevented members from applying for jobs in the district. The organization claimed that the local mind-set was "sterile, steeped in parochialism and self-destruction," and that parents encouraged students to display "open hostility to learning, curse teachers, and destroy school property." In addition to harsh living conditions, the MTA contended, teachers on Nantucket faced "'unreasonable' teaching assignments, parental harassment, 'vicious' public rumors, an unsympathetic school committee, lack of public respect, and improper supervision." The state's department of education took a moderate approach to the standoff, promising not to "become involved in the activities of professional teaching groups" but also to keep the schools open with nonunionized teachers if necessary. The Nantucket school committee won in the short term: In subsequent years it fired Minnich's successor rather than give him tenure and dismissed a teacher for marrying an African American man. Only when concerned parents began sending their children to mainland schools did community leaders work to improve relations with the school faculty.[26]

At the national level, the NEA's use of sanctions faltered in 1967, when Florida legislators refused to raise school spending and remained intransigent in the face of thousands of teacher resignations. The union had to scale back its funding demands and hundreds of teachers lost their jobs. By the end of the decade, the failure of statewide action forced the NEA to shift its attention back to local districts and to loosen its position on strikes. Without the threat of work stoppage, collective bargaining had largely failed to improve working conditions, contract violations, or low pay. Local associations began to defy strike injunctions and pushed the national leadership to embrace a more confrontational defense of teachers' rights. Rising militancy might have jeopardized the NEA's professional reputation but it also dramatically increased membership, which exceeded two million by the mid-1970s. Teacher strikes soon became a fixture of municipal politics, occurring at a rate of over a hundred a year.[27]

Strikes were rare but not unheard of in small school districts.[28] Although they remained illegal in most states, between 1960 and 1975 there were almost five hundred work stoppages in districts with two hundred teachers or fewer (see figure 9). Some of these were part of statewide actions, taking place in working-class suburbs of Pittsburgh, Detroit, or other strongholds of organized labor. Others had causes as diverse as the communities themselves, but usually resulted from some combination of overcrowding, poor working conditions, and rising professionalization rather than salary or benefits alone. Finally, and significantly, most occurred immediately after a community experienced school consolidation or an influx of suburban growth.

An early strike took place in Portola Valley, a rural district south of San Mateo, California, with only eight grades and thirty teachers but a growing number of commuters from a nearby defense plant. In 1960, the district narrowly voted to fire its superintendent, a proponent of residential development and progressive

Strikes of Two Hundred Teachers or Fewer, 1960–75

FIGURE 9.   Teacher strikes occurred in small districts all over the country, although they were concentrated in the Northeast and Midwest.

teaching styles, both points of contention with the farmer-dominated school board. In response, the faculty staged a one-day protest strike. Their demonstration divided the community. The board members who orchestrated the superintendent's removal were voted out of office, but other residents sued the teachers (twice) for violating their contracts.[29] Similarly, shortly after the resort town of Union Beach, New Jersey, opened its first high school to accommodate a rise in year-round residents, the school board denied a social studies teacher tenure without explanation. The New Jersey Education Association responded with sanctions, encouraging resignations among the district's faculty and hampering the recruitment of replacement teachers. New Jersey's Supreme Court took the board to task for its behavior but nevertheless upheld an injunction against the union, concluding that sanctions were no different than a coordinated strike.[30]

In 1967, New York State passed the Taylor Law, which allowed public employees to organize and established protocols for mediation and fact-finding. However, the law prohibited strikes and ultimately granted municipal authorities the right to impose unilateral settlements, ensuring that power still resided with the school board. The next year, the faculty of the recently consolidated Greenburgh school district voted to affiliate with the state teachers' union. One teacher recalled that contract negotiations had previously been an informal, amicable affair. But any hope of a "negotiations 'honeymoon' was shattered [during] the next contract talks," she continued, "when we had to deal with a hired board negotiator, and felt really taken advantage of." Unwilling to cede further ground on salary or bargaining rights, and frustrated at the board's stonewalling, Greenburgh became one of several Westchester County districts to challenge the Taylor Law. In 1973, the teachers waged a successful thirteen-day strike, for which they were severely fined, but they also won a ten percent raise and formal grievance procedure.[31]

One of the era's most infamous strikes occurred in Hortonville, Wisconsin, a community of about fifteen hundred residents located in the Fox River Valley, near Appleton. In 1973, control of the town's public schools still rested with the old timers, a group of farmers and small industrialists that included owners of the local paper mill and toy factory. Like most towns in the valley, one observer quipped, "the money was in the mill, and the mill controlled the school board, and the rest of the people . . . were employees of the mill." However, an increasingly white collar workforce and expanding suburbs had begun to strain these provincial politics. The local high school, built to accommodate consolidated rural districts in 1960, proved unequal to subsequent population growth in the adjoining town of Greenville, where young families and Appleton commuters filled new subdivisions. Overcrowding soon forced high school art classes to meet in the elementary school, and administrators planned to lengthen the school day by two hours to accommodate double shifts. Frustration mounted on all sides as rural voters—still a majority and upset with their rising property taxes—rejected school bond referendums three years in a row. Teacher salaries fell almost a thousand dollars below those in Appleton, and the district began the 1973 school year without a contract.[32]

The newly formed Hortonville Education Association (HEA), which represented all eighty-four of the district's teachers, pressed the board for an impartial fact-finding session throughout the fall. Once convened, however, both sides rejected its recommendations. The board did not present an acceptable contract until early February, at which time the HEA insisted that the terms extend for two years to prevent similar stalling in the future. When the board refused, the teachers demanded binding arbitration. The board refused that as well. "We would not go to binding arbitration," declared the board president, Roger Weihing. "People in the school district are the ones that pay the taxes, they elect us, they should be the ones that tell us how they want the schools run." Union members accused him of cloaking obstinacy with principle, grumbling that rural districts would rather cling to the concept of local control than bargain with their teachers. As the rhetoric escalated, meetings grew long and tempers short, and the teachers struck on March 18, 1974.[33]

At the time it was illegal for public employees to strike in Wisconsin, but the practice was becoming increasingly common. In 1959, the state was the first in the nation to allow collective bargaining for public employees. A 1971 revision of the law mandated good faith bargaining but included no penalties for school boards that did not comply, leaving the threat of an illegal strike as a last resort for teachers. From 1972 to 1974 there were over three hundred Wisconsin districts with outstanding contracts through October, thirty of which suffered official strikes. A WEAC negotiator remarked that although "farmers had acted the same way" in two small-town strikes the previous year, both communities had resolved their differences in a matter of weeks. Everyone expected a similar outcome in Hortonville, but hopes for a quick resolution proved illusory.[34]

After substitute teachers monitored classes in late March, the schools closed for three weeks while the union picketed and the board scheduled disciplinary hearings for breach of contract. When the HEA refused individual hearings, the board obliged them by firing all eighty-four members at once and reopening the schools with replacement teachers, primarily young or recently retired women lured by the promise of a forty-five dollar daily stipend. The picket line grew tense with the appearance of these "scabs." Five hundred teachers from around the state forfeited their spring break and traveled to Hortonville in a show of solidarity. Rather than simply circling the school, they marched downtown, obstructing traffic and occupying local businesses. The police arrested seventy-one strikers by mid-April.[35]

The town already harbored a general hostility to the teachers, three quarters of whom lived outside the district and held tenure of less than ten years. To many residents the arrival of more "outsiders" represented an organized offensive against local prerogative. Rumors spread that the strikers condescendingly referred to the board as "those farmers," that they were intent on "wrecking the community" and were "talking about crippling our little village." One man recalled that "a big shot in the W.E.A . . . came in here, stood right in front of the high school and said, 'We're going to bust this little town right in two. This little village is going to be nothing but a scarecrow nest in two years'" (see figure 10).[36]

Numerous residents, informed by right-wing pamphlets, said that they saw "the influence of [community organizer Saul] Alinsky" in the teachers' bargaining tactics. "Teachers in Hortonville [had] been attending meetings," a mill owner ominously recalled, "as many as five meetings a week, and after that experience they all started thinking the same. . . . A lot of people were using that word, 'brainwashed'—that very word." He believed that "[union] leadership was manipulating these teachers, and that the strike didn't speak to working conditions at all but to leadership manipulation." Many townspeople blamed a hazily

FIGURE 10.   Supporters of the school board watch teachers picket in Hortonville, Wisconsin, in 1974. The standoff between teachers and local residents frequently verged on violence. (Courtesy of the Wisconsin Education Association Council)

defined "leadership" for starting the strike, saying that "'they' . . . were going to have a strike in Appleton, but the Appleton school board capitulated, and so they chose Hortonville," or that "'they' lost in Wisconsin Rapids and they thought they'd win in Hortonville because they thought it was a smaller community." A high school senior agreed that HEA members "became radical" because they were "being advised" by outsiders. With a metaphor that would have set his English teacher's teeth on edge, he proclaimed that they "were guinea pigs [who] got sold up the river!"[37]

A group of unemployed youths soon took matters into their own hands and formed the Hortonville Vigilante Association—its name a parody of the union's— to "defend" local bars. Striking teachers found their houses vandalized, with porch lights shot out, rocks thrown through windows, and car tires slashed.[38] Some vigilantes began brandishing broom or axe handles and unloaded guns while making forays into the HEA's headquarters. The county sheriff arrested one of them for sending threatening letters and religious messages to the leader of a pro-union parent group, shortly after a local minister had issued a sermon and pamphlet calling down "divine punishment" upon the strikers.[39] On March 25, a school board member named Floyd Meyer made a frustrated attempt to exit the school parking lot and hit the HEA's chief negotiator with his car, for which the man was briefly hospitalized. At least two other picketers also reported automobile collisions. As the overwhelmed sheriff's department struggled to keep the peace, it deputized officers from five surrounding counties and even pleaded for a mobilization of the National Guard.[40]

The acrimony made for tense working conditions. Every morning, Hortonville's replacement teachers met in an empty barn along the highway, where a convoy of farmers would guard their cars and drive them to and from the schools, which they entered on foot and under guard, subjected to a barrage of invective from the strikers. The arrival of strange, inexperienced teachers ensured that the atmosphere within the classroom was almost as chaotic as without. One group of third grade boys, although sharply divided on the validity of the strike itself, expressed a universal dislike for their new teacher and bragged about throwing clay at her. A team of negotiators found the elementary school "destroyed from the inside out," with bulletin boards knocked down, filth on the science room floor, modeling clay strewn around, and thousands of dollars of broken equipment. High school students, too, engaged in widespread vandalism.[41]

Most of the strikebreakers quit under the strain, some after a single day, and the school board faced a perpetual shortage of qualified instructors. Two hundred and forty replacements were used to fill the eighty-four positions, some coming from distances of eighty miles or more. State Superintendent Barbara Thompson voiced strong support for the board. Although she denied that the DPI supplied them with lists of replacements—pointing out that her department's job was merely "to carefully check the replacements' certification"—she did not do that either, repeatedly waiving state certification requirements.[42] In April 1974, a group of parents, mostly from suburban Greenville, withdrew forty-nine students from the school system to attend an alternative school operated by striking teachers. They also mounted a taxpayers' lawsuit to force arbitration and an amicable reopening of the schools.[43]

As spring came, the controversy became the purview of the courts. On May 6, the Outagamie County Court ordered the district to rehire all the teachers for the final month of school but allowed the school board to list any teachers it would not ask back the next year: "a decision," protested the HEA, "that in effect . . . busts the union." The teachers appealed to the Wisconsin Supreme Court, which maintained the illegality of the strike but agreed with the union that the board did not have the right to fire teachers without due process. The school board appealed that decision to the U.S. Supreme Court, which reversed it again, finding that a democratically elected board was well within its rights to fire illegal strikers, whether or not it was negotiating with them at the time and regardless of bargaining customs.[44]

Although the issue was decided in favor of the Hortonville school board and local control, it is usually remembered as a victory for labor. Wisconsin's governor cited the Hortonville conflict as "evidence that the present law prohibiting strikes by public employees does not work" and threatened that future strikes "would extend the crisis to the boundaries of the state." With his backing, the legislature passed a law requiring mediation and arbitration in future labor disputes.[45] All the same, the Supreme Court decision represented a valuable precedent for Hortonville. When the replacement teachers hired during the Hortonville strike tried to form a new union, the board squelched the effort. In fact, the town's teachers did not reestablish union affiliation until 2003, and then joined the WFT rather than WEAC. Anecdotal evidence suggests that the court decision also stemmed the tide of union organizing in other towns, and that school boards became more aggressive negotiators in the years after Hortonville. From farming communities to the Milwaukee suburbs, several union members recall local conservative groups trying to intimidate them with the warning, "Remember Hortonville!"[46]

Conclusion

Just as the Hortonville strike faded, a similar incident wracked Plaistow, New Hampshire, a quickly growing rural area near the Massachusetts border where, from February to December 1974, the faculty of the Timberlane Regional School District sustained the longest strike in U.S. educational history. Although the district's salaries were near the state average, the teachers' association struck for rights of collective bargaining and outside arbitration. Its leaders complained that school board members clung to "a 1930s concept that they [had] the right to be judge, prosecutor, and jury" rather than engage in professional mediation. The board retorted that if "some third party" interfered with town politics, voters would "lose control [and] the good old apple pie image of home rule is going out the window." After a contentious round of negotiations, the board replaced the strikers with substitutes and the state department of education permanently decertified them, following guidelines established after a strike in Salem, New Hampshire, the year before. The board's most outspoken supporters seem to have been farmers, but many townspeople divided on the strike's legitimacy. As one woman remembered, the issue "split the community . . . [and] it changed friendships."[47]

New Hampshire courts ruled in favor of the board in multiple decisions, finding that elected representatives had the right to fire illegally striking teachers and were not obliged to submit to arbitration. Beyond the particulars of the case, however, the judiciary offered some hope to other teachers' unions: In April, for instance, the New Hampshire Supreme Court revoked the permanent decertification of strikers and dismissed the state's contention that injunctions should automatically apply at the outset of a strike. In hopes of avoiding future incidents, the state legislature soon expanded provisions for collective bargaining and, as in Hortonville, the incident became a nominal victory for labor. Yet in Plaistow itself the outcome was less encouraging. None of the strikers were rehired after their suspension. Although their replacements formed another bargaining unit, the school board limited its negotiating power to salary and benefits, making no provisions for binding arbitration. Political analysts also credited the reelection of the conservative governor, Meldrim Thomson—who had won a first term on his own reputation as a combative school board member—to his outspoken support of the Timberlane board.[48]

The mixed legacy of the Timberlane case is representative of public labor law generally during the 1960s and 1970s. In the face of growing teacher militancy, legislation that permitted collective bargaining but prohibited strikes seemed increasingly unworkable, yet state and federal judges struggled to craft a new jurisprudence to handle union disputes. They generally sought to preserve local democratic control while reining in overzealous school boards and legislators. By the late 1970s, many state judges cited the Timberlane decision—together with earlier rulings from Holland, Michigan (1968) and Westerly, Rhode Island (1973)—when weighing penalties for illegal strikes.[49] The emerging consensus was that states could prohibit strikes, but that school boards could not summarily fire teachers, and that courts were bound to issue injunctions against strikers only in cases of fraud or violence. The result, predictably, was a more permissive attitude, and in many states more permissive legislation, toward striking.[50]

Courts also began to subject school boards to outside arbitration more regularly. For example, in 1974, the Vermont Supreme Court compelled the town of Danville to accept an arbitrator's recommendations in a contract dispute, a measure already stipulated in the district's contract but ignored under the assumption that courts would defer to local officials. The Massachusetts Supreme Court likewise ordered mediation for a teacher who was arbitrarily denied tenure in the Danvers school district, northwest of Salem. "Although a school committee may not surrender its authority to make tenure decisions," the ruling asserted, "there is no reason why a school committee may not bind itself to follow certain procedures precedent to the making of any such decision." These rulings did not explicitly shift power from school boards to labor unions—they merely sought to ensure fairness and compliance with established procedures—but the effect was the same.[51]

Courts established other professional protections as well. In Lockport, Illinois, the construction of two new schools in the early 1960s met resistance from local voters, who rejected a bond referendum and, after it eventually passed, voted down the taxes necessary to staff the schools. When the teachers' union printed letters to the local newspaper criticizing tight-fisted school board members, the board fired Marvin Pickering, a signatory, for insubordination. In 1968, the U.S. Supreme Court reinstated him, ruling that the First Amendment gave teachers the right to speak about school board policy publicly and without reprisal, so long as their comments did not impede student learning or demonstrably hurt faculty morale.[52] By the early 1980s, cases from exurban communities in Texas and California established similar precedents for the abolition of "captive audience meetings," which school boards frequently used to bully teachers and discourage union activities but which state courts found impermissibly coercive. Whereas courts had once equated a well-ordered democracy with the fealty of public workers, by the late 1960s the excesses of small-district school boards seemed to contradict acceptable labor practices and demand judicial intervention on the workers' behalf.[53]

Yet notions of fairness remained malleable in a rapidly changing legal environment. While indiscriminate treatment of teachers seemed increasingly indefensible, efforts to restrain school boards and respect traditions of local control required repeated reversals and clarifications. To cite one example, in 1972, the New York Court of Appeals wrote that labor arbitration was "part and parcel of the administration of grievances" and had to be honored by both teachers and board members. But just five years later, the same court reversed course. In a case out of Liverpool, a small town near Syracuse, it found that arbitrators "[did] not carry the same historical or general acceptance" as school boards and that it was not satisfied with "the efficacy of arbitration as a means for resolving controversies in government employment." Only gradually, in a series of minor rulings, did New York's judiciary apply arbitration rules to local school boards.[54]

Federal courts also vacillated on the appropriate balance between worker protection and local democracy, particularly as Nixon and Ford appointees made the judiciary more conservative. Typical was the Supreme Court's handling of the Fair Labor Standards Amendment (FLSA) of 1961, which extended federal wage standards to workers in schools and hospitals and was strongly supported by teachers' unions. In *Maryland v. Wirtz* (1968) the court upheld the amendment, writing that so long as legislation "established only minimum wages and maximum hours . . . and did not otherwise affect the manner in which schools and hospitals were managed," it was subject to federal regulation under the commerce clause. In *National League of Cities v. Usery* (1976), however, a more conservative group of justices reconsidered, arguing that the FLSA "impermissibly [interfered] with the integral governmental functions of such bodies" and would, in practice, "displace the states' freedom to structure integral operations in areas of traditional governmental functions." The court would later reverse course again, with *Garcia v. San Antonio Metropolitan Transit Authority* (1985), reestablishing the supremacy of federal labor laws, but the issue of local control remained contentious when applied to public workers.[55]

Teacher unionization had by the 1970s become a clarion call for American conservatives. The rising influence of organized labor prompted some of them to abandon the public schools altogether—one more reason to send children to private schools or to homeschool them.[56] For others, the issue demanded revitalized political activism, a reassertion of popular sovereignty against private interests. Fueled by corporate donors, conservative think tanks and lobbying groups expanded their campaigns against public employee unions, which they denounced as undemocratic.[57] These campaigns yielded remarkable results. During periods of economic hardship—which, research suggests, have been nearly constant for working-class families over the past thirty years—voters proved quite willing to curtail the bargaining rights of public workers. Indeed, rather than attributing economic insecurity to the decline of private-sector unions, many voters turned against the benefits afforded those in the public sector, evident in the expansion of right-to-work legislation and statutory limitations on government workers' bargaining rights.[58]

Whether those remedies will neutralize unions remains to be seen, but the centrality of public sector unionization to today's political debates underscores the significance of labor law in the 1970s. As subsequent chapters explain, unions would become a cornerstone in liberal campaigns to equalize school funding and professionalize curricular selection. But opponents could adopt similar strategies and legal precedents to advance their own agenda. Once courts gave teacher organizations an advantage over local school boards, conservatives began turning to higher levels of government to check them. At the same time, they formulated new arguments for parental authority, laying claim to the same rights of conscience and contract that teachers used to establish professional autonomy. The result was a greater role for states, individuals, and courts in debates about school finance and curricular reform, but a greatly diminished role for local school boards. More than any other factor, it was the sudden success of teacher unions that made conservatives abandon local control as a means of ensuring the public good in education.

THE FIGHT FOR FUNDING

In 1897, Deerfield, Illinois, a farming community just outside Chicago's North Shore suburbs, decided to take advantage of new state subsidies encouraging rural high school construction. Like many other towns it formed a union high school district, the loosest form of secondary school governance, which preserved the area's one-room schoolhouses and independent elementary school boards. Sixty farmers tried to secede from the district rather than pay taxes for any high school at all, but the state department of education denied their petition. The farmers' brief, seemingly futile act of protest could stand in for hundreds like it at the turn of the twentieth century. As state governments expanded provisions for secondary schooling and raised requirements for school funding, they met widespread resistance from rural communities, where local control and outdated facilities kept taxes low. Yet even in rural areas like Deerfield, new sources of state funding created sufficient incentives and threats to begin modernizing public school systems and strengthening government oversight.[1]

Interesting in this case, however, was the persistence and evolution of rural opposition. In 1949, another group of Deerfield residents tried and failed to secede from the high school district. "Home rule of one of the district's two schools was [again] a factor," noted the *Chicago Tribune*, as was the belief that the town, now a mixture of farms and affluent estates, paid "more than a fair share" of taxes to support expanding, middle-class suburbs to its south. Yet the second secession effort signaled a subtle shift in the town's politics, as farmers cooperated with wealthy suburbanites to limit development and property taxes through the local control of education.[2]

The nexus between population growth, taxes, and school district autonomy became even clearer a decade later, in 1959, when Deerfield made national news for rejecting a racially integrated housing tract. The municipal board had initially approved the project but, after learning the details and fearing integration's effect on home values, subsequently condemned the land to build a park. Like many affluent suburbs, Deerfield had stringent requirements for lot sizes and green space, and the municipal board framed their decision as a zoning issue. When the developer brought a court challenge, however, they backtracked and claimed they needed the land for a new elementary school instead. No one found these excuses convincing at the time and nor should we now, but it would be a mistake to dismiss them simply as cover for racism. The school excuse becomes even *less* convincing when interpreted in the context of Deerfield's broader development strategy. For while most towns could plausibly claim that increasing enrollments during the baby boom required the construction of more schools, to do so in Deerfield was to reverse cause and effect. Limited school facilities provided a pretext to keep not only black but working- and middle-class families out of town, and Deerfield gladly preserved locally funded, nineteenth-century buildings through the mid-1960s. Even when real estate developers promised to pay for additional classrooms, the board refused to grant them permits. Turning down school expansions became almost an annual rite in Deerfield, occurring at least three times in the years before the integrated development was proposed. Thus, while racial exclusion was one means to preserve home values in Chicago's borderlands, small, locally funded schools were an equally important tool for managing growth: They kept property values high and the demand for public services low. Control over school funding and construction was vital to protecting Deerfield's self-determination and character, and through them its socioeconomic advantages. In this light, the persistence of earlier resistance to new school buildings, centralized administration, and higher taxes takes on lasting significance.[3]

The dynamics at work in Deerfield played out across the country during the postwar period. Thousands of towns preserved small, decentralized school districts to limit development and shield valuable property from taxation. In the process, however, they also perpetuated widely different levels of school funding and educational quality. Liberal policymakers implemented a series of reforms to overcome this sort of parochialism, including school district consolidation, which widened tax bases and diffused resources more broadly; state aid to education, which sought to mitigate disparities between local property values; and, ultimately, the redistribution of tax revenue from rich to poor districts. Scholars have documented these efforts in great detail, usually focusing on the successful expansion of state power in the former cases and its failure in the latter. Implicit but often unelaborated in their analyses has been the consistent effort of small communities—initially rural areas, but also wealthy suburbs and vacation communities—to stall consolidation and evade or overturn equalization plans. As was the case with race-based busing and teachers' unions, in the mid-1970s suburban communities appropriated traditions of rural education to preserve the primacy of locally funded schools, creating a coalition of convenience against urban interests and reinforcing the inviolability and inequality of school district boundaries.

District Consolidation and Equalized Funding

Although it remains difficult to correlate levels of school funding with specific academic outcomes, state governments have long acknowledged a general relationship between money and educational quality and have sought to provide public financing sufficient for an educated citizenry. They have struggled to do so, however, within the narrow framework of local control. Resistance to public school systems during the nineteenth century required states to extend their power gradually, with legislatures initially devolving taxation to local school districts and merely compelling them to establish tax rates within statutory minimums and maximums.[4] Individual school boards decided how much to tax property-holders and what level of education was appropriate for their communities' children. With disparate property values and different appetites for spending between communities, this arrangement yielded predictable disjunctions between state interests and local means. Many rural districts simply operated one-room schools until the year's budget ran out—for four, five, or six months at a time—and shuttered them in years when taxes ran short or teachers were unavailable.

Even if they wanted to provide quality education, communities with low property values had to tax themselves at much higher rates to achieve the same level of spending as wealthier neighbors. Disparities in land values were made worse by inconsistent tax assessments. Although uniformity clauses in most state constitutions required taxation of all property at its full value, county assessors, who were locally elected and largely unregulated, usually undervalued the holdings of homeowners and farmers through a practice known as "fractional assessment." Assessors also left tax assessments unchanged for years at a time, "a practice that was good for most homeowners when the market was strong and homes were appreciating in value," notes the economist Isaac Martin, "but bad for those homeowners, often poor or black, who lived in areas of declining property values" and were steadily overtaxed. The sum of these practices was a chaotic system of land valuation that shrank the tax base available to school districts and—by confining taxation to pockets of widely different affluence and population—undermined educational equality between districts, as well.[5]

The most incremental way to increase educational capacity was for state legislatures to set minimum standards for an acceptable education and then help districts meet them. As Ethan Hutt has observed, debates about academic quality have almost always returned to these statutory minimums—an uninspiring way to value schooling, perhaps, but also an unambiguous, practical expression of the state's priorities and expectations.[6] As states began to mandate new facilities and longer attendance periods, reformers complained that low property values in rural districts made "the burden of [financial] support . . . greater than many communities can meet; with the maximum [rate of] taxation allowed by law they are unable to meet the minimum demands of the state." Rather than lowering its expectations, they contended, "the state places itself under obligations to help its poorer members to comply with demands which are for the general good."[7] A flyer from the League of Wisconsin League of Municipalities captured the sentiments of many taxpayers in the early twentieth century (see figure 11). It depicted a gang of state officials at the schoolhouse door, voicing increasingly aggressive demands. "The state decides how much you must spend," they say. "Education is of state-wide concern." "You must do this with your schools." "I can compel your school to . . ." When the schoolmaster asks where the money will come from, they vanish. Some residents resented any state intrusion into educational policy and would have gladly forgone subsidies simply to be left alone. Others did not mind the new regulations but demanded financial support to meet them. Either way, it became clear that if states expected to reap the rewards of public education they would have to step forward and pay for some part of it themselves.[8]

The initial step was distributing grants to allay the costs of teachers, textbooks, and equipment, offering a degree of assistance to districts with small tax bases. Dozens of states had implemented these basic subsidies by the 1910s. However, if a state's goal was to improve the *uniformity* of children's education, flat grants did nothing to close the gap with wealthy areas. As long as local property taxes comprised the bulk of school revenues, districts with valuable real estate could generate more money (with lower tax rates) at any level of funding, easily overtopping state aid to provide their students with extra resources.

Reformers recognized the shortcomings of flat grants almost immediately and by the 1920s had begun to devise more comprehensive systems of state aid.

FIGURE 11. A 1940s cartoon advocates state aid to schools in Wisconsin, both as a form of tax relief and as compensation for increased state supervision. (Courtesy of the Wisconsin Historical Society)

The most common, usually described as "equalization" or "foundation" plans, sought to provide modern educational facilities and uniform tax rates without usurping local initiative. They did so by leaving structures of local taxation in place but setting guaranteed minimum valuations to address disparities in property wealth. As long as districts taxed themselves at a prescribed rate, the state would make up the difference in revenue to the level of the guarantee, using proceeds from sales taxes or other levies. Foundation plans ostensibly achieved equalization by providing an "adequate" amount of spending per pupil across all districts in proportion to their need, and almost every state adopted some version of the system between the 1930s and the 1960s.[9]

Underlying these plans, however, were Byzantine allocation formulas, prone to the tinkering and obfuscation of state legislators. Final versions usually included basal subsidies that provided some aid to every district, regardless of need, and provisions that promised steady funding from year to year, regardless of shifts in wealth or population. Flat grants for textbooks and teacher salaries continued as well, redundant at best, and often pernicious in their obstruction of real equalization between rich and poor districts. By the early 1960s, one study found, seventy percent of state aid in Massachusetts was distributed on the basis of an " 'equalizing formula' . . . which purports to give more dollars to poor districts than to rich," but in fact "the correlation between the rate of state support and local ability was so slight that the state could actually have done as well if it had . . . distributed its largesse in a completely random fashion, as by the State Treasurer throwing checks from an airplane."[10]

Inequality was likely to persist even if the new foundation plans had been administered fairly. Aligning guaranteed valuations and minimum participation requirements with the richest districts would have made state aid universal and forced every community to make a proportional effort to qualify, mitigating disparities and achieving true equalization (albeit at great cost to the state). Instead, as Rachel Tompkins notes, funding was usually based on the property value of average districts and "never kept pace with anyone's idea of adequate spending for education," obliging almost every locality to tax itself above the state guarantee. Thus, in most states, local taxation still covered the majority of per pupil expenditures, a system inherently favoring the wealthy. "From California to Maine to Florida," Tompkins writes, "the so-called equalization plans did not equalize."[11]

With dependence on local property values thwarting hopes for equalization and a shift to statewide taxation politically unpopular, liberal policymakers decided to work within existing policy frameworks, particularly school district consolidation. Rather than jeopardizing the principle of local taxation they simply created larger localities, spreading pupils and costs over ever-wider swaths of land. Of course, in order to be effective, consolidation also had to be fairly drastic. Vermont legislators estimated that a uniform property valuation of $15,000 per pupil would require centralizing the state's 278 school districts into only eight. In Nebraska, where the number of districts halved between 1955 and 1965, rumors flew that "the bureaucrats would really like to see . . . one huge statewide school district—run out of Lincoln." School consolidation promised economies of scale and a more rational, equitable system of property taxation, but that equity unavoidably came at the expense of small, locally controlled school districts.[12]

It was with its eye to fiscal parity that the California legislature, in 1964, took up a bill to combine the state's 1,585 independent school districts into only 350 county and metropolitan zones.[13] The bill's sponsor, a Democratic assemblyman named Jesse Unruh, sounded paternalistic when asked about potential resistance. "Inoculating tribes of primitive people against disease is not always easy," he inveighed. "Their witch doctors can be expected to object. . . . [Nonetheless], schools do not exist for 'local control.'" Conservative legislators did object and managed to remove the mechanism for compulsory consolidation, but the bill's fate was never in doubt. By providing extra funding for reorganized districts, requiring a simple majority vote rather than the approval of all the districts affected, and imposing area-wide taxation even on those districts that refused to reorganize politically, Unruh promised that the law "[achieved] nearly all of the reforms mandatory unification would have achieved."[14]

Perhaps the most interesting feature of the Unruh bill debate was how little attention opponents paid to the rural districts that the bill ostensibly targeted. By the mid-1960s, commentators seemed to regard the "massive reduction in rural districts" as a foregone conclusion; it was the consolidation of districts in and around cities that generated real discussion. "Designed to equalize as much as possible the taxable wealth behind the schoolchildren of the state," one observer wrote, the Unruh bill "may be said to illustrate a law: that the larger district favors the poor, and the poor tend to favor the larger district." The prospect of forced annexation to large urban districts terrified residents of affluent suburbs. Communities like Newport Beach, which shared a high school with the more populous Costa Mesa but maintained its own elementary schools, launched massive protests against the law. Max Rafferty, the state superintendent and an outspoken conservative, claimed it would yield "European style centralization" and "would wipe out [school] boards, to be replaced by monstrous bureaucracies."[15]

More common was the measured reaction of a state senator from Ojai, a semi-rural community at the north end of Ventura County, who opposed the bill's coercive methods but ultimately supported its promise of increased state aid. "The bill is a breakthrough," he wrote. "It recognizes that the already overburdened property taxpayer must be helped by increasing the State's share of school finance." Districts such as Ojai were resigned to consolidation by that time and assumed that increased state support would not only achieve equalization but lower property taxes. That sentiment seems overly optimistic in light of subsequent events. For state funding, apportioned on a foundational basis, did not overcome inequalities between districts and (as will be discussed in the next chapter) areas like Ojai soon soured on the notion that increased state support would in itself provide property tax relief. The number of independent districts in California did fall by almost a third over the next five years, but the one thousand that remained were still three times as many as Unruh had proposed. Disparate spending levels remained entrenched.[16]

The Rise of School Funding Litigation

Lingering inequality in educational spending became the subject of numerous lawsuits during the late 1960s. Central to the adjudication of these suits were competing interpretations of local control and its ability to provide adequate public education. Generally speaking, liberals interpreted funding as a determinant of equal educational opportunity—the constitutional standard established in *Brown v. Board of Education*—and assumed that equal per pupil spending required larger districts and a stronger state role in school finance. From their perspective, the correlation between educational spending, local property values, and school district boundaries was a form of blatant discrimination against the poor and children of color. Conservatives were committed to local control despite its apparent inequalities and worried that state subsidies would undermine local decision-making. Their defense of existing funding formulas, crafted in response to liberal court challenges, was more varied but no less effective in its legal rationale. Conservatives denied that spending alone improved academic quality or that connections between a family's wealth, race, and place of residence were sufficiently precise. The following section explains these two positions in the context of court decisions in California and Texas—and with particular attention, in the latter case, to the lingering impact of rural educational policy on relevant case law.

Legal challenges to school funding formulas proceeded along lines identified in *Rich Schools, Poor Schools* (1968), a book by the educational researcher Arthur Wise. Wise began with the simple question of whether unequal funding violated the Fourteenth Amendment's promise of equal protection under the law. Reviewing a range of Supreme Court decisions over the previous fifteen years, from *Brown v. Board of Education* (1954) to *Baker v. Carr* (1962) and *Harper v. Virginia Board of Elections* (1966), he found that the court had repeatedly struck down impediments to civic participation, particularly regarding education and voting. In this context, he argued, the persistence of local property taxes, with their segregative and chaotic effects on school quality, seemed blatantly unconstitutional. "[If] negroes cannot receive different treatment from the state because of their race . . . indigent criminals cannot receive different treatment from the state because of their indigency . . . voters cannot have their votes valued differently because of where they happen to live . . . [and] cannot be prevented from casting their ballots because they cannot afford to pay a poll tax," he asked, "can children receive substantially different educational opportunities solely because of their parents' economic circumstances or where they happen to live?"[17]

In 1968, a group of Mexican American parents from a comparatively poor section of Los Angeles posed the same question in a lawsuit against the California Department of Education. Under the state's existing foundation plan, they contended, they paid higher tax rates than neighboring districts while their children only got "the same or lesser educational opportunities," an outcome that denied them equal protection.[18] Three years later, in *Serrano v. Priest* (1971), the California Supreme Court ruled in their favor. In a multipart ruling, the justices followed Wise's argument to the letter. They cited *Brown v. Board of Education* and subsequent cases to establish that education was a fundamental interest of the state and that wealth, like race, was a "suspect classification," deserving of strict judicial scrutiny.[19] They acknowledged that a district's wealth was not synonymous with an individual's—that wealthy families could perhaps live in property-poor areas—but countered that the state had more or less admitted to a correlation between property wealth and social class. Even without such a correlation, they continued, it was silly to rely on the haphazard distribution of valuable property to assure adequate educational funding. How could the state's interest in a uniform school system possibly be served when the taxable wealth of two districts in the same city could vary by a factor of fifteen?[20]

The justices acknowledged that a federal court, in *McInnis v. Ogilvie* (1966), had declined to overturn a similar funding system in Illinois, and that the U.S. Supreme Court had affirmed its decision without hearing arguments. But they argued that the plaintiffs in *McInnis* had erroneously tried to align methods of school finance with the "educational needs" of pupils, too vague a standard for the court to enforce. In *Serrano v. Priest*, the California Supreme Court found the issue much clearer. Rather than trying to quantify students' educational needs, the court flatly stated that any system that "produces substantial disparities among school districts in the amount of revenue available for education" violated the equal protection clause. The justices concluded that money was what mattered and that California's system of school funding was unconstitutional until it actually achieved equalized expenditures.[21]

The *Serrano* decision sent tremors through legislatures and departments of education around the country. Because most states had similar funding systems, their courts and (eventually) the U.S. Supreme Court might now reach similar conclusions. As other cases worked their way through the judicial system, governors and legislators frantically convened studies on school finance reform. Yet they struggled to understand how they could neutralize local disparities in property wealth without dissolving public education altogether, on the one hand, or funding it entirely at the state level on the other. Widespread support for seemingly unconstitutional systems of local funding left lawmakers at an impasse.

A potentially workable solution came from Harvard researchers John Coons, William Clune, and Stephen Sugarman, in a book entitled *Private Wealth and Public Education* (1970). The authors reiterated that unless a state pegged foundational aid to its wealthiest district, lower determinations of "adequacy" would allow property-rich districts to exceed state aid at the expense of poorer ones. The same phenomenon occurred if, as in California, states allowed localities to voluntarily surpass the maximum tax rate. Greater dependence on local revenues would always benefit the wealthy. Rather than "despair of any middle path," however, they argued that equalized funding simply required raising guaranteed expenditures to the level of the wealthiest district, an approach they described as "power equalization." As under existing foundation plans, "for every level of local tax effort permitted by statute, the state would have fixed the number of dollars . . . that the district would be empowered to spend" and would "guarantee that this number of dollars will be available to the district." Unlike existing foundation plans, however, the state would enable the poorest districts to generate as much money as the wealthiest at every tax rate, based solely on local effort and irrespective of how much the latter taxed themselves.[22]

Because of the steep, possibly exponential costs that this plan would impose on state governments, several states coupled proposals for power equalization with new limits on local taxation, putting a ceiling on the amount of funding they would need to supplement. Some even developed systems of "negative aid," in which districts that raised more revenue than others at a certain tax rate would have their surplus collected and redistributed. Just as power equalization offered poor districts an incentive to tax themselves at high rates (as many already were), negative aid discouraged rich districts from outspending their neighbors. Both left local voters responsible for adequately funding their schools. Thus, while the new equalization model was imperfect in many respects—it did not actually guarantee equal funding, for instance, and reduced the measure of educational quality to the amount of money spent—Coons and his colleagues wrote that "it is probably feasible; it is vastly superior to any existing system; [and] it preserves most [aspects] of the existing systems."[23]

The first test for power equalization came in Texas, which in the late 1960s was proceeding through the same debates and lawsuits as California. Here, too, the politics of school finance were closely tied to the history of rural school consolidation—indeed, one cannot understand the persistence of local school funding, in Texas or elsewhere, without recognizing the impact of rural education.

Texas first overhauled its system of school funding during the 1910s, when it established independent school districts for urban areas; rural "common" districts, operated under the supervision of county boards and taxed on county land valuations; and a state textbook fund, distributed on a flat, per pupil basis. These reforms resulted in a political standoff during the 1940s, however, as small, rural districts began to demand a greater share of state funds and larger districts insisted that school aid continue based on the number of students enrolled. A group of legislators known as the Gilmer-Aikin committee tentatively resolved the dispute by increasing state aid to rural areas but making it contingent on district consolidation, higher teacher salaries, and a nonelected state superintendent, all of which were signed into law in 1949.[24]

It took some creative parliamentary maneuvers to get these measures past rural representatives, who secured concessions that would have a significant impact on Texas school administration over the subsequent twenty years. First, the state board of education remained much larger than the Gilmer-Aikin committee had suggested—with twenty-one members rather than nine—and its voting districts remained unchanged for decades, skewing in favor of rural areas as urban populations grew. Also, while the Gilmer-Aikin law ordered the closure of thousands of "dormant" districts—tax havens that did not operate schools—in practice there were laughably low thresholds for compliance. The law defined dormancy as two consecutive years without classes, for instance, so the Provident City Independent School District, which sat atop $28 million in natural gas reserves, served three children in 1965, closed in 1966, and reopened with two children in 1967. Under the assumption that consolidation would soon phase them out, the Gilmer-Aikin law also provided extra money for rural districts that were too property-poor to meet funding requirements without exceeding Texas's maximum tax rate. Only ten such districts actually existed by the 1960s, but wealthy exurban and agricultural areas began to exploit the loophole, creating a "legal fantasy" in which they listed themselves as unincorporated rural districts still dependent on undervalued county assessments. By 1968, nearly one hundred of these districts were receiving $3.3 million in tax credits annually. Outside Port Arthur, the West Orange-Cove school district, with a booming petrochemical industry and property valuation three times the state average, received $259,000 (see table 2).[25]

These abuses indicate the growing confluence between the interests of wealthy rural and suburban areas, both of which opposed any effort to tax land at its full value, attach their property to poor, neighboring communities, or redistribute local revenue elsewhere in the state. Needless to say, both groups also opposed

TABLE 2. In Texas, wealthy districts misrepresented their tax bases to claim subsidies intended for poor rural areas.

CLAIMS FOR TEXAS MAXIMUM TAX RATE EXEMPTION, 1963–68	
YEAR	NUMBER OF DISTRICTS
1963–64	28
1964–65	34
1965–66	74
1966–67	82
1967–68	99

state campaigns to equalize school funding through district consolidation between the 1940s and 1960s. In 1965, they managed to halt a proposal for a redistributive negative aid program. Despite their lobbying, however, in 1967 the Texas legislature began to shift tax credits from rural to urban districts, and in 1968, following a dire report by the governor on the inadequacies of small schools, it pushed for another round of rural district consolidation.[26]

Texas's poor rural communities remained divided on the 1968 consolidation proposal. Some welcomed its promise of tax savings, while others were willing to tax themselves at higher rates to maintain their independence.[27] Wealthier rural and suburban areas had nothing to gain from larger districts or more state funds and were staunchly opposed. The latter areas became the backbone of a number of anticonsolidation organizations. The most powerful was the Texas Small Schools Association, which organized large-scale letter-writing campaigns and voter drives against the consolidation bill. Another group, the Little Red School House Committee, mobilized ranchers, oil companies, and rural landowners against the proposal's assessment reforms, which would have raised taxes in many rural areas. Yet rather than focus on tax rates, the School House Committee emphasized the benefits of small school districts and invoked the rhetoric of local democracy, arguing that consolidation would "virtually wipe out 865 community centers" and that "mere bigness is not an absolute guarantee of excellence." The legislature ultimately bowed to political pressure and rejected the consolidation plan. To address concerns about unequal tax bases it merely extended existing provisions for rural pupils to attend schools outside their district, allowing students unsatisfied with local funding to seek opportunities in neighboring communities through the use of tuition-based transfers.[28]

The degree to which transfers mitigated disparate property values and the means by which they did so became a significant point of disagreement in the legal battle over school funding. Like the rural property tax credit, voluntary pupil transfers had become something of a legal fantasy in Texas, originally passed for the benefit of rural districts that did not operate high schools but later employed by both suburban and urban districts that did. In 1971, a district judge named William Justice found that voluntary transfers were enabling children from an air force base in San Felipe, Texas, a poor, predominantly Hispanic district, to enroll in the adjacent Del Rio schools, which were whiter and significantly better funded. Citing Supreme Court precedents prohibiting transfers to perpetuate racial segregation, Justice halted the program and ordered the consolidation of the two districts to achieve racial balance. There was some distance, however, between the logic of his decision and that of the original complaint: San Felipe had not objected to the transfer policy on racial grounds but simply because it lost revenue paying students' out-of-district tuition. The case had significant implications for later arguments about money and educational equality, since it interwove them with elements of racial discrimination and made questions about student transfers and district consolidation as applicable to cities and suburbs as to rural areas.[29]

Once the Del Rio consolidation order went through, another Texas district asked to join the ruling and have their district consolidated with a wealthier neighbor. The Edgewood Independent School District, encompassing a Mexican American section of San Antonio, also contained an air force base and little commercial property, consigning it to high taxes and poor schools. Demetrio Rodriguez and several other parents had already filed a suit against San Antonio and the state board of education for denying their children equal educational opportunity on the basis of property wealth. With that case pending, their petition for consolidation with the San Antonio school district was denied. But their victory would come soon enough. Four months after the *Serrano* decision, a panel of federal judges found in the Edgewood parents' favor, repeating the California Supreme Court's findings that education was a fundamental interest, wealth was a suspect classification, and local taxation was an unconstitutional basis for school finance.[30]

As in the *Serrano* and Del Rio cases, the initial decision in *San Antonio v. Rodriguez* blurred distinctions between class and racial discrimination. Edgewood was not merely poor but an identifiably Mexican American district, and for that reason opponents understood the ruling as threat to the economic and racial integrity of surrounding suburbs, with consolidation and race-based busing its logical endpoint. "We're getting a real groundswell against enforced consolidation around the state and around San Antonio," remarked one school superintendent, of which race-based busing, rather than equalized funding, seemed to be "the most controversial dilemma." *Rodriguez* prompted suburban districts from around the state to form the Texas Association of Suburban Schools, an organization (like its rural counterparts) opposed to the forced consolidation of any school district.[31] The Association of Suburban Schools was even willing to increase state funds to inner-city schools in order to prevent the consolidation of metropolitan districts. Many suburbanites hoped that allocating resources through a system of preferential funding would offset the push for consolidation and the sort of racial and socioeconomic integration that it portended.[32]

The U.S. Supreme Court made that compromise unnecessary (or at least less urgent) when it heard *Rodriguez* on appeal in October 1972. Rather than disallowing the connection between local property values and school funding, the court reinforced it, finding no constitutional right to equal educational funding between districts. Several justices warned that changes to existing funding plans would inevitably lead to overweening state control and the dissolution of district boundaries. They gave the notion of power equalization short shrift in oral arguments. Instead of recognizing the Coons team's proposal as a means to preserve decentralization and local initiative within a more equitable system, Justice Lewis Powell in particular "suspected that [it] would lead to more centralized authority over education" and that upholding the lower court's ruling "would mean that only absolute equality in per student funding would satisfy the Equal Protection Clause," although the plaintiffs had expressly avoided such reasoning.[33]

Powell might have misinterpreted the implications of power equalization, but he correctly identified imprecision in the plaintiffs' conflation of individual and district wealth and of class and racial discrimination. It was true that the ten Texas districts with per pupil valuations above $100,000 had the highest family incomes and the lowest percentage of minority students, while the four districts with per pupil valuations below $10,000 had the lowest family incomes and the most minority students. Yet what was clear at the extremes became muddled in the middle. For example, districts with a $30,000 to $50,000 valuation per pupil actually had *lower* median incomes than those with a $10,000 to $30,000 valuation. Meanwhile, those in the $50,000 to $100,000 range had higher concentrations of minority students, a reminder that per pupil expenditures already tended to be higher in at-risk urban areas than in many suburbs. Whatever the general trend, Powell recognized that there was no rigid correlation between property wealth, spending, and race.[34]

Powell drew further support for this position from voluntary student transfers, the same policy that had framed William Justice's earlier ruling in Del Rio. While Justice had seen transfers as an urban ploy to thwart desegregation and thus considered district consolidation an appropriate remedy, Powell learned about the practice from one of his clerks, Larry Hammond, who had attended a poor school district on the outskirts of El Paso, which, because it lacked a high school, bused its students into the city. Providing rural students access to secondary education had been the original purpose of the Texas transfer program and, Hammond explained to Powell, it underscored the imperfect connection between family and district wealth. As long as educational policies encouraged student mobility and parental choice, they precluded the sort of static, suspect class necessary for strict judicial scrutiny of poverty. Despite occasional misuse, transfers represented a longstanding compromise to guarantee quality education *without* consolidating school districts. They offered justification for Powell's commitment to local control of schools.[35]

The majority decision in *San Antonio v. Rodriguez* (1973) overturned the lower court's ruling and contradicted *Serrano* on almost every point. Powell wrote that the Texas system did not hurt " 'poor' people" as a distinct class and did not "impermissibly interfere with the exercise of a 'fundamental' right or liberty," since education was not enumerated in the United States Constitution. Thus, he argued that the case did not merit strict scrutiny of the law and cautioned that any dispute dealing with "the most delicate and difficult questions of local taxation, fiscal planning, educational policy, and federalism . . . [required] a more restrained form of review." After these preliminary pronouncements, Powell proceeded with an extended paean to the local control of education. "In an era that has witnessed a consistent trend toward centralization of the functions of government," he wrote, "local sharing of responsibility for public education has survived . . . [due to] the depth of commitment of its supporters." Part of that commitment was a valid impulse "to devote more money to the education of one's [own] children" than to others', and to participate "in the decision-making process that determines how those local tax dollars will be spent." Powell conceded that the plaintiffs had offered power equalization as a means to *encourage* such participation, unconstrained by wealth, but again seemed to misunderstand the method's basis in local effort, writing that "Texas may be justified in believing that other systems of school finance, which place more of the financial responsibility in the hands of the State, will result in a . . . lessening of desired local autonomy," and that there was "no justification for such a severe denigration of local property taxation and control." Powell thought Edgewood's poverty was unfortunate but that it did not rise to the level of illegality and should not threaten local democracy.[36]

In upholding the Texas foundation system the Supreme Court did not preclude more comprehensive measures for educational equity; it merely established that there was no constitutional right to equal expenditures or extra-local taxation. The issue went back to state courts and legislatures, which often divided on the next steps to take. Texas, for example, increased state support but maintained its foundational basis, and enough inequality to raise subsequent court challenges in the 1980s and 2000s. Meanwhile, the California Supreme Court reaffirmed its original findings in *Serrano v. Priest*. In *Serrano II* (1976) the justices not only upheld but strengthened California's new funding system, finding that provisions in the state constitution required legislators to equalize both tax capacity and per pupil spending in public education.[37] A handful of states followed California's example, but most used the *Rodriguez* decision to preserve foundation systems and the role of local funding. In either case, school funding remains politically fraught. States frequently fall out of compliance with court mandates, new lawsuits take years to assemble, and judges struggle to parse the constitutionality of funding formulas without infringing on legislatures' power to set policy and control public spending.[38]

Rural Division on "Negative Aid" Formulas

In the wake of the *Rodriguez* decision, Rachel Tompkins, the expert on rural educational policy, wrote: "Two major groups have been most adamant about local control—one suburban and one rural. That, however, does not make them allies today on matters of state school finance." Tompkins argued that rural and suburban areas' common defense of localism was a legacy of the early twentieth century, when consolidation offered them little economic gain and threatened to weaken their political power. By the 1970s, when almost all rural districts had to some degree merged and suburban districts had grown increasingly wealthy, their alliance against state funding weakened. Suburbs now sought to guard their wealth, Tompkins implied, while rural districts, increasingly dependent on state aid, became less worried about its coercive effects. Her formulation was generally correct, but with an important caveat. There were a growing number of areas with few permanent residents but valuable land assessments—vacation communities, for instance—that remained nominally rural but aligned with suburbs on issues of school finance.[39]

The two types of rural opinion were particularly evident in Door County, Wisconsin, the peninsular "thumb" of the state jutting into Lake Michigan. The city of Sturgeon Bay bisected the county, geographically and culturally. South of it one found grain farms and a primarily rural population; to its north, orchards and small fishing villages mixed with posh retreats for Chicago vacationers. Historically, southern farmers had refused to raise taxes for municipal services while northern towns prided themselves on well-funded schools and libraries, often receiving endowments of books and artwork from resident millionaires. Although the state's 1959 consolidation order was unpopular in both areas, the south grudgingly combined its one-room schools into a regional high school district—the most economical choice under the circumstances—while

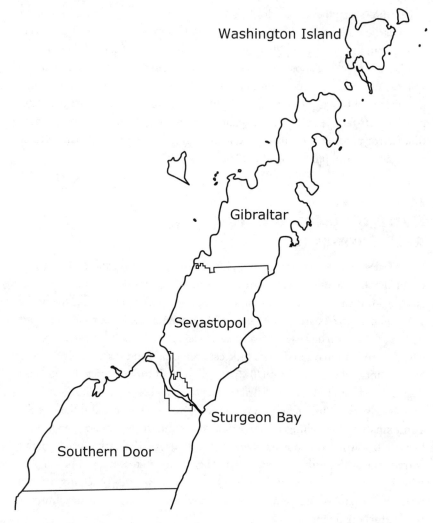

FIGURE 12. The school districts of Door County, Wisconsin. Attempts to consolidate districts north of Sturgeon Bay failed when vacation communities used local control to safeguard property wealth.

the north's small but comparatively wealthy communities kept their schools separate.[40]

By 1962, a drive north from Green Bay proceeded through five very different districts (see figure 12). One first passed the Southern Door regional high school, a large building praised as "a model in [district] reorganization" for its ability to offer classes in agricultural science.[41] Then came the Sturgeon Bay city school system. After that was Sevastopol, a farming community that had refurbished its tiny high school to comply with state building standards and very much wanted to keep it under local control. Then came Gibraltar, an exurban area at the peninsula's tip with four elementary districts and a union high school. Finally, there was remote Washington Island, which operated the state's smallest high school district. The persistence of these small northern districts undermined the state's preference for large tax bases and comprehensive high schools, but DPI officials assumed that the area's growing population would soon complete the consolidation process. It did not work out as they hoped.[42]

In 1964, suburban commuters tried to detach an elementary school from the southern edge of the Sevastopol district, complaining that Sevastopol High School provided only "a rural education . . . with Vo Ag and related courses" and that their children would be better served by the Sturgeon Bay schools. Sevastopol board members objected that such a partition would lower their district's assessed valuation, leading to full annexation by the city and inevitable school closures. "The city would not have been interested in helping us build our grade school centers," they wrote, "and we would not have been satisfied to pay a city tax rate and keep our one-room schools as they were." The secession failed, but Sevastopol, eager to repay the cost of its new high school, suggested that parents' dissatisfaction might abate with the creation of a single district north of Sturgeon Bay. Such a merger would increase its own revenues with property taxes from the loosely organized vacation communities to the north.[43]

Predictably, the Gibraltar district wanted none of it. A second group of newcomers on Sevastopol's *north* side soon petitioned to detach another elementary school, arguing that "the small high school is going to be a detriment in the very near future," and that splitting Sevastopol in half, with the south end joining Sturgeon Bay and theirs joining Gibraltar, would be more appropriate. Contrary to the wishes of the state superintendent, however, they had no intention of building bigger elementary schools or turning Gibraltar into a K–12 district. Instead, the gambit was a means to preserve small schools and local taxation. If the parents had succeeded in joining the Gibraltar district, their elementary schools would have had two rooms and four teachers between them, what one board member described as "a very nice teacher-pupil relationship." Nor would they have been subsumed under the Gibraltar high school board: Votes to consolidate the union district were tabled after failing for two years in a row. Thus, the peninsula's three northern districts remained warily intact following statewide consolidation. The most rural, Sevastopol, resisted annexation to the city but was unable to enlarge its tax base, while the wealthiest, Gibraltar and Washington Island, were able to maintain independent elementary schools and local taxation.[44]

Similar dynamics reappeared in 1971, when, following the *Serrano* decision, Wisconsin governor Patrick Lucey convened a task force to study equalized school funding.[45] In 1973, the group's recommendations produced legislation that raised the state's share of school expenditures from thirty-one to thirty-nine percent (still twelve percent below the national average), set lower guaranteed valuations for K–8 than K–12 districts (encouraging the consolidation of union high schools), and imposed negative aid requirements on a handful of districts whose valuations exceeded the state guarantee. Door County's truly rural districts, Southern Door and Sevastopol, which relied on modest farmsteads for tax support and had already consolidated their high schools, welcomed the proposal for its increased state subsidies. Gibraltar and Washington Island, with a union high school and the highest property values in the state, respectively, lobbied strongly against it.[46]

All twenty-three of the state's negative aid districts were either Milwaukee suburbs or quasi-rural towns, where suburban concerns about rising taxes mixed easily with rural fears of district consolidation.[47] Sure that "consolidation [would] be the only alternative" if taxes rose, a number of resort towns coordinated a letter-writing campaign to "preserve the integrity of the community school system and to save our schools from eventually being dissolved into surrounding districts." The mayor of Green Lake admitted that communities like his were "basically tourist areas with high priced land and lake frontage property." Because many of their residents were retirees on fixed incomes, however, he argued that the equalization plan "[smacked] of socialism" and represented the "erosion of local control."[48] A woman from Hubertus, a small town northwest of Milwaukee, expressed similar sentiments. "Should the rural and small city people be penalized for living in the country or [in a] community which strives to hold down taxation?" she asked. "Rural government (which includes schools) is cautious how citizens' money is spent. . . . Perhaps City Government should take lessons."[49]

Setting a high bar for guaranteed valuation ensured that consolidation and negative aid would affect only a handful of districts, but they happened to be the ones with the most political clout. Even without the votes to repeal the new system of state funding outright, conservatives in the legislature managed to nullify the most important provisions. In 1974, the state senate passed a bill extending home rule to rural towns in matters of taxation, education, and public services. Critics objected that the law had less to do with farming communities than with suburban areas—"spiritually and economically urban but politically defined rural"—which feared annexation to cities. One reporter noted that it would give "families in higher income brackets tax advantages that the residents of the adjacent cities do not enjoy . . . [as] the well-to-do migrate to the quiet and comfort of the country and leave urban problems to the resolution of the less affluent." The following year, the assembly modified the negative aid law as well, raising the level of guaranteed valuation from $75,000 to $102,000 per pupil, narrowing the list of negative aid districts from twenty-three to five.[50] Finally, following the *Rodriguez* decision, the Wisconsin Supreme Court overturned the school finance formula itself. In *Buse v. Smith* (1976), the court found in favor of the five negative aid districts, including Gibraltar and Washington Island, ruling that "while the state's power over education is extensive, there remains some [standard of] local control." State support for schools merely needed to be "as nearly uniform as practicable" and was not required to achieve absolute equality between districts.[51] The justices acknowledged the right to a free education, but they argued that the framers of Wisconsin's constitution had expected communities, rather than the state, to take primary responsibility for its funding. Applying a local tax to a state purpose, as the equalization formula did, violated the state's code of uniform taxation.[52]

Buse v. Smith was the first state-level case after *Rodriguez* to reverse negative aid provisions, and by using the widely recognized uniformity principle to do so, it became as generally applicable against statewide funding as *Serrano* had been in its support. Over the subsequent decade numerous other states used prohibitions against statewide taxation to invalidate negative aid formulas, preventing the redistribution of wealth from rich to poor school districts. Thus, once again, as rural politics converged with those of the suburbs, invocations of tradition and community control provided a convincing rationale for conservative judges to limit state regulation of schools. Those rulings could be applied in any number of contexts; they found purchase almost anywhere there was property wealth to defend. But they began in a particular sort of place: where economic privilege and skepticism of government adhered to lingering structures of local democracy, where school districts remained small and towns thinned into fields.[53]

Conclusion

State support for education expanded greatly but not steadily over the course of the twentieth century. In fits and starts legislatures increased subsidies to local school districts, trying to modernize public education with new buildings and textbooks, better teachers, and wider course offerings. Complicating the process, however, were underlying questions about the purpose and structure of state aid. How much education were states supposed to provide their citizens, and how much of the cost could be shouldered by local taxpayers? Was state revenue meant to address specific categories of need, such as textbooks, or was it supposed to mitigate funding disparities between districts more broadly? If the latter, how completely were states supposed to close the gap, and for whose benefit, schoolchildren or taxpayers? Answers to these questions differed from state to state and from year to year, but they coalesced around the notion of minimal standards. In school finance, minimums were first codified in statutory tax rates during the nineteenth century, which established a floor for local support but proved unequal to the task of modernizing and equalizing school facilities. By the mid-twentieth century, most states had implemented foundational aid to supplement local revenues, but again limited their support to insufficient levels of adequacy. Increasing the state's share of school finance has been one of the signal changes in educational politics since then. Even in states that rejected a right to strictly equal funding, courts have found gross inequalities or inadequate state support to be unconstitutional. Legislatures have grudgingly begun to craft more equitable systems of school finance, reducing the responsibility of local taxpayers to fund their schools. Yet that change has been incremental and generally ineffective, with states struggling to meet rising standards of adequacy, the public skeptical about schools' use of state funds, and almost no one willing to prevent localities from exceeding state guarantees. The trend toward state-financed school systems seems simple enough, but its details remain maddeningly complex.

By the mid-1980s, Deerfield, Illinois, had grown to nearly twenty thousand residents and built several new elementary and junior high schools. The debates about residential development, zoning, and school funding that had wracked the town twenty-five years earlier diminished as the area grew larger and more diverse. Yet those debates persisted farther out, along the edge of suburban settlement just north and west of Deerfield. Decades of farm consolidation in the village of Harvard, for instance, ended abruptly as young families "fleeing the chaos of contemporary urban life [and] the anonymity of suburbia" bought five-acre plots and "a whole colony of country-gentleman airline pilots" took advantage of the town's proximity to O'Hare International Airport. The municipal board in Libertyville, declaring that its residents were "willing to pay [more] for a quality of life," used tax revenues to purchase vacant farmsteads on the outskirts of town, which it sublet to gardeners or converted into golf courses rather than develop as subdivisions. "What's going to take root is a new attitude on [residential] growth here," said the town supervisor. "We've been laboring under the illusion that all growth was a sign of progress. That's a myth." When developers challenged similar land-preservation initiatives in the village of Long Grove, the town petitioned the state for home-rule status. " 'They've made the debate that we have not had the authority [to limit housing development]," said the village president. "But under home rule there is no debate at all." In case after case, land use controls allowed towns to limit development and preserve an affluent, quasi-rural charm.[54]

Attempts to slow in-migration through limited school capacity also remained widespread. Many of the communities northwest of Chicago still operated union districts with separate elementary and high school boards, sharply segregating local tax revenues and perpetuating scores of small elementary schools. In 1985, when Republican Governor James Thompson tried to slip a bill through the state assembly tying state funding to harsher consolidation requirements, the bill's most vocal opponents came both from rural school districts in southern Illinois and from the northern suburbs of Chicago. Commentators noted that these areas differed in the character of their opposition. Rural districts downstate feared losing state aid if they refused to consolidate, but were more worried about losing community coherence if they submitted. Suburban districts, which "enjoyed high assessed valuation and received very little revenue from the state aid formula," opposed consolidation mostly "as a means of preserving their elite position . . . ignoring the growing educational, financial, and racial problems plaguing the remainder of the state." Nevertheless, the groups united around the principle of local control of education.[55]

Support for consolidation and increased aid to schools came from both of Illinois's political parties, as well as business interests, large suburbs, and some poor rural areas. A Republican governor introduced the bill and shepherded it through a Republican legislature as part of a broader platform of lower taxes and greater academic accountability. Unfortunately for them, most of the areas affected by consolidation were also solidly Republican, and just as alienating teachers' unions could sabotage a Democratic campaign, the Republican Party misjudged the degree of resistance from crucial segments of its constituency. Grassroots groups from the affected districts attracted sympathetic media coverage while withholding contributions from Republican lawmakers. Sensing an opening for the 1986 gubernatorial election, Democrats tried to turn school consolidation into a wedge issue, with the challenger, Adlai Stevenson III, calling the law "dictatorial and ambiguous" and declaring that "a school isn't bad [just] because it's small." Governor Thompson soon reversed course himself, denouncing mandatory consolidation and urging lawmakers to repeal the law. Ultimately, anticonsolidation activists convinced all major stakeholders to soften their positions on the issue, and legislators frantically reversed their votes. District reorganization plans became voluntary rather than mandatory, and of the fifty-nine submitted that year, fifty maintained the status quo.[56]

The failure of the 1985 bill was merely the latest manifestation of Illinois's commitment to the local control of schools. After shuttering its smallest districts and most of its one-room schoolhouses during the 1940s, the state struggled to effect subsequent closures: In the 1980s it still had the third most districts in the nation behind California and Texas. In *Cronin v. Lindberg* (1976), the Illinois Supreme Court found no right to equalized funding between districts—the case cited *McInnis v. Ogilvie* and *San Antonio v. Rodriguez*—and its legislature left school spending entirely to local discretion. In each of these arenas the confluence of rural and suburban interests seemed to represent a unified commitment to localism.[57] But the 1985 consolidation campaign, which had started at the behest of the Tax Federation of Illinois and right-wing pundits promoting academic "excellence," also suggested that that position was growing more tenuous, even among conservatives. Fewer and fewer communities could argue, as the wealthiest did, that local control alone ensured low taxes and high standards, and as those issues became central to school politics, even districts that opposed consolidation began to clamor for increased financial support. Thus, while *Rodriguez* remained an impediment to equalized school funding, in Illinois and elsewhere, an educational politics focused on state action would soon undercut the conservative defense of localism.

TAX REVOLTS

In 1978, two years after the California Supreme Court reaffirmed its commitment to equalized school funding in *Serrano II*, the state's voters passed Proposition 13, a constitutional initiative that checked rising land assessments, capped property taxes, and required a legislative supermajority to approve future tax increases. The measure seemed to set off a nationwide "tax revolt," in which thirty-seven other states imposed statutory or constitutional restrictions on property taxes, leaving lasting scars on municipal budgets, particularly those of school districts. Some historians have argued that the tax revolt of the late 1970s was a reaction to equalized school funding; that suburban voters, resentful of the redistribution of local tax revenues to other socioeconomic or racial groups, withdrew support for public spending altogether. There is some truth to that claim. As demonstrated earlier, many suburban communities had invoked local control to resist equalization, particularly when it involved limiting or confiscating the money that rich districts spent on their children's education. But assuming a link between equalized funding and tax revolts raises thorny questions about how historians understand causation. For the antiequalization hypothesis cannot account for tax revolts that predated redistributive policies; nor does it explain why, even in states that rejected equalized school funding, conservative voters abandoned local taxation in favor of statewide spending mandates, implicitly *increasing* their dependence on state aid and undermining the basis for local control of schools.

Opposition to equalized funding is at best an incomplete explanation for statewide tax revolts during the 1970s. Revolts mounted over several decades and were less a reaction to a particular funding scheme than to the professionalization of property assessment and school spending, which threatened local control over the collection and disbursement, respectively, of tax revenues. Grassroots antitax movements in California, as well as in places like West Virginia, Oregon, Wisconsin, and New Hampshire, began during the early 1960s, predating equalized school funding formulas. In each of these cases tax revolts began as local attempts to reclaim authority over school administration, with protesters exerting leverage through strategies of "voice" and "exit": either empowering voters to restrain spending through democratic means such as the referendum, or allowing individual parents to take their tax money away from the public schools. These attempts were particularly effective on the suburban fringe, where they seemed to offer the greatest degree of tax relief and faced the least resistance from teachers' unions. By exerting leverage at the state level, however, unions and other interest groups soon squelched local experiments with "voice" and "exit." Only as these alternatives failed did conservatives resort to statewide spending limits, surrendering their commitment to local funding in order to restrict property taxes.[1]

Seen in this light, Proposition 13 was not the beginning of the tax revolt but its compromised conclusion. The principle of local taxation enshrined in *San Antonio v. Rodriguez* became worthless when decoupled from democratic participation and voters' ability to limit expenditures: Local control was no match for the phalanx of certified assessors, unionized faculty, school administrators, and state officials using state power to push and pull school budgets higher. With local boards unable to resist calls for more spending, conservatives turned to new, extra-local restrictions to achieve their policy goals. Thus, even as local control made gains in court it began to lose at the ballot box.

The Meaning of Proposition 13

Scholars have debated the origins of Proposition 13 for decades. Their terms of disagreement vary across disciplines, but most disputes focus on the measure's seemingly disproportionate response to rising property taxes. Rather than temporarily curbing tax rates or expanding exemptions for needy landowners, Proposition 13 imposed drastic, permanent limits on the state's ability to raise revenue. One group of scholars interprets that severity much as contemporary activists did, as a necessarily dramatic demonstration against an unresponsive state bureaucracy. In the words of one voter, "I always felt that there was a lot of wasted effort. They [public officials] could learn to economize more." The other side contends that anti-tax sentiment should not be taken at face value but is better understood as an implicit rejection of redistributive social policies: in short, that the language of spending cuts concealed unsavory racial and class resentments.[2]

There is certainly evidence to support the latter position. In *My Blue Heaven* (2002), Becky Nicolaides demonstrates that taxes were the primary political concern of working-class homeowners in Los Angeles throughout the twentieth century. In the 1920s, voters in the South Gate neighborhood repeatedly rejected recommendations to consolidate or reorganize their school district for fear of tax hikes. Many had built their own modest homes and feared losing them in economic downturns. They even accepted limited racial integration as a means to lessen school spending. By the early 1960s, however, the efforts of city and state officials to fully desegregate and better fund neighborhood schools through centralized administration alarmed local voters. Working-class whites "began agitating for more power in school affairs, asserting their right to community control," Nicolaides writes. Suggestions of race-based busing "revived talk of separating [South Gate] from the Los Angeles district altogether," a move that would ensure "'home rule' in school decisions," "better use of tax revenue," and a racially homogenous student body. In 1963, a movement called the Taxpayers Rebellion organized over one hundred community groups across the state "to vote out of office those government officials who ignore the wishes of the people to cut the cost of government." Thus, Nicolaides argues, fifteen years before Proposition 13, "'taxes' became a coded reference to civil rights and programs for minorities, an excellent local example of the national trend that saw an overlapping of race and taxes as political issues."[3]

Although the rhetorical link between race and taxes is undeniable in California and nationally, there remains significant imprecision in our understanding of the shift from local to state-level tax revolts, leading many scholars to overemphasize racism and underestimate local activists' stated desire to curb bureaucracy.[4] For example, Nicolaides extends the anti-tax sentiment of Los Angeles homeowners in the 1960s to voters in twenty-two other counties, despite the fact that few communities in rural or suburban California faced the school integration that she cites as its cause. Other reasons these voters might have had to cut local tax rates go unmentioned.[5]

Histories of Proposition 13 often rely on similar generalizations, characterizing a broad-based grassroots campaign with suggestive, selective references to suburban racism. In an early account of the tax revolt, for instance, economist William Fischel dismisses claims that government bureaucracy was unresponsive to voters' interests, citing a lack of local austerity measures as evidence of voter satisfaction. Instead, Fischel writes, "something had changed the political climate" in the mid-1970s to energize support for Proposition 13. He deduces that the source of discontent was the system of equalized funding implemented after *Serrano v. Priest II* (1976), which redistributed tax revenues from richer to poorer school districts. But that conclusion becomes less convincing when one recognizes that widespread austerity movements *were* already gripping California by the early 1960s, and that tax limitation was popular in many of the same districts that benefited from equalized school funding.[6] In *American Babylon* (2005), Robert Self makes a different but similarly flawed argument about the meaning of Proposition 13. Self concludes his analysis of racial politics in Oakland with the claim that Proposition 13's "equation between property taxation and wasteful state bureaucracy was entirely ideological, because property taxes had (and have) little to do with state government financing." According to Self, conservative activists intent on cutting welfare mistakenly crippled their own children's schools instead.[7] By ignoring the fact that schools themselves were a major component of the "state bureaucracy," however, Self bypasses the simple, explicit reason for the tax revolt for a more tendentious argument about coded racism and unintended consequences. None of these historians are wrong in their analysis: Issues of redistribution and race played an important role in the passage of Proposition 13. But it is important to emphasize that local schools were neither new nor in any way incidental to anti-tax campaigns in California. To the contrary, while proponents of Proposition 13 could have easily "posed as defenders of local control against a redistributive mandate imposed by the state . . . they did not. Instead, they posed as defenders of the beleaguered taxpayer against state and local governments—*including* school districts," and in the process jettisoned their defense of local control.[8]

Proposition 13 derived from two sources of discontent, both related to the loss of local political autonomy. The first, thoroughly outlined by Isaac Martin in *The Permanent Tax Revolt* (2008), was land assessment reform. Before the 1960s, nearly all tax assessors were locally elected and used their position to curry political favor, whether through fractional assessment, in which property was valued below its market rate, or through the unrevised transcription of tax rolls, which offset rising land values. Although some commercial interests benefited from these practices, Martin notes, "the most favored constituency was actually homeowners, who were a big, stable, and potentially loyal voting bloc." Localized assessment functioned both as a subsidy and safety net for taxpayers unwilling to withstand rapid shifts in the market value of their property, particularly those with high fixed costs (such as farmers) or low fixed incomes (the elderly). At the same time, inconsistent assessments compounded disparities between local property values, especially in rural areas, and thwarted attempts at uniform spending on schools and other community services. As was the case with school consolidation, liberals' efforts to standardize or centralize the process were frequently voted down by rural legislators. California inched toward assessment reform between 1958 and 1964, with strong support from the California Teachers Association and other educational interests, but efforts repeatedly stalled in the face of rural resistance. Only legislative reapportionment and a highly publicized corruption trial against the San Francisco assessor induced the California legislature in the mid-1960s to pass bills requiring larger jurisdictions, uniform formulas, and professional certification for assessors. These reforms made property taxes fairer, Martin notes, but they also "took away the informal social policy that had protected homeowners," who for the first time found their property assessed at full value and their taxes rising with the state's bullish real estate market.[9]

Into the breach strode Howard Jarvis, a Los Angeles businessman who in 1968 tried to gather enough signatures for a statewide limit on property taxes. He was unsuccessful, but threw his support behind a similar effort by the Los Angeles county assessor, which over the course of five years would have eliminated funding for "people-related services" such as education and welfare, and limited funding for "property-related services" like streets, police, and fire protection to a one percent property tax. That measure failed as well. The legislature instead passed a more modest "homestead" provision to accommodate poor and elderly homeowners, exempting the first $750 of property values from taxation. Undaunted, Jarvis launched two more campaigns for tax limits during the early 1970s, each of which failed by a narrower margin. Proposition 13, his fourth attempt, succeeded on the strength of strong grassroots lobbying and thousands of individual donations. As home values continued to spiral upwards, the one percent limit that had seemed ludicrous a decade before became a constitutional mandate.[10]

As drastic as Proposition 13 was, however, it was neither a rejection of equalized educational funding nor of taxation in general. For one thing, similar measures passed in states that *rejected* equalization. Even in California, proponents of tax limitation often came from the same rural areas that benefited from equalization formulas and had little exposure to racial integration. Martin argues that Proposition 13 merely reestablished, constitutionally and statewide, the financial surety that homeowners had long sought through informal practice. "The tax rebels were not opposed to government action," he concludes. "They *wanted* government to redistribute income in order to protect them from income shocks that resulted from the rising price of housing. The tax revolt, in short, was a social protectionist movement—much like the movements of farmers, workers, and poor people that gave rise to the first welfare states."[11] The historian Thomas Goebel offers numerous precedents for that argument, documenting similar attempts to streamline property taxes through grassroots initiatives during the 1930s.[12] What had changed in intervening decades was that middle- and working-class families now needed protection not only from corporations or political machines, as they had earlier, but from the very bureaucracies they had installed to counteract those groups. State auditors and assessors were supposed to prevent moneyed interests from receiving preferential treatment from local officials—a practice roundly denounced as "tax dodging"—but not to extend their scrutiny to practices that helped homeowners and the ostensibly deserving middle class.[13]

A similar shift toward professionalization and bureaucracy had taken place in the public schools. As state departments of education sought to increase and standardize school funding, they threatened the informal privileges of local taxpayers. School district spending in California more than doubled between 1967 and 1978, outpacing increases in personal income and consumer prices and beating the national average by twenty percent, with much of the money padding higher teacher salaries and new administrative positions. Analysts cited a rash of expensive new regulations, and noted that "the well-staffed, highly educated, and very activist California legislature also contributed to [a] proliferation of programs and experiments in the state's schools." A wry estimate put "the elapsed time between the appearance of an idea in a national education journal and its legislation into the California State Education Code" at about three months.[14] Taxpayers were hardly ignorant about where their money was going, and many specifically supported Proposition 13 as a means of imposing educational austerity. The same polls that showed hostility to welfare programs also suggested that voters "clearly preferred cuts in education over cuts in other essential local services, since the latter were . . . felt to provide better 'value for [the] money.'" When asked to address Proposition 13's potential impact on schools, Howard Jarvis assured audiences that "cuts to education would not be serious since schools aren't teaching anyway," an unsubtle dig at poor discipline and falling test scores; and insofar as "schools by law [had] first call on the state dollar," he argued that the equalization required by *Serrano* "can best be implemented by passage of [Proposition] 13, with the state assuming the burden of educating students." Thus, Jarvis actually *supported* equalized funding across the state, on the understanding that local funding decisions allowed teacher unions to pressure school boards and increase spending. His alternative was firm funding limits and statewide scrutiny, which would ensure that "fat [was] trimmed but essential services [not] endangered."[15]

Many voters seemed to agree with that diagnosis. The problem was not so much that they had to share revenues with other districts but that they had lost the ability to limit tax collection and expenditure even in their own. Whereas local control had once ensured lower taxes, the combination of assessment reform, union bargaining, and state regulation left local boards overmatched, with stronger inducements toward spending and fewer opportunities to register disapproval. The equalization formula in *Serrano II* worsened this trend, but it was not its source. The number of California towns voting down school bond issues had already jumped by the mid-1960s, and by 1978 many voters considered tax limitation the only way to check rising school expenditures.[16] In the little town of Placerville, California, east of Sacramento, letter-writers ascribed school spending problems to the formation of a union high school district in the 1950s and the corresponding increase in bureaucracy. "It's said proposition 13 will destroy local control," one wrote, "but that's already lost." "What scares the opponents [of Proposition 13]," declared another, "is that they may find out the people don't want all the so called services forced on them. . . . For the first time in the 15 years I have been voting I see an opportunity to have some control over my elected officials' spending." Other rural districts used Proposition 13's budget constraints to fire superintendents and staff and return to a "back-to-basics, mandated-programs-only staffing pattern."[17] In these sentiments lies an aspect of the anti-tax movement often overlooked. Tax limits were partly an effort to protect homeownership, as Martin argues, but they were also a means to return government spending to the purview of local voters.[18]

Property Taxes and Political "Voice"

The same factors affecting California were at work in dozens of other states. Signs of a nationwide tax revolt were already palpable in 1974, when political scientist Joel Berke noticed that Americans seemed to be defunding their schools. Voters had rejected only eleven percent of proposed school bonds in 1960, he pointed out, but thirty-three percent in 1965 and fifty-two percent in 1970. What had prompted the increase? For Berke, the answer was simple: "referenda on school budgets and bond issues make education questions among the few opportunities voters have to register, explicitly and directly, their dislike of higher taxes."[19] That statement is undeniably true but it also allows two possible interpretations that, although not mutually exclusive, speak to conflicting historical understandings of the tax revolt. The first interpretation, much like Fischel's and Self's analysis of Proposition 13, takes Berke to mean that school budget referendums stood in for a more general resistance to taxation during the 1970s—that voters targeted school spending simply because it was closest at hand and provided an appealingly direct, if slightly misguided, release for broader political dissatisfaction. A more persuasive interpretation takes opposition to property taxes not as a response to remote state and federal politics but to the increasingly remote administration of local schools themselves. As voters were denied "voice" in professional systems of school administration, rejecting tax increases was one of the few policy levers left to them. Cutting off funding became a means to re-claim not only control of spending but also of personnel, curriculum, and other aspects of school governance.

The professionalization of public education was one of the primary reasons that property taxes rose so dramatically during the postwar period. Spending on schools doubled during the 1950s and tripled during the 1960s, as secondary education became increasingly linked to college attendance, jobs, and social mobility. Class sizes fell over the same period and teachers' salaries rose significantly faster than those of other professions. Although administrative costs remained low in absolute terms, they also rose thirty-fold, from $133 million to $4.3 billion a year, with the sharpest increases occurring between 1965 and 1975. Local taxpayers shouldered the majority of these cost increases until the mid-1970s, when campaigns for equalized funding and tax relief shifted a larger portion of school finance to state and federal governments.[20] Yet individual states still varied widely in their commitment to equalized funding. Many in the Northeast and Midwest remained largely dependent on local revenues, and even those that increased state aid (like California) found that doing so did not necessarily restrain spending.[21] Interlocking policy structures, what political scientists would later describe as "iron triangles," had formed between state legislators, departments of education, and professional organizations, with each arm pushing for greater centralization and bureaucracy in public schools and, in the process, across-the-board increases in school funding.[22]

Outside of cities, the nexus between professionalization, spending, and property taxes remained closely tied to issues of school district consolidation. Proponents of consolidation believed that larger districts would not only widen tax bases but, by empowering teachers and superintendents and putting budget decisions in the hands of centralized school boards, would also encourage higher expenditures. When enough districts had consolidated to tilt the political balance in their favor, city and state policymakers could force the last holdouts to submit to the taxes and spending necessary for their vision of an adequate, modern system of public education.

During the 1950s, for instance, West Virginia passed the Better Schools Amendment, which enabled county boards of education to assess land at its full value and raise tax rates unilaterally when bonds failed, leaving them less dependent on local assessors or public approval to raise revenue.[23] Rural legislators balked, objecting to new taxes generally and especially to those that would build modern, centralized school buildings rather than refurbish outlying schools. They responded to the Better Schools Amendment with a second law requiring sixty percent majorities on all school funding referendums, ensuring that most bonds did fail and daring school boards to exercise their taxing power.[24] Although requiring supermajorities for local bonds and levies certainly returned power to the voters, their goals in exercising that power were less clear. Did local control of school funding represent a legitimate commitment to community-based education, or was it merely an excuse to shield rural voters from higher taxes? Those questions have always been present in educational debates, and they can be difficult to untangle. A telling example occurred in Preston County, West Virginia, between 1973 and 1976, when voters rejected four straight school bonds. The first three bonds, which would have closed rural high schools outright, lost by wide margins; a fourth included a plan to preserve the schools and lost only narrowly. The difference between the first three votes and the last suggests that many of the county's rural voters were not simply rejectionist but were willing to fund community-based schools, although the failure of all four bonds means that there were obviously not enough of them.

Ultimately, consolidating West Virginia's rural high schools required the passage of a second Better Schools Amendment, which provided millions of dollars for county boards to build new schools without levying bonds or raising property taxes. As the educational researcher Timothy Weaver noted, the second amendment represented "financial and regulatory control at the state level" rather than at the local level, enlarging "an already sizable, insulated bureaucracy of professional educationists impervious to populist control" and allowing boards "[to] accomplish by default what [they] could not accomplish through the ballot." Weaver characterized West Virginia's anti-tax movement primarily as an educational conflict between poor, rural communities trying to retain control of their schools and wealthier cities and towns trying to close them. From his perspective, the state's school consolidation battles were simply being reprised as tax revolts.[25]

The funding conflicts that Weaver described were most pointed on the metropolitan fringe, where the effects of suburbanization on land values and school facilities put a financial strain on farmers and other large property holders. Yet tax rebels were never confined to the latter groups. In South Umpqua, Oregon, in 1976, voters also rejected four budget referendums, closing the schools for weeks and attracting national news coverage. At the time, the press blamed the conflict on rural lumbermen who, commentators presumed, doubted the necessity of "'exotic' courses" at the high school or a local preschool program operated by the Experimental Schools Project, and were "delivering an ultimatum to the schools to reduce taxes." After conducting fieldwork in the community, however, several Experimental Schools researchers were surprised to find that their most vocal antagonists were not lumbermen. They were newly arrived exurbanites.[26]

South Umpqua had gained over a thousand residents between 1970 and 1973, a quarter of them from out of state. The area had previously sustained the lowest property valuation in Oregon and spent about one hundred dollars less per pupil than the state average. But four percent annual population growth, coupled with higher land assessments, increased taxes by fifty percent over five years. Studies of similar Oregon towns found that residential growth posed unique challenges for rural municipalities, which could not offset infrastructure costs with the kinds of fees imposed on industrial or extractive development and so transferred costs back to homeowners through property taxes.[27] Yet the newcomers in South Umpqua did not recognize their own responsibility for rising taxes. If anything, they opted "to 'out-Oregon the Oregonians'" in their resistance to educational spending. They organized community groups to exploit residual resentment over school consolidation (which had happened only a few years before) and redirected it toward other causes, including the school budget, objectionable curriculum, teacher tenure, and "socially distant" school leaders. As one observer noted about the failed bond issues: "Leaders of the opposition cheerfully agreed that the budget was not the issue, but its defeat was the most direct means of controlling school policy. The issue of morality turned out to be, in part, a mechanism for gathering people with a wide variety of anxieties about the schools into a common cause. . . . Lack of either representation or direct participation in school leadership was at the base of the [South Umpqua] taxpayer revolt." Thus, as in many other areas of the country, exurbanites used tax limitation as a means to regain control of personnel and curriculum decisions, taking advantage of lingering resistance to consolidation and, by using the language of local control, downplaying their differences with potentially hostile rural residents.[28]

South Umpqua eventually became part of a statewide campaign for constitutional limits on property taxes. Oregon's voters had rejected a plan to abolish property taxes in 1973 but only narrowly turned down a similar measure in 1978. To ease political discontent, the legislature slashed $705 million in tax obligations by lowering local thresholds for school funding. Unlike in other states, however, it did not offset these cuts with increased state aid.[29] As the economists Fred Thompson and Mark Green point out, Oregon was perhaps the least disciplined state in the country in its support for public education. Between 1950 and 1989, foundational aid swung from as much as fifty-five to as little as nineteen percent of total school spending, and during the recession of the late 1970s it fell from forty-five to twenty-eight percent in only a few years. These oscillations put a disproportionate burden on local taxpayers to keep schools open—particularly in poorer districts such as South Umpqua, which were most dependent on state aid—so that instead of preventing tax revolts, the cutbacks at most forestalled them. In 1990, Oregon voters passed Measure 5, a constitutional amendment restricting property tax increases to 1.5 percent annually, with school taxes gradually reduced to 0.5 percent increases. Ironically, the anti-tax movement that began as an assertion of local control did not allow localities to override these limits.[30]

Wisconsin responded much earlier and more deliberately than Oregon to the problem of rising property values. In 1964 it became the first state in the country to enact a homestead tax credit, a "circuit breaker" that offset property tax payments for low-income and elderly homeowners.[31] Yet that provision did not help farmers, many of whom saw their land values increase tenfold during the 1960s as a result of assessment reform and suburban encroachment.[32] By 1970, perceptions of a property-tax crisis prompted a search for more drastic solutions, exemplified by the creation of the Wisconsin Property Owners League (WPOL), whose fifteen thousand members subscribed to the tax theories of the nineteenth-century economist Henry George. Under George's land-value tax, property would be assessed at a low, flat rate based on the value of the land, regardless of structures or improvements.[33] Proponents believed that this simplified structure would unleash competition for sites near urban centers and promote intensive development, eradicating the twin problems of urban decay and inflationary real estate speculation at the city's edge. The WPOL's proposals for land-value taxation did not attract mainstream support and were voted down repeatedly between 1971 and 1977. In 1979, the Wisconsin attorney general tried to put the issue to rest by ruling that adoption of land-value taxes violated principles of uniform taxation. The WPOL launched a last campaign to amend the state constitution, but that also failed.[34]

Despite its unsuccessful attempts to overhaul the state's tax structure, the WPOL was actually quite influential with other, small-scale reforms. In 1974 voters approved a constitutional amendment for the differential assessment of agricultural land, one of the group's secondary demands, and in 1977 the legislature passed the state's first farmland preservation tax credit.[35] The organization also tried to increase voters' control over their tax revenues by turning its attention to school spending. In numerous publications, members argued that suburban sprawl and school construction had become mutually reinforcing, and together were the cause of rising property taxes. As tax hikes pushed urban residents to buy cheaper land in the countryside, they pointed out, the result was "falling enrollment in the central schools," which suddenly struggled to retain staff and maintain buildings, and "an overload in the schools in the developing suburbs," which were forced to raise taxes to accommodate the surplus students. Most politicians sought to offset these problems by increasing state aid to education, but the WPOL complained that aid lagged years behind rapidly shifting populations and did nothing to address the root problem of unplanned suburban development.[36] The WPOL's plan to use land-value taxes to slow residential growth and reverse the trend toward school consolidation attracted hundreds of followers in exurban areas.[37] In both 1972 and 1975, the WPOL chapter in New London, Wisconsin, tried to dissolve its unified school district in favor of an old-fashioned common district, which would have shifted control of the annual budget from the school board to the voters at large on a referendum basis. Chapters in dozens of other towns refused to remit tax revenues to their school districts and instead put them in escrow accounts as a means of protest.[38]

Many Wisconsin voters felt that a return to basic education and local control of spending would settle the property tax problem. Speaking to a crowd of five hundred residents, the city assessor of Fox Lake pointed out that in the five years since its reassessment, the area's valuation had almost doubled. "Seventy-five percent of the property tax is spent in the school districts," she added, although because of the introduction of unionized teachers and administrative bureaucracy, "I am not saying that it is spent on education."[39] In 1972, when Governor Lucey convened the Doyle Commission to investigate the cause of rising property taxes, the commissioners were barraged with questions and complaints about school expenditures. A mother in Kimberly, Wisconsin, voiced a common sentiment when she wrote that "additional state financing is . . . viewed by most educators as the green light for increased salaries and more relaxed spending." Contrasting her small school district with the larger one in nearby Appleton, she argued that although "higher salaries, modern equipment, and supplies have caused the cost of education to rise drastically, *it does not follow that more dollars will guarantee higher quality education.*" She continued:

> The "local control" issue . . . should be strengthened. The concept is already almost diluted out of existence by the effects of the teachers' unions, state agencies, courts, legislature . . . . Parents, after all, have the inherent right to govern and guard their children's education. With all the regimentation of requirements and "professionalism-in-the-name-of-education," the parent has been steadily excluded from the school process . . . and [yet] still expected to wholeheartedly finance more of the same. . . . The aware and protesting local taxpayer seems to be most effective in controlling costs and educational misdeeds.[40]

Here was a quintessential conservative critique of school reform at midcentury—the suspicion of rising bureaucracy, professionalism, and teacher militancy combined with demands for more parental control and basic education—held together with a commonsense argument about local control over school spending. It was a call for increased political voice.

Unfortunately, in the wake of the *Serrano* decision in California, increasing local control over funding (and thus school districts' dependence on local property values) was not on the agenda of either Wisconsin's Democratic or Republican parties. Both assumed that the only feasible way to control taxes and maintain adequate spending for education was to increase state funding further. Members of the Doyle Commission privately admitted that the state would merely "pay lip-service to local control" while pushing to improve assessment practices and centralize school finance. Yet they were forced to acknowledge what the mother in Kimberly had emphasized: that tax cuts were unlikely while teachers and administrators clamored for a greater share of state aid to education. "Increasing the [state aid] guarantee . . . assumes that school boards will choose to lower taxes rather than to increase spending," one member of the commission wrote, but "considering that many educators strongly believe they should be spending more and considering teachers' bargaining, this may not be a safe assumption."[41]

The solution to profligate teachers' unions was not a return to local control but a bipartisan agreement combining increased aid with statewide spending limits. In 1973, the Doyle Commission recommended a one-year freeze on school spending, with increases limited to the rise in a district's assessed valuation. They reasoned that limiting expenditures would rein in property taxes and, combined with more revenue from the state and negative aid provisions, would further equalize spending between districts. The legislature complied with the commission's recommendations on the latter issue—increasing state subsidies to public education and implementing a negative aid formula—and exceeded them on the former, imposing a one-year spending limit of fifty-five dollars per pupil. The effects of spending controls seemed marginal at first: School property taxes fell only two percent in 1973. When the controls lapsed, however, tax rates immediately rose fourteen percent. In 1975 the legislature imposed more stringent, permanent limits, holding districts to nine-and-a-half percent cost increases annually.[42] Thus, just as California would four years later, the Wisconsin legislature moved to placate angry voters by lessening reliance on property taxes but also restricting local control over school budgets.[43]

There was some preservation of local autonomy. School districts in Wisconsin remained more dependent on property taxes than they did in other states, for example, and the legislature rejected subsequent constitutional amendments tying spending to growth in the state's gross income.[44] But such was the new political landscape that interest groups found their positions on local control suddenly reversed. Many conservatives abandoned the rhetoric of localism to ensure fiscal discipline across the state. As a school board member in Pewaukee complained, "Suburban communities such as ours are forced to pay higher costs than most Wisconsin schools because teachers and other workers demand and get more money here. . . . Therefore, we cannot accept out-in-the-state [rural] costs as a criterion for us here if we are to continue to operate." "We believe you will be representing this area," he wrote to his assemblyman, "by asking for an increase in the [amount of] cost control limitation rather than a lowering of it."[45]

Meanwhile, in an effort to protect salary increases, teachers' unions became outspoken champions of local control, specifically appealing for the right of some districts to tax themselves at higher rates than others. "Under the proposed cost controls," a WEAC representative observed, "even if the local taxpayer and school district want, they would be prohibited from increasing expenditures on behalf of their students. This kind of prohibition limits democracy. . . . Currently some Wisconsin school districts spend as little as $600 per pupil and some as much as $2,000. If the people living in the $600 per pupil district wished to spend $2,000 per pupil—it would take 42 years to catch up under the proposed cost controls." With school boards "empowered to make all decisions on the *minimum* standards of the educational program . . . and the state setting an unrealistic and stringent maximum for spending," it warned, "this mixture of state and local control of education accomplishes the worst possible results."[46]

Over subsequent decades both sides sought to expand the aspects of state regulation that suited their interests. Unions kept lobbying to increase state funding and end local spending controls, while conservatives tried to reduce state funding and leave the controls in place. The result was predictable tinkering by the legislature and DPI but, by and large, a move away from the cause of local control and a failure of grassroots movements to reclaim direct political "voice." Similar forces would hinder attempts to lower property taxes through parental choice and the ability to "exit" local public schools.[47]

Property Taxes and Political "Exit"

Often underlying local tax revolts was the assumption that bigger school districts, while perhaps more equitable, were also more wasteful. Critics claimed that consolidation had created an educational monopoly unresponsive to the will of taxpayers and parents. Some insisted that the most effective way to reestablish popular sovereignty and cost efficiency was to break that monopoly by issuing vouchers to parents and allowing them to enroll their children in any public or private school that had space. This sort of "exit" policy would presumably foster competition for students and impose market discipline on school spending, edging schools toward the competitive educational model that had existed before the rise of public education in the nineteenth century.

Vouchers were first proposed by University of Chicago economist Milton Friedman, in 1955. Friedman was generally hostile to government interference in markets, but he acknowledged some degree of state responsibility in education. Even within a free-market system, he observed, government was necessary to enforce contracts and punish fraud or coercion. Other circumstances also merited limitations on individual choice and exchange.[48] Friedman contended that a democratic government needed to police at least three aspects of public schools: It had a responsibility to compel attendance, prevent exclusion, and ensure that schools met basic standards of accreditation. Beyond those minimum thresholds, he continued, "it is more difficult to justify . . . the actual administration of educational institutions by the government, the 'nationalization,' as it were, of the bulk of the 'education industry.' "[49]

Friedman argued that as school administration became increasingly constrained by state and federal regulation, it lost variety, vitality, or any real accountability to parents. If parents were dissatisfied with local schools, their only alternatives were to enroll their children in private schools or to relocate to a new community, neither a feasible option for most families. Friedman suggested that loosening the allocation of public funding through vouchers would force "a wide variety of schools [to] spring up to meet [consumer] demand" and allow parents to "express their views about schools directly," not through "cumbrous political channels" but simply by moving their children and the attendant state funds from one school to another. Doing so would ensure the closure of all but the most responsive schools and, significantly, would once again "make the salaries of school teachers responsive to market forces . . . [giving] educational authorities an independent standard against which to judge salary scales." Essentially, vouchers would render politics redundant, reinterpreting local control at the level of the individual consumer rather than of the community as a whole.[50]

Friedman's proposal percolated for over a decade, engendering opposition from teachers' unions, who worried that competition would allow schools to introduce nonunionized labor; as well as civil libertarians, who worried about public money going to parochial schools; and many civil rights groups, who had already watched Southern whites use vouchers to evade desegregation orders. Vouchers drew support from an even more eclectic group, including free-market ideologues, Catholics seeking state support for parochial schools, and some parents of color and their left-wing supporters who were tired of struggling against racism and bureaucratic dysfunction in large, inner-city schools. By the late 1960s the federal Office of Economic Opportunity (OEO) considered using vouchers to improve integration and student achievement in urban schools, and allocated money to a team of Harvard researchers, led by the sociologist Christopher Jencks, to study their feasibility. The team's final report won the approval of the Nixon administration, and in 1970 the OEO launched pilot programs in several school districts. The Jencks team assumed that the program would be most popular in urban areas, where the effects of bureaucracy and racial stratification were most pronounced. But in fact only a few cities opted to join the program, and their participation was circumscribed and short-lived.[51]

The two longest-lasting experiments with vouchers appeared outside of major cities, in exurban districts in New Hampshire and California. This was an unexpected development, since so many people bought suburban or rural homes specifically "for the schools" and, having exercised choice through the real estate market, seemed to have little interest in loosening ties to their school district. But it was even more surprising because Friedman himself had specifically excluded outlying communities from his original proposal, arguing that their populations were too small to sustain multiple, reasonably-sized schools and thus the competition necessary to protect individual choice.[52]

Those assumptions overlooked other characteristics that made rural and suburban districts amenable to vouchers. Small, homogenous communities were more likely to buy into the program than were cities, and comparatively weak teachers' unions meant less organized opposition. "Exit" also had longstanding precedents in rural areas, where single-school or inoperative districts paid tuition for students to attend high schools of their choice. In the wake of unpopular school consolidations, some hoped to return to that system. In Wisconsin, for example, the same farm bureaus that solicited antiunion literature in the early 1960s also read the libertarian pamphlet *Private Schools for All* (1959), while the state's first legislative proposal for vouchers came from an assembly candidate in rural Portage County. Finally, rural and suburban districts were especially susceptible to the era's growing tax burden and welcomed new methods of controlling costs. Their hope was that under a voucher system "local control would be returned to the parents" while taxpayers saved money through increased competition for students.[53]

One can imagine the appeal of such a program to the residents of New Hampshire, where a report revealed that rising school costs had nearly doubled the state's property taxes between 1940 and 1965. For years state bureaucrats had pushed through contentious school consolidations with promises of tax savings. Now they switched course, admitting that consolidation was not so much a matter of "economy [as] of equal educational opportunity," meaning that consolidated schools would provide better facilities, programs, and teachers, but at a higher cost. The tax burden would be more evenly shared within consolidated districts—towns with fewer than a thousand elementary students had, theretofore, spent anywhere between $195 and $750 per pupil at the same tax rates— but the trend toward higher taxes was indisputable. In 1966, rising taxes led to the formation of the New Hampshire Public School Association, an anticonsolidation group that promised "to preserve those special values of democratic control by duly elected local officials" and to check "the wild-eyed demands of the education lobby" that threatened "the imminent bankruptcy" of the state. Like its counterparts elsewhere, the organization attracted support from farmers and lumbermen as well as residents of outlying suburbs and vacation areas. Its first chairman was the future governor Meldrim Thomson.[54]

In most of rural New Hampshire opposition to consolidation and higher taxes was "voice"-based, comprised of school board takeovers and anti-tax campaigns. Typical were incidents in the Groveton–Stark school district, in North Stratford, where after the closure of one-room schools in the early 1960s voters rejected reassignment to a larger supervisory union or inclusion in a regional high school. The area welcomed its first superintendent with three years of budget cuts and, in 1967, required him to file financial reports for public review. In 1968, voters expanded the school board from three to five members to include more conservatives, who promptly fired the superintendent in order to "keep expenditures low while maintaining . . . a good, traditional program in the 'basics.'"[55] A number of other towns withdrew from their supervisory unions altogether, citing high tax rates, while board members across the state tried to limit expenditures by reclaiming control of personnel decisions from principals and superintendents.[56]

Voucher-like programs had a long history in New Hampshire, and many rural districts continued to send their students to neighboring towns on a tuition basis.[57] Notably, however, it was not these districts that enrolled in the federal pilot program. Fourteen of the seventeen districts that participated were rural, but just one was located in the state's sparsely populated north. Most were exurban communities in the rapidly growing south, where, as the historian Jim Carl points out, thousands of people had moved for the "low taxes and charming geography." The two men most responsible for New Hampshire's participation in the voucher program were themselves newly arrived residents. One was Governor Meldrim Thomson, who had moved to the state during the 1950s. The other was Milton Friedman, who summered in New Hampshire from 1950 to 1967 and owned a home just across the Vermont border until the 1980s, from which he cultivated relationships with state policymakers—most importantly Secretary of Education William Bittenbender, who cast the deciding vote in favor of the program—and members of Dartmouth University's economics department. While New Hampshire was not the ideal setting for the experiment, both Friedman and the supervisors at the OEO recognized that it was the most ideologically receptive environment they were likely to get, and they threw their support behind the program. For its part, the state initially tried to implement a faithful facsimile of Friedman's proposal, allowing students to attend public or private schools of their choice.[58]

The second prominent experiment with vouchers took place in the Alum Rock union elementary district, at the east edge of San Jose, California. Alum Rock was idiosyncratic in both its history and demographics: It was an agricultural area undergoing rapid urbanization, annexed by the city of San Jose in the 1950s but still undergoing development a decade later. The district encompassed dozens of schools and served sixteen thousand children, over half of them Mexican American, African American, or Asian American and nearly as many living below the poverty line. The area's valuation was less than a third of the state median and it required high property tax rates to maintain adequate schools. Thus, by 1970, Alum Rock was a landscape of poor, racially diverse suburban sprawl, bearing little resemblance either to the gritty urban segregation that OEO reformers had envisioned or to the small exurban districts described elsewhere in this chapter.[59]

Alum Rock nevertheless merits a place in this discussion because of the reasons it adopted vouchers. For twelve years the district had remained loosely organized politically but tightly regulated by its superintendent, who kept each school on lockstep schedules, leading to low teacher morale and cost overruns. When the superintendent William Jefferds took over in 1968, he proposed greater autonomy for local communities and saw vouchers as a means to further that goal. Teachers in Alum Rock were divided between the NEA and the AFT, and loosely enough affiliated with both organizations to ignore national opposition to vouchers; they agreed to the program in hopes of greater independence and community involvement in the schools. Finally, rapid population growth made the area's voters receptive to experimentation. As one researcher noted, the threat of shifting school enrollments was less daunting for a district that experienced thirty percent pupil turnover annually. Moreover, the experiment promised to ease the budget deficits and tax hikes caused by the new arrivals. Six schools in Alum Rock ultimately decided to accept voucher students.[60]

The experiments in New Hampshire and California lasted three and five years, respectively, and both concluded by 1976. As it turned out, there were significant impediments to putting vouchers into practice, even outside of cities. First was the cacophony of grassroots interests they had to accommodate. David Cohen and Eleanor Farrar point out that the OEO plan was "a complex and cumbersome creation" because it had "to promote freedom of choice, equality, and due process all at once, while radically revising public schools." These goals required complex layers of regulation, including extra financial incentives to enroll poor children and lotteries that both allowed students to choose schools and schools to choose students. Together with preliminary safeguards against racial imbalance and unqualified instructors, as well as constitutional prohibitions against the inclusion of parochial schools, these filters diluted the market dynamics that Friedman had originally proposed. The plans also took for granted that "political power in . . . education [was] centralized and monolithic," and that empowering parents would quickly bring school boards, administrators, and teachers into line. Experience proved otherwise. Even administrators sympathetic to parental choice balked at rapid shifts in enrollment and staffing, while teachers' unions continued to mobilize their members against the project altogether.[61]

Vouchers were an intriguing reform because they cut across entrenched interests, but they were vulnerable for the same reason. Political constraints prevented them from becoming panaceas of academic innovation or cost control, and whatever moderate benefits they produced were not enough to outweigh mounting opposition from unions and the educational establishment. Much of their grassroots support dissipated when the simplicity of the thought experiment gave way to the necessary complexities of implementation, and ultimately, Carl argues, it was an impatience with local politics that prompted subsequent voucher advocates to turn directly to state legislatures and "[bypass] local school districts as possible allies."[62]

Thus, hopes of regaining local control through exit failed. Vouchers remained popular with conservatives and some liberals, but political and constitutional impediments prevented further experimentation until the 1990s. Few cities have adopted them even since then, and those that have are urban districts like Cleveland and Milwaukee, which have often had the plans imposed on them by conservative legislatures (whose districts they do not affect) rather than local decision makers. As is the case with education reform overall, school choice programs have moved away from local government even as they remain bound by its constraints: State and federal initiatives for choice and mobility in education have greatly expanded, but most still limit students to public schools within a single district.[63]

Conclusion

Tax revolts began as a platform for a wide range of conservative positions, based on the assumption that almost any discontent with local schools could be registered through funding cuts. By the mid-1970s, however, calls for tax relief increasingly clashed with those for local control, suggesting a conflict of conservative values. While the Supreme Court, in *San Antonio v. Rodriguez*, argued that statewide funding schemes would inevitably and unacceptably impinge on local governance, many legislatures began moving in that direction voluntarily, citing school boards' inability to resist the spending demands of unions and state bureaucrats. For most states, tax and expenditure limitation offered the most effective solution to the problem, promising the lower taxes that conservatives demanded and the greater reliance on state aid that liberals had long advocated.[64]

Unfortunately, like most political compromises, tax limitation agreements did not always play out according to expectations. Nominal increases to state funding, for instance, failed to achieve the sort of equalization that liberals envisioned. A study in 1972, years before Proposition 13, found that statewide spending limits had already "sharply [limited] the degree of local board autonomy in the majority of states," but also that there was "little direct relationship between the percentage of state aid provided and the degree of state restrictions on the operation of school boards." That is, "local control [was] limited whether states [invested] a lot or a little in school support," and once local spending was under control many legislators proved unwilling to replace it with state funds. With or without equalization formulas like the one in California, legislatures proved far more willing to constrain local expenditures than to supplement them.[65]

On the other hand, tax limitation failed to curb teachers' salaries to the degree that conservatives had hoped. When California governor Jerry Brown imposed a pay freeze on all public employees in the wake of Proposition 13, the California Teachers Association sued for an injunction, arguing that the action violated home rule provisions allowing individual districts to set salaries. The California Supreme Court found in the union's favor, weakening Proposition 13 supporters' claims that tax-starved districts would cut back on teacher salaries rather than on integral academic programs. A study conducted five years after Proposition 13 found that "pressures to maintain and augment teacher salaries remained very high during this time" and created "a structural barrier to flexibility in resource allocation within school districts." As judges in other states issued similar decisions, local control became a means for unions to sidestep statewide limits on school spending. Many voters maintained a consistent commitment to the principle of community governance, but both business interests and teachers' unions began to invoke local control opportunistically, while at the same time competing for power at higher levels of government.[66]

Some of the effects Proposition 13 had on California's system of public education were more predictable. Previously a national leader in primary and secondary school funding, by the mid-1980s the state had fallen below the national average, and although the devastating cuts to teacher and administrative salaries never materialized, districts did scale back library services, summer school, adult education, and other supplemental programs.[67] Academic outcomes were mixed: The general distribution of standardized test scores remained unchanged, but several studies documented modest increases, especially in poor areas. Researchers also found that districts that reduced their administrative staffs became more attentive to student achievement, suggesting that Proposition 13 "did impose effective political constraints on decision makers in some, if not all, school districts in California."[68]

Perhaps the most overlooked legacy of Proposition 13 was its effect on rural school districts—some of its strongest proponents but also the victims of its greatest depredations. The primary appeal of Proposition 13, its seemingly equitable mechanism of tax limitation, actually disadvantaged rural districts in subtle but profound ways. For instance, the law allowed reassessment of property values only after a sale, ensuring areas with frequent residential turnover a higher tax base than those where landholders had longer tenure, as in agricultural or mining areas, where assessments fell far below market value.[69] Proposition 13 also reorganized structures of tax collection, stripping nearly sixty-three hundred local agencies of the right to levy property taxes and reassigning that responsibility to the state's fifty-eight counties. County-wide taxation further disempowered outlying communities, which struggled to maintain their portion of revenues even as low, uniform tax rates forced them to improve economies of scale further than they already had. Shifting the administration of school finance to the state department of education likewise allowed urban areas to lobby for regulations and funding streams that favored large districts. All of these changes threatened to complete, under conservative auspices, the campaign of school consolidation that liberals had begun seventy-five years earlier, as the number of school districts in the state continued to shrink.[70]

In 1983, a coalition of rural superintendents formed the California Small School Districts' Association, an advocacy group to oppose consolidation and preserve funding for small schools. Similar groups had formed decades before to defend rural school districts, but they had benefited from legislative overrepresentation and a broad grassroots coalition. By the 1970s, rural political power had diminished and conservative voters had rallied around their homes rather than their schools. The Small School Districts' Association lobbied for special subsidies and administrative flexibility for rural districts (with mixed results) but it could not reinstate the voluntary spending levels necessary to sustain many small districts. Proposition 13 had created a policy environment in which conservatives turned their backs on local control.[71]

THE BATTLE OF IDEAS

Whatever else one thought of Mitchell Quelhurst, the man was a perceptive homebuyer. Hundreds of other New Yorkers had moved to Bennington, Vermont, in the early 1960s, seeing only covered bridges and a picturesque women's college. Not so Quelhurst. "This school problem," he wrote to the *Bennington Banner* after visiting the area in 1961, "involves far more than appears on the surface. It actually comes into the realm of the four freedoms," and as a prospective resident it troubled him. Referring to Franklin Roosevelt's list of American liberties, he implied that the local school board was infringing on citizens' freedom of speech—as well, perhaps, as their freedom from fear.[1] Bennington had induced surrounding towns to join a union high school district in 1959, but guarantees of rural overrepresentation seemed to embolden rather than placate conservative board members. Towns north of the city repeatedly petitioned to form their own high school, tried to secede from the district's supervisory union, and—despite criticism that they lacked "adequate facilities for physical education, industrial arts, home economics, science or music"—insisted on returning their seventh graders to one- or two-room elementary schools rather than busing them into town.[2] The high school's first principal remained controversial more than a decade after his departure. The second, resigning after a tense term, recommended dissolving the district "for the kids' sake." A third resigned less than a year after his hiring, amid allegations of corruption.[3] School administrators reported shouting matches, bomb scares, and death threats on almost a monthly basis between 1960 and 1976.[4]

Over the same period, the district was rocked by numerous censorship campaigns. *Tropic of Cancer* came under fire in 1962, "The Zoo Story" in 1970, *Ms.*

magazine in 1974, and *Go Ask Alice* in 1976. Angry parents and board members framed their objections to these titles in democratic terms. "Believe it or not, we are not prudes," wrote one mother. "We are the so-called middle-class, hard work-ing, taxpaying type and we are *very* concerned that our child can go to school and check a book out of the library that we would not let her buy or read." She continued, "Because I disagree with a school librarian's judgment [I am not] automatically wrong. I am not criticizing Mrs. Plumb's character. . . . but not she or anyone else except my husband and I have no right [sic] to control my child's environment." Another protester wrote, "They call this protecting the rights of people to read what they choose. In our opinion . . . they are trying to take away the right of a parent to guide a minor child." A local teacher, exasper-ated at the prospect of the school board determining her lesson plans, responded, "Are we professionals or not—and where is the line drawn?"[5]

The conflicts in Bennington were not unique. Similar cases of censorship in-undated postwar American towns, and the vast majority of them revolved around the same question: Did teachers or parents have the right to control what children learned?[6] Nowhere was the issue more fraught than in exurban commu-nities, where teachers' professional status remained tenuous and demographic change allowed diverse constituencies to adopt the rhetoric of "parents' rights." During the 1960s and 1970s, an eclectic group of farmers, middle-class migrants, and wealthy businessmen came together to protest what they considered undemocratic policies of curricular selection. Theirs was a paradoxical vision of democracy—invoking majority rule while casting parents as aggrieved minori-ties, and frequently banning schoolbooks in the name of higher academic standards—but it was one that nevertheless cohered in the face of expanding professionalization. At the local level, parent coalitions secured favorable but narrow outcomes in court rulings and school board elections, while at the na-tional level they galvanized campaigns for Christianity and patriotism in schools. In conjunction with conservative organizations like the John Birch Society (JBS) and the Council for Basic Education (CBE), rural and suburban activists devel-oped a common interest in school curriculum and employed the language of local control to reclaim power in a radically changed educational context.

Curricular Reform and Its Opponents

When commentators discuss curricular disputes they usually ascribe them to one of two causes. Some assume that controversy results from a particular dis-agreement about what children should learn, and that if one were to change the books, subjects, or methods at hand, it would quickly resolve the problem.

Others argue that curricular controversy is in fact irresolvable because it reflects a clash of worldviews, with fundamentally different notions of morality or freedom at stake. Although both of these interpretations are to some degree accurate, the roots of curricular conflict frequently lie elsewhere, in changing structures of school governance and realignments of political power. When new laws or systems threaten customary methods for determining course content, they lay the groundwork for particular subjects to be challenged or for philosophical differences to flare up. Thus, controversy is never simply a question of what children should learn or which educational philosophy should prevail; it is ultimately a struggle between parents, educators, and other interest groups for institutional authority.

In the early 1900s, two reforms began the transfer of curricular control from parents and school boards to teachers, librarians, and the state. The first was an expansive interpretation of compulsory attendance laws, which created new legal grounds to limit parental influence in the classroom. The second was school district consolidation, which helped professionalize teaching and modernize coursework, also at the expense of parental involvement. These changes would set the terms of debate for a century to come, framing curricular reform as a competition between local democracy and professional autonomy.

The historian Stephen Provasnik documents important legal connections between compulsory attendance laws, which required a child's presence at school, and subsequent laws for compulsory education, which prescribed particular subjects of study. During the nineteenth century, before states required school attendance, the common law framed public education as a contract between school authorities and individual parents. Parents did not have to enroll children in the public schools, but if they did so they had no right to challenge school administrators on issues of attendance, discipline, or rules. The only significant influence they retained was over the content of a student's learning. If parents did not want their children to learn bookkeeping, Greek, or any other subject, most states accepted a note to that effect as legally binding. During the 1910s, court rulings compelling school attendance threatened that arrangement. Specifically, by upholding attendance laws under "police power" provisions— provisions that usurped parental authority in the interest of society as a whole rather than that of any particular child—many courts allowed state legislatures to mandate not only students' presence at school but the type and number of courses they took there. In the process, parents lost the power to tailor their children's courses of study. These rulings did not create an educational Leviathan overnight. Some courts still allowed parents to withdraw their children from particular classes, while subsequent cases imposed other limits on state power—preserving the ability to attend private schools, for instance.

Overall, however, the principle of state control accrued greater power to teachers, superintendents, and state departments of education, and limited parents' ability to shield their children from content that they deemed objectionable. Part and parcel with the professionalization and funding mandates described in earlier chapters, state officials began to exert a new degree of control and compulsion in curricular decisions, standardizing course requirements and textbooks, raising standards, and narrowing the influence of parents and school boards. As the historian Newton Edwards notes, there was ultimately little doubt that the state could "prescribe what studies the child shall pursue in the interests of good citizenship."[7]

School consolidation further weakened parental control over course material. In the early 1900s, when local school boards had final say in curricular decisions, school reformers assumed that teachers in small districts stuck with basic reading, writing, and arithmetic as a result of board intimidation or a lack of the disciplinary training and up-to-date equipment that more modern courses required. Reformers promised that larger districts could provide hands-on learning in mechanical arts, driver education, and home economics—courses suited to an increasingly complex, industrial society—as well as bring new approaches to traditional academic subjects.[8] While nineteenth-century schoolbooks like the *McGuffey's Readers* had disciplined students' minds through phonics drills and nurtured their souls with a vaguely Protestant nationalism, progressive educators, armed with new research in child development, argued that phonics bored students and led to high rates of attrition. They sought to make reading more accessible through "look-say" or "whole language" techniques, in which children memorized simple words and deduced meaning from context before trying to sound out words unfamiliar to them, and through the use of nursery tales, fantasy, and age-appropriate fiction, which would appeal to students' interests.[9]

In other subjects, too, educators tried to incorporate new developments in the natural and social sciences. Chemistry and biology courses encouraged field study and experimentation, while history gave way to social studies, an amorphous field organized around social problems like class conflict, environmental degradation, and racism.[10] By the 1960s, educators were redesigning classes along even more conceptual lines, from the explicitly theoretical methods of the "new math" to the integrated humanities approach of "Man: A Course of Study" (MACOS), which infused history and literature with insights from anthropology and psychology. The same impulses led to the development of comprehensive sex education, which discussed human sexuality not only in terms of social hygiene but, depending on students' ages, as a matter of emotion, pleasure, and personal choice. Schools adopted these reforms at different times, to different degrees, and for many different reasons, but the general trend was clear. Over the course of the twentieth century, curriculum was increasingly designed and selected by professional teachers and librarians rather than parents, and most children's textbooks and homework assignments looked markedly different than those of previous generations. All of these changes depended on the new buildings, centralized school boards, and larger, professional faculties created by school district consolidation.

Curricular reform encountered two types of conservative pushback, which historians have generally characterized as "radical" and "respectable" resistance.[11] The radical approach relied on emotional appeals or conspiracy theories to mobilize citizens and browbeat educators. From the 1920s, when the American Legion burned subversive textbooks and the Scopes' "monkey trial" prompted many states to forbid the teaching of evolution, to the 1970s, when emerging networks of Christian fundamentalists accused the MACOS program of advocating cannibalism, curricular controversy stood at the front line of the culture wars.[12] Right-wing propaganda firms scrutinized almost every area of study, including biology, health, literature, history, reading, and mathematics. The ensuing controversies, fed with money from corporate interests, provided a means to undercut teachers' unions and flood schools with free-market or antienvironmental literature.[13] The most famous "radical" propagandist in the 1950s was a fascist sympathizer named Allen Zoll, whose National Council for American Education supplied tracts for most of the era's major censorship campaigns. Zoll achieved notoriety in 1950, when a group of disgruntled parents in Pasadena, California, used his pamphlets to force the resignation of superintendent Willard Goslin, the president of the American Association of School Administrators and an outspoken supporter of school desegregation, whom they accused of communism and brainwashing.[14] Similar conflicts broke out in Denver, Houston, and several other cities in the wake of the attack, establishing a pattern of threats and community intimidation that long outlasted the McCarthy era.[15]

A more measured, "respectable" critique of the schools came from conservative intellectuals, who eschewed the radicals' methods but agreed with them that progressive educators posed a threat to academic quality. Under the guise of professionalism, they cautioned, progressives had deflected scrutiny of the pragmatist philosophy underlying their reforms, particularly the notion that curriculum must reflect all aspects of human experience and adapt to evolving truths. Critics deemed these assumptions indeterminate and dangerously relativistic. Mindful of children's malleability under totalitarian regimes, they questioned whether state-sanctioned education could mold citizens without first embracing moral certainty. They also blamed progressives for promoting anti-intellectualism and mediocrity in the classroom, evident in the alleged gap between the rigorous math and science coursework of the Soviet Union and the insipid "life adjustment" and "hobby" courses gaining ground in the United States. For many conservatives, the sanctity of the individual and the safety of the nation demanded a return to academic excellence.[16]

Respectable conservatives found a receptive audience for their message. Educational exposés became almost a cottage industry during the early 1950s, when books like *Crisis in Education* (1949), *Educational Wastelands* (1953), and *Why Johnny Can't Read* (1955) climbed the best-seller list.[17] In 1956, Mortimer Smith, the author of *And Madly Teach* (1949), founded the CBE in Washington, DC, which quickly became the leading advocate for a return to traditional coursework. Smith recognized that in an era of consensus politics it was natural (and for progressive educators, beneficial) to conflate any criticism of the status quo with more radical social movements. Thus, while the council's membership was comprised mostly of writers and professors—including such well-known liberals as the historians Arthur Bestor and Richard Hofstadter—Smith went out of his way to "preserve [a] disinterested, scholarly character and avoid any association in the public mind with groups and individuals of questionable reputation or motive."[18] He wrote: "We don't want to get into any arguments about . . . whether the Bible should be read in public schools or whether the economics professor at Podunk Teachers College is advocating socialism but [we are] opposed in principle to the Professional Education party now in charge of public education."[19] When one of the CBE's supporters favorably compared the organization to the ultraconservative John Birch Society, Smith demurred, writing that the society had "set back not only the cause of honest political debate in this country but also the cause of effective conservatism." When the California Teachers Association implied a connection between the two groups, he dismissed it as an attempt "to besmirch the critics of education" with a kind of "reverse McCarthyism."[20]

From Smith's perspective, insinuations of censorship or anti-intellectualism were simply politically motivated attempts to impugn a respectable organization. Yet the boundary between radical and respectable conservatism was not always clear, and examining their points of overlap is crucial to understanding the formation of a broad-based movement for parents' rights. While Smith considered hot-button issues a distraction and insisted that the CBE could not be held responsible for the actions of misguided individuals, it was often his own ambiguity that misguided them in the first place. The CBE's clipped denunciations of censorship were far outweighed by the scorn it heaped on professional educators, and the vague appeal of "back to basics" allowed supporters to avoid specific questions about the phrase's meaning or their own methods. All sorts of conservatives cheered the CBE's confrontational rhetoric. Russell Kirk endorsed the organization several times in the *National Review*, as did a number of right-wing newsletters.[21]

One of the council's earliest members was Phyllis Schlafly, the future antifeminist scion, who asked for tips on homeschooling her children.[22] Other grassroots groups solicited the organization's advice just before launching censorship campaigns—in Anaheim, California, in 1961, for example, and Sarasota, Florida, in 1962.[23]

The CBE drew particular attention for its support of Max Rafferty's campaign to become the California state school superintendent, in 1962. Rafferty, a school administrator near Los Angeles, was quickly becoming a cult hero to conservatives. His campaign denounced progressive education both because it left students vulnerable to "red psychological warfare" and because "cold-eyed, sadistic, perverted punks . . . spend a good many years in programs designed to teach effective social living," although such programs had not "noticeably adjusted our current crop of juveniles."[24] Rafferty's alternative was stricter discipline and a return to rigorous academics. Unsurprisingly, he won not only the support of the CBE but of ultraconservative organizations. Mortimer Smith and others repeatedly asked why Rafferty did not distance himself from such groups. A CBE member from San Francisco noted that she had "a bad time here over the extreme right and John Birch charge" and pleaded with Rafferty's headquarters for a strong denial but "made no progress." Although Rafferty won the election, she continued, his intemperate remarks and a slew of school board takeovers allowed teachers' unions to deflect even respectable criticism of the schools "with sneering, condescending rebuttals that the critics were John Birchers and ultrarightists."[25] These claims had sufficient basis for the CBE to pointedly tout exceptions to the rule, such as a standards-raising principal in Little Lake, California, who, for once, could "not be dismissed" with such charges.[26]

The leadership of the CBE itself encompassed both apologists for and opponents of censorship. While Arthur Bestor denounced the "smear tactics" of Allen Zoll, for instance, Harold Clapp, Bestor's colleague at the University of Illinois, praised Zoll for doing a "highly commendable job," saying that he would "probably not go quite so far [with charges of socialism] but the difference is only one of degree."[27] The council's sole sponsor for its first two years was the William Volker Fund, a libertarian philanthropy which, in addition to supporting basic education and free-market economics programs, financed Harding College in Arkansas, the distributor of *Communism on the Map*, *Operation Abolition*, and other right-wing propaganda films.[28]

Even the CBE's official literature was unclear when it came to the role of grassroots activism in educational reform. One of its pamphlets took the little town of East Greenbush, New York—an exurban area near Albany—as a model of community involvement. In 1957, a group called the Greenbush Taxpayer's Association took over a school board meeting and proposed cutting everything from algebra to foreign languages, shouting down scientists from a nearby research institute and booing anyone introduced as "doctor." The CBE acknowledged that "some of [the Association's] leading spokesmen dealt in bombast and sometimes took extreme positions." However, the increased scrutiny also improved communication between the public and the school board. The board appointed liaisons to investigate community complaints, the taxpayer's association moderated its demands, and as if by magic the district's budget doubled over the next five years. The pamphlet concluded that confrontation was a necessary step toward cooperation and better-funded schools.[29] Unsurprisingly, right-wing groups interpreted this explanation as an endorsement of their own methods, and the CBE remained a popular site for conservative networking. Notwithstanding Smith's claims to the contrary, the organization's ambiguity and ecumenism provided intellectual cover for far more reactionary viewpoints than his own.

Conflicts such as the one in Greenbush occurred throughout rural and suburban areas. While school consolidation increased teachers' professional status, small districts still had few safeguards for academic freedom, making censorship and budget cuts an easy way to reassert community standards. But the problem went beyond the small-mindedness of small towns, especially when suburban newcomers got involved. The sociologist James Coleman found that newcomers to rural areas often demanded more control of textbook selection than they had exercised in the city, believing that their education and level of interest entitled them to direct authority over their children's schooling. Unfortunately, he wrote, these demands had "few formal channels for expression" and were "not recognized as fully legitimate by administrators themselves," leaving rapidly growing towns "ripe for controversy and conflict."[30] Caught at the crossroads of rural decline and suburban ascendance, teachers and administrators in small districts were trying to establish their professional status while making concessions to angry parents, for whom book banning became a blunt but effective means of reclaiming local control. By the 1960s, the convergence of radical, respectable, rural, and suburban conservatism yielded expansive campaigns against professional influence in education, often beginning in areas where school consolidation remained unfinished.

Building a Movement

A case study in rural Wisconsin offers particular insight into the relationship between school consolidation, suburban growth, and campaigns for parents' rights. During the early 1960s, just as its legislature was completing the painful process of district consolidation, a series of small-town censorship campaigns broke out across the state, attracting attention from national media outlets as well as from Wisconsin's educational and civil liberties organizations. These incidents were connected by some common characteristics. Most took place in recently consolidated school districts and drew support from both farmers and incoming suburbanites. But even more significantly, and in ways that contemporaries did not recognize, they were connected by the right-wing networks to which the latter group belonged. It was suburbanites' access to media, money, and political power that transformed a rearguard action against rural school consolidation into a new, nationwide battle for parents' rights.

Wisconsin was not the only state experiencing censorship campaigns, but it was certainly at the forefront. When the right-wing pamphleteer Allen Zoll retired in 1953, most of his followers joined the American Council for Christian Laymen (ACCL), a subsidiary group operated out of Madison, Wisconsin, by Zoll's assistant, Verne Kaub.[31] Kaub took up the work with gusto. He exchanged lists of suspicious textbooks with patriotic groups; published *Communist-Socialist Propaganda in American Schools* (1953), a widely read indictment of the National Education Association (NEA); and began selling reprints of *McGuffey's Readers*, which had fallen out of classroom use sixty years earlier but were enjoying a revival in conservative circles for their embodiment of old-fashioned patriotism and phonics.[32] In 1958, Kaub was one of twelve men present at the founding of the John Birch Society, after which he secured funding from its founder, Robert Welch, as well as from the Liberty Lobby, the Bradley Foundation, and the Milwaukee industrialist William Grede, one of the Society's officers.[33] Kaub cofounded "We, the People," another supplier of right-wing literature, and maintained contact with other propagandists, including Billy James Hargis, an evangelical broadcaster in Tulsa; Gerda Koch in Minneapolis; Kent and Phoebe Courtney in New Orleans; and Dan Smoot in Dallas, whose newsletter ran two articles on Kaub and the *McGuffey's Readers* in 1960 and 1961. In short, Kaub was an integral link between the conservative networks of the McCarthy era and those of the emerging "New Right."[34]

Kaub's activism first bore fruit in Twin Lakes, Wisconsin, a small village near the Illinois border, ten miles east of Lake Geneva and about an hour away from Milwaukee and Chicago. As early as the nineteenth century, the town's mixture of urban proximity and rustic charm had solidified economic ties to both cities. In the summer its lakes provided recreation for tourists, and in the winter, ice for the meatpacking industry. The ebb and flow of this seasonal economy persisted until the 1950s, when new highways improved access to the area, allowing a growing number of city dwellers to put additions on their cabins and add insulation for year-round residence. Wives remained in Twin Lakes to raise children, while their husbands endured daily or weekly commutes to white-collar jobs in the city. Between 1945 and 1960, the town's population grew from six hundred to over fifteen hundred people and required repeated additions to its single school.[35] A one-room wooden schoolhouse, erected in 1904, was replaced by a sturdier, four-room brick structure in 1951. The town added two more classrooms over the next five years, bringing the total to six, with eight teachers. Nevertheless, by 1960, two hundred first- to eighth-grade students crowded the school's single hallway, forcing several classes to meet in the firehouse and post office while a new facility was built. That building would become the cause of considerable controversy.[36]

In 1961, Twin Lakes' five-member school board began to reflect the town's demographic changes. Dennis Beula, the board president, welcomed three newly elected members: John Pfeiffer, John Collins, and William Smeeth. All four were recent transplants—middle-class professionals working in Milwaukee and Chicago. All had children enrolled in the district's school and, according to several commentators, all were "angry young men." They were mostly upset with the local principal, whom they blamed for poor student discipline. Given the overcrowding and ad hoc accommodations, the charge undoubtedly had some basis. For these fathers, however, the problem would not improve with the opening of a new building, it would only grow worse. Indeed, the problem was larger than the principal's disciplinary skills; it resulted from the demoralizing effects of progressive education, which both the building and the principal embodied. As in other exurban communities, population growth required the modernization of school facilities but seemed to threaten democratic control in the process.[37]

Few of the changes seen in larger districts by midcentury had actually come to Twin Lakes, which like most small towns lacked the staff or facilities to abandon its traditional academic programs. The school had not done away with grades or subject fields, nor had it incorporated hands-on learning or employed counselors to facilitate the "adjustment" of its students. It had, however, become increasingly professionalized over the previous years and threatened to become more so with Wisconsin's district consolidation order. While the town voluntarily sent its children to the regional high school, paying tuition on a per pupil basis, consolidation would make that arrangement mandatory. It would also dilute the school board's control over curricular and personnel decisions. Many parents worried that as professional educators gained control of their elementary school they would prioritize "fancy buildings and 'busyness' courses" rather than high academic standards. Some of them felt that the process was already underway, since the faculty had adopted look-say reading instruction rather than phonics.[38]

The loss of the phonics program particularly upset William Smeeth, the fourth board member, and compelled him to run for office. Smeeth had only moved to

Twin Lakes a few months before the election, though he had become increasingly interested in educational issues since reading about the Allen Zoll controversy in Pasadena a decade before. In a way, Zoll's objections to progressive education accounted for Smeeth's very presence in Twin Lakes. Disgusted with the look-say reading program at his daughter's school in the Chicago suburbs and tired of his job as an insurance executive, Smeeth resolved to open a private academy based on phonics, a "highly classical" curriculum, and old-fashioned American values. "We [would] start the day with a prayer and raise the flag and salute it," he imagined, and parents, rather than teachers, would discipline their own children. Unfortunately, he had neither the facilities nor the enrollment necessary to open his school in Illinois. So in 1960 he moved to Wisconsin (where the chartering laws were more flexible) to try again.[39]

Smeeth had connections to a range of conservative organizations, many of which provided him with philosophical and financial support. He met William Grede, the head of the John Birch Society in Milwaukee, through a church study group in 1960. He also had a friend in the education department of the William Volker Fund, which gave him funds for a nationwide survey of phonics programs, including visits to conservative private schools in Maryland, Colorado, and California. The Volker Fund put him in touch with Mortimer Smith of the CBE and Robert LeFevre, the founder of the Freedom School (later Rampart College) in Colorado, an academy that conducted two-week seminars on libertarian ideology and activism. Grede sponsored Smeeth's attendance there just a few months after he moved to Wisconsin.[40]

Thus, Smeeth arrived in Twin Lakes brimming with "radical educational ideas" and was eager to implement them. When Dennis Beula approached him about running for the school board, he quickly accepted, becoming the first candidate in memory to campaign for the position. Throughout the spring of 1961, Smeeth gathered small groups of residents in his living room or on his pontoon boat, passed out refreshments, set up an easel and blackboard, and said, "I don't believe in politics, but here is what I stand for. Don't vote for Bill Smeeth unless you believe in these four points!" The points were phonics, parental authority, Christianity, and Americanism in schools. They won him a seat.[41] Once elected, Smeeth arranged a special meeting with Beula, Collins, and Pfeiffer, but did not inform William Thorsen, the fifth board member, who was out of town that week. The four men met several more times during the first month of school. Uncomfortable with his exclusion, Thorsen asked to see the meetings' minutes. Beula explained that the meetings were only for the newly formed "academic committee," and closed to Thorsen and the public. "I don't think the people would be interested, anyway," he promised.[42]

People became interested by the end of September, when the board distributed an article by right-wing author Dan Smoot to faculty and parents. The article noted that, like Twin Lakes, towns all over the country were getting new school buildings, but that given the laxity of modern teaching, "a child who spent six years in a one-room, one-teacher school, diligently disciplined to a thorough study of *McGuffey's [Readers]* would emerge a far better-educated person."[43] With the article came the abrupt announcement that Twin Lakes teachers would no longer "discuss the United Nations . . . the governments of other countries or any current issues," eighth graders would not take health class until the board eliminated any "over-emphasis on sex," and all reading instruction would use the 1879 edition of *McGuffey's Readers.*[44]

Twin Lakes was the first public school in the country to revive the *Readers,* which had been out of circulation for decades, and parental complaints brought the county superintendent to town by the end of the week. She found teachers unsure about what to teach, resistant to the *Readers,* but afraid of the board. She reported the situation to the state superintendent, Angus Rothwell, and wrote a letter to Smeeth, warning him not to inject politics into the school curriculum. Smeeth responded by barring any further visits by state inspectors and ordered Twin Lakes teachers to avoid contact with the press. Rothwell, annoyed at the board's defiance, threatened that the DPI had "the power, if their program doesn't meet our standards . . . to withhold state funds." Overnight, the story became national news.[45] *The Wall Street Journal, Time,* and *Newsweek* ran stories, and NBC News came to board members' homes for interviews. Editorials on both sides of the issue appeared as far away as California.[46]

Rothwell had been superintendent for barely six months and was bewildered by the whole situation, suddenly a laughingstock among colleagues who could not understand why anyone would challenge professional authority or the value of modern textbooks. If he hoped for a quick restoration of professional control, however, he severely underestimated his opponents. Dennis Beula cited Wisconsin statutes granting the board, not the state, supervision over the school and the power to "adopt all the textbooks necessary for use in the schools." When Rothwell countered that the *Readers* violated a prohibition of sectarian material the board simply tore out or pasted over the few biblical passages.[47] Meanwhile, people wrote in from around the country, cheering the board's action. After two weeks of political pressure, Rothwell broke the impasse and agreed to allow the *McGuffey's* as secondary readers in conjunction with modern phonics texts.[48]

The residents of Twin Lakes, however, remained too sharply divided to accept that compromise. While many families supported the board, a group called the Taxpayer's Alliance filed a lawsuit for its removal, citing "subversion" and "arbitrary methods." In addition to adopting the *Readers* without public comment, the group alleged, the four board members had strong-armed subsequent meetings, cut off debate, and brought in speakers critical of "the present state of education." The neighboring Randall township schools demanded transfer to another municipality, alarmed that "the same group . . . in Twin Lakes [had] infiltrated the Wilmot high school district." There were further insinuations about the influence of "extremist organizations," for whom, the local principal warned, "Twin Lakes could be a testing ground."[49]

Despite similarities with right-wing takeovers elsewhere, the principal's intimation that Twin Lakes was part of an orchestrated, external attack was unfounded—or at least oversimplified. The discontent in Twin Lakes derived from local conditions and was advanced by local actors. Dennis Beula's widow remembers, "None of that political stuff: Dan Smoot, John Birch, none of that was on our minds!" Even William Smeeth, with numerous friends on the far right and connections to a network of conservative educators, recalls being "*very* conservative, but not political" at the time.[50] Nor had any of the board members ever heard of Verne Kaub, operating only an hour away, when they selected the *Readers*, although as the source of the Dan Smoot article he was ultimately the inspiration for their use. Thus, while the board members drew on a range of external resources, their actions were not nearly as conspiratorial or centrally coordinated as their opponents supposed.

Nevertheless, local and national networks entwined as soon as the story broke. Kaub began to counsel the board and wrote public and private letters in its support.[51] Board members, in turn, began directing interested letter writers to Kaub, as did some sympathetic newspaper editors around the state.[52] At the same time, the Wisconsin Schools Association (formerly the Wisconsin *Rural* Schools Association, the anticonsolidation group) released pamphlets denouncing the "Democrat technique for stripping local officials of local control over local affairs" in Twin Lakes.[53] In early November, Twin Lakes residents learned that Sidney DeLove, the president of a right-wing organization in Chicago, had offered to recompense any funds lost in the *McGuffey's* gambit. DeLove also gave the keynote speech at the launch of the school's new "Americanism versus Communism" program.[54]

Although national organizations had not selected Twin Lakes as a testing ground, they welcomed the publicity of the Taxpayers' lawsuit and celebrated when Judge Eugene Baker ruled in the school board's favor in the spring of 1962. Comparing the board members to "crusaders," the judge noted that "in this burning desire to establish a system, which some would call old fashioned . . . they were not always diplomatic in dealing with the views of others in their own community." However, he unequivocally ruled that "the school board . . . has the absolute right and duty to select the textbooks. The particular duty of the State Superintendent (as far as texts are concerned) is to exclude all sectarian books and instruction. . . . Other than that he has no direct duty with respect to controlling the textbooks." The verdict was a firm rejection of the state's curricular authority, and the board quickly consolidated its gains by firing the principal and all but one of the district's teachers. The acrimony initially hurt *McGuffey's* advocates in the town council election, but Beula and Pfeiffer declared victory when they won a close reelection to the school board in July. As a local matter, the Twin Lakes incident settled down soon after that. The new principal demonstrated his competency and the new teachers were satisfied with phonics-based textbooks. In a few years, the *McGuffey's Readers* were no longer assigned for reading instruction.[55]

Twin Lakes had far-reaching effects on educational activism in Wisconsin. The board members' wives formed a statewide organization to pressure the Department of Public Instruction (DPI) into adopting phonics texts, and several cited their participation in the dispute as the impetus to volunteer for Barry Goldwater's presidential campaign in 1964. In 1965, the Wisconsin Chamber of Commerce invoked the Twin Lakes incident to lobby against the Elementary and Secondary Education Act, and Verne Kaub used it to promote sales of his *McGuffey's Readers* and to make connections with other right-wing groups.[56] William Smeeth used the publicity from Twin Lakes to open his private school, the Academy of Basic Education (now Brookfield Academy), just outside Milwaukee. In addition to using *McGuffey's Readers*, the academy taught Christian morals and free-market ideology. An advertisement in the *National Review* said it was "unlikely that state-trained teachers would qualify" for positions at the school: One taught wearing "I'm For Barry Goldwater" sweatshirts, while another became an editor of the conservative *Wisconsin Report* and was active in later censorship campaigns.[57]

It seems that the only group that did not make use of the Twin Lakes controversy was the Council for Basic Education, which never commented publicly on the events in Wisconsin and likely knew little about them. However, much like the Rafferty campaign in California, the Twin Lakes controversy raises intriguing questions about the relationship between respectable groups like the CBE and more extreme conservative activism. How would the Council have responded, one wonders, if it were confronted with the situation in Twin Lakes? Would it have denounced the board members as censors "setting back the cause of responsible conservatism," as it did the John Birch Society? Would it have supported the adoption of the *McGuffey's Readers* as a courageous stand for basic education? Or would it have refrained from taking a position altogether? The available evidence is thin, but enough exists to support all three possibilities.

The only direct reference to Twin Lakes in the CBE's correspondence puts the organization at odds with the school board and its allies. Shortly after the story broke, Verne Kaub sent the council several newspaper clippings, together with a letter proudly describing the *McGuffey's Readers* as "one small facet of the general agitation for basic education." Mortimer Smith did not respond to this letter. Instead, before filing it, he took a red pencil and wrote the words "Crackpot Group" across the top. Like the Birch campaigns in California, he interpreted Twin Lakes as an instance of right-wing extremists seeking approval for censorship and sensationalism.[58]

Yet even as Smith denounced these "crackpots," he unknowingly developed a close relationship with their leader, William Smeeth. Smeeth had admired Smith's writing since 1949 and was an early member of the CBE. He first met Smith in March of 1961, in Washington, DC, where they discussed his plan to open a private school.[59] When Smeeth moved to Wisconsin a few weeks later, his wife wrote to Smith for information about district consolidation and its effects on curriculum. She hoped that by providing "facts and figures on districts who have 'integrated,'" the CBE could prove that "[parental] control of the schools . . . is lost completely." However, the council took no official position on the consolidation issue, and a staffer apologized that he could not help in the matter. Mortimer Smith, on vacation at the time, never saw the letter.[60] If he had, he might have recognized his new friend as the source of both Verne Kaub's "crackpot" letter and later correspondence from other towns in rural Wisconsin. As it stands, however, there was no communication between the two men until 1963, after Smeeth had moved to Milwaukee. That spring, as Smeeth's Academy of Basic Education got off the ground, they began working together closely. Smith traveled to Wisconsin at Smeeth's request, visited the academy, and lectured at the Round Table Club, a group of businessmen interested in educational issues. He helped coordinate a similar visit by Max Rafferty six months later and supported Smeeth over the coming years as he expanded his enrollment, organized a network of conservative private schools, and edited a textbook on grammar.[61]

Mortimer Smith might not have seen anything contradictory about this relationship, even if he were aware of Smeeth's past. After all, one could easily support the actions of the Twin Lakes board but not the propagandists that they attracted, or oppose its zealousness in a public school while supporting the same measures in a private school. However, it is unlikely that Smith could parse the issue so neatly, especially since William Smeeth made none of these distinctions himself. From Smeeth's perspective, there was no clear division between radical and respectable conservatism: He believed that one could simultaneously embrace the methods of McCarthyism and the intellectual position of its staunchest opponents. The juxtaposition of Smeeth's association with "crackpots" and

Smith's rejection of them speaks to the irony and ambiguities of conservative opposition to progressive education reform. Commitments to academic rigor, Christianity, and parental choice created strange bedfellows during the 1960s, joined, however tentatively, in their support for local control.

Local Democracy and Parents' Rights

Twin Lakes encouraged a slew of other Wisconsin towns to challenge their schools' curriculum. Some of these towns were linked to Verne Kaub and William Smeeth through right-wing networks; all were undergoing the same process of suburbanization and school consolidation. One example was Eagle River, a vacation and logging community in the far northern section of the state, which saw its population skyrocket during the 1950s, mostly with newcomers from Chicago.[62] High school enrollment increased by twenty students in 1960 alone, and the faculty grew from fourteen to twenty-one by 1964.[63] School growth did not come easily to the area. In 1960 and 1961, when high school principal Win Abney solicited federal funds for his math and science departments, the board twice rejected his proposal for fear of government control.[64] In 1961, a Syrian national addressed the high school student body in support of the United Nations, only to be castigated by a city alderman for "[pouring] into the minds of our children the idea we should abandon our American heritage." The Rotary club also berated elementary school teachers for combining traditional phonics with inferior look-say and learning-by-doing instructional methods. The most dramatic confrontation, however, came in 1962, when the town received national media attention over a John Birch Society struggle for control of its school board and the contents of its high school library.[65]

Eagle River was one of the first towns in Wisconsin to experience Birch Society agitation. Ben Tuttle, a retired engineer and real estate agent, was a prominent member of the Vilas County Republican Party when he founded Chapter 136 in March of 1961.[66] Tuttle had been a personal friend of Senator Joseph McCarthy and established the string of patriotic "McCarthy clubs" that would later supply the infrastructure for the state's Birch Society network.[67] By 1961, the local chapter had grown to forty members and, according to a *Vilas County News-Review* survey, enjoyed the support of at least fifteen percent of the electorate.[68] Tuttle, who also served as school board president, hosted screenings of right-wing films in the high school auditorium and invited conservative speakers to lecture at the American Legion hall.[69]

Tuttle had been in contact with Verne Kaub since 1960, when the two served on the board of We, the People, the right-wing activist organization. He was fully informed about the Twin Lakes affair and by the summer of 1962 he was in contact with William Smeeth as well.[70] Tuttle saw both symbolic and practical value in the *McGuffey's Readers* dispute, and he planned to use the Twin Lakes court decision to expand school board power and conservative values in Eagle River. In September 1962, he sent the JBS home office a report entitled "A Case History of Eagle River: How Birchers Took Over School Board."[71] The report has been lost, but its contents become apparent with a summary of the 1962 school board election, in which Everett Hoover, a local real estate broker, challenged Tuttle for the presidency. Tuttle won an easy reelection but also received a scathing public letter from his opponent, who accused the Birch Society of sabotaging his campaign with slanderous rumors.[72] Hoover further warned that "Birch-printed hate propaganda" had been placed in the high school library. The *Vilas County News-Review* ran a quick response from Verne Kaub, in Madison, who proclaimed such materials "a welcome change from the tenor of the content of textbooks [supplied by the] National Education Association." Following his success in Twin Lakes, Kaub argued that denying Eagle River students access to conservative magazines impinged on their civil rights.[73]

At the seating of the new school board, Tuttle appointed a three-man committee to investigate the John Birch issue. The chair was Frank Carter, a sympathetic judge, whom Tuttle directed to Kaub for more information. During the inquiry, Carter used legal maneuvers to weaken the charges against Tuttle and went on long digressions about the links between liberal library holdings and juvenile delinquency. Afterward, Carter refused to write a joint report, Tuttle requested one from him alone, and the two published their version of events before the other committee members could submit dissenting views.[74] Tuttle coordinated these actions in a series of letters with Kaub, and he used the Twin Lakes ruling to reserve the board's right to choose library materials.[75]

These were all common Birch Society tactics, as was the subsequent mobilization of church, veterans', and women's groups to support the board. In March, the town's American Legion post insisted on the removal of "obscene and lascivious" titles from the school library and the appointment of a parents' committee to screen future book and magazine purchases.[76] In the meantime, Tuttle and Kaub disseminated several hundred copies of Judge Carter's report. Kaub even sent one to William F. Buckley, editor of *The National Review*, with a private note promising that it would "tickle him pink."[77]

Most of the state's newspapers condemned the Eagle River parents' committee as a front for censorship. Unaware of the connection between the two incidents, the editor of the *Vilas County News-Review* warned that it would soon become "an issue as widespread as the bitter squabble over the McGuffey's readers" in Twin Lakes. The NEA's national office despaired that the situation in Eagle

River would be "nonsense . . . if the basic issues—education and censorship— weren't so serious. Teachers, and not amateurs," the organization contended, "should determine their source materials."[78] The Wisconsin Education Association Council, the state library association, and the National Council of Teachers of English coordinated a lobbying campaign, while small businesses in Eagle River formed a citizens' committee to support Principal Abney and unseat Tuttle in the 1964 school board election. They succeeded, and the controversy gradually subsided.[79]

As Eagle River debated library materials, in Princeton, Wisconsin, near the center of the state, a school board member named Sam Garro tried to ban the novel *1984*. After a contentious vote overturned the ban, Garro claimed he had raised the issue to embarrass the principal, who had been ineffective with student discipline. The principal apologized, but pointed out that school consolidation had pushed high school enrollment from 135 to 168 in two years. He promised to add more staff but said that he "shuddered a little thinking about next year's discipline problems, with four new teachers on faculty."[80] Garro's support came primarily from farm families who were angry about their lack of representation on the newly consolidated school board, so the board took steps to remedy that problem as well: After voting down the censorship motion, two members offered to give their seats to rural representatives. What board members did not understand was the source of Garro's own dissatisfaction. He was the town dentist, not an angry farmer. Nor, despite his use of their pamphlets, was he one of the anticommunist "kooks" or rabid tax-cutters that were commonly associated with right-wing agitation. In fact, upset that Princeton was "sacrificing good education for monetary reasons," he wanted to *raise* the school's budget and to hire new math and science teachers. Like many other basic education advocates, Garro believed that talk about new teaching methods and expanded facilities had not actually improved instruction and thus, counterintuitively, saw the threat of censorship as a way to air legitimate questions about educational quality.[81]

Similar dynamics played out in Edgerton, a town ninety miles to the south, where the consolidation of rural districts and the arrival of the interstate highway also led to overcrowding.[82] In 1962, charges of collusion and favoritism accompanied the closure of six one-room schoolhouses and the construction of a new elementary school. Parents were even more upset when Edgerton's bookish superintendent refused to hire a profane, chain-smoking football coach to whip the high school team into shape. In a show of community control, the school board overruled him and hired the man anyway. The situation reached a head early in 1963, when a group of mothers confronted the school board about controversial books read in the senior English class, including *1984*, *Of Mice and*

Men, and *Crime and Punishment*. Dissatisfied with the school's initial deferral to teacher discretion, the mothers wrote a series of letters to the local paper lamenting the immorality of modern education and their apparent inability to change it. One, a poem, read:

> Don't cry, you're only parents
> You ain't got a thing to say
> Cause the good old superintendent
> And the school-board got their way.
> Soooooo—Give me back my sexy books, Mom
> You fought and lost the war
> Cause the Bible, God, and Prayer, Mom
> Fall outside the school-room door.

Another letter insisted that the books were written by men "inspired by communism, and will have the result of demoralizing our country." A local attorney accused board members of accepting illegal gifts from textbook companies, and demanded that they sign a moral code.[83] Shortly after these letters were published, the mothers discovered that the *McGuffey's Readers* decision in Twin Lakes had given school boards rather than administrators the power to choose curriculum. They launched a telephone campaign to "pack" that month's board meeting, which drew five hundred people and widespread news coverage.[84]

A supporter of the board blamed this agitation on a "pressure group whose only interest is the glorification of athletics" and wrote that board members were "being persecuted . . . to force their resignations in order to pack the board in the spring elections with 'friendly members,'" although whether friendly to football, "decent" literature, or some other agenda he did not say. Edgerton's superintendent complained that right-wing organizations were trying to set a precedent that "instead of satisfying a professional colleague . . . all teachers would be hired and fired not by the superintendent but by the board." The high school principal agreed that control over employment was the "bigger problem under this whole thing." It was no coincidence, he argued, that the English teacher under attack was the head of the local teachers' union.[85]

Ultimately, moderates prevailed. Parents backed away from the charges of bribery and favoritism, and the football coach was fired when the Badger Athletic Conference threatened to sever relations over the matter. The school board stood firm on the issue of book selection but agreed to schedule two English classes, only one of which would read the controversial titles.[86] As the turmoil subsided, the author August Derleth, a resident of Sauk City, Wisconsin, chuckled, "The cruel fact—cruel for the would-be censors—is that every book condemned . . . has been read, as a result, by ten and twenty times the number of young people who were meant to be 'protected' from them." "Can anyone doubt," he asked, "that a majority of the citizens, young and old, of Edgerton . . . has read *The Catcher in the Rye*?"[87]

Derleth intended to expose the futility of censorship, but from the perspective of an Edgerton parent he missed the point. The real question was not whether students should be allowed to read a particular book but whether their teachers or their parents had the authority to make that decision. At issue in Edgerton was the exercise of power in a decreasingly democratic institution. Parents supported book banning not out of provincialism or prudery but to voice their dissatisfaction with school administration and reassert control over their children's learning. Although they did not reclaim the right to fire teachers or choose curriculum directly, for many of them the board's compromise constituted a small success. Throughout the 1960s, other rural districts continued to invoke local control against the administrators and state bureaucrats who wanted to professionalize their schools. A grassroots campaign secured a state law mandating area-wide rather than town representation on school boards, "[assuring] closeness of board members to the people," while similar censorship campaigns appeared in Fond du Lac, Minocqua, and other Wisconsin communities.[88]

Conclusion

As debates over parents' rights roiled Wisconsin, similar issues yielded the era's most violent curricular conflict, in Kanawha County, West Virginia. In the late 1960s, the county school district, with the city of Charleston at its center, approved a list of new textbooks, including the MACOS curriculum and several other titles with multicultural approaches to literature and history. At first, the books attracted little notice, even when a dispute over sex education prompted Alice Moore, a minister's wife from the affluent suburbs of west Charleston, to run for school board under a banner of moral reform.[89] The trouble only began in the spring of 1974, when the district disbanded its curriculum committee (composed, in part, of parent representatives) and appointed a select group of educators to approve textbooks. Moore seized the opportunity to circulate petitions against the new books, which she claimed advocated racial hatred and a "secular humanism" that threatened Christian faith.[90]

Tens of thousands of parents signed the petitions that summer. When school started in September, parents held fifteen thousand children out of classes, roughly twenty percent of the district's enrollment. Many opened their own Christian schools in garages and church basements, using *McGuffey's Readers* and textbooks "discarded as too old [fashioned] by other states."[91] Over the next few months their strike attracted support from a range of right-wing groups, from the Heritage Foundation to the Ku Klux Klan. At the height of the strike, hardline protesters dynamited elementary schools and peppered empty school buses with buckshot. Parents who supported the textbooks found their cars firebombed, while the county sheriff arrested school board members for contributing to the delinquency of minors. The rancor finally quieted in December, when the school board president resigned, the district reinstated parent representatives to the curriculum committee, and new protocols allowed students to opt out of morally or religiously objectionable classes. The incident nevertheless became a catalyst for a new wave of conservative activism nationwide, resulting in the rise of groups like the Moral Majority and the highest number of censorship campaigns since the 1950s (see figure 13).[92]

Unfortunately, while many scholars have located the origins of the New Right in Kanawha County, few have made an effort to uncover the origins of the controversy itself. Most pick up the story in 1970, with Alice Moore's election, and explain earlier problems in the district with hazy references to the fundamentalist worldview or timeless "mountain culture" of rural protesters.[93] In *Reading Appalachia from Left to Right* (2009), Carol Mason goes a little further, comparing the textbook controversy with the area's Communist-led coal strikes in the 1930s. Yet she too contends that the 1974 incident moved away from class conflict to a "newly emerging" cultural politics, an explanation which—like Thomas Frank's diagnosis of conservative voting patterns in *What's the Matter With Kansas?*—implies misdirected rural resentment, a sort of false consciousness that vilified educators rather than sources of economic inequality.[94]

That analysis elides forty years of policies hostile to the local control of education, of which the dismissal of parent representatives was merely the last example. When one replaces essentialist notions of cultural difference with an actual examination of school administration between the 1930s and the 1970s, the events in Kanawha County become less a knee-jerk reaction to modernity than a successful campaign of political resistance, very much in keeping with earlier coal strikes. That the campaign transcended class and geography, encompassing suburban housewives and self-described "hillbillies," suggests not that the latter were duped but that conservative activists successfully identified and narrated a democratic vision that liberals had long since forgotten.

Falling tax revenues forced West Virginia to reorganize school districts along county lines in 1933. The change lowered administrative costs and widened tax bases enough to assure teachers a paycheck, but it also transferred personnel decisions to county boards, notorious seats of graft. Teaching remained a patronage job, and outlying neighborhoods frequently got the least qualified can-

FIGURE 13.   Children join the textbook protest in Campbells Creek, West Virginia, in 1974. Local residents resisted both the content of the books and the lack of control in their selection. (Courtesy of the Charleston Newspapers)

didates. In Kanawha County, rural parents' only means of influencing district policy became the bond referendum required for new construction funds, which they frequently rejected. Starving the district financially allowed rural areas to maintain older systems of local control within the county structure, keeping dilapidated one- and two-room schools in operation through the mid-1950s. City dwellers, corporations, and the West Virginia Education Association objected to this veto power, noting that "once rural areas [were] now populated suburbs," and that thousands of students were trapped in schools "never designed for that number." Their solution was the Better Schools Amendment of 1958, which enabled the county board of education to reassess land values and raise taxes to close substandard facilities.[95]

Opposition to the Better Schools Amendment was strongest in coal-mining communities east of Charleston, particularly Campbells Creek, where a history of corruption and neglect had left residents wary of the county board.[96] School consolidation remained an ongoing and divisive issue in the area. Although the total number of elementary schools in the county was falling fast—of the 285 operating in 1945, only ninety-seven survived to 1975—as late as 1960 there were still fifty-eight one- or two-room buildings dotting the county's hills and hollows. Few residents regarded their closure as an improvement: Crumbling infrastructure could suspend school bus service for weeks at a time, forcing children to walk up to three miles to consolidated elementary schools. Under the new building program, Campbells Creek would lose its middle school altogether, meaning even longer bus rides for students and less supervision by area residents.[97] The Better Schools Amendment narrowly passed, but for years to come the district superintendent attributed bond failures to voters' resistance to consolidation. Stripped of their neighborhood schools, the antagonism of rural residents represented not an innate clash of worldviews but a simple bid for local control and, by extension, good government.[98]

The same factors made Campbells Creek the epicenter of the textbook protests ten years later. As an NEA investigation concluded, it was because of "the absence of adequate voice to influence the decision-making process" in district schools that "the textbooks became a trumpet for voiceless people."[99] Contemporary commentators ridiculed the protesters' conspiracy theories and hysteria, but at the heart of the matter were legitimate questions about parents' rights and the failures of large-scale, liberal school administration. To the residents of Campbells Creek, teachers and board members were still "outsiders" despite being West Virginia natives and were no more trustworthy for their credentials. One high school student acknowledged that she supported the textbooks in principle but chafed when she heard district administrators saying, " 'Trust us. We've been educated.' " Surely their qualifications did not extend to the teachers in her school, the ones with criminal records and reputations for drunkenness? She quipped that philosophers might speculate about when theft is justified, but "you don't want second-grade teachers that got arrested for shoplifting teaching that kind of thing."[100]

For all of its inflammatory rhetoric and political posturing, the Kanawha County protest basically revived older questions about the role of community morals and local political power in education. Just as one cannot understand the local significance of the West Virginia conflict without recognizing the decades of uneven, inequitable reform that preceded it, the incident's national resonance is inseparable from the longstanding erosion of parental control over curriculum. Revitalized Christian fundamentalism and new political networks may have fanned curricular debates during the 1970s, but in case after case the sparks came from lingering disputes over school consolidation. Rural residents had the strongest incentive to challenge professional educators, so conservative activists built their case for parents' rights on rural notions of democracy. Whatever paradoxes underlay the resulting campaigns—the overlap of radical and respectable critiques, for instance—it was their rootedness in place and past that enabled the Right to craft a new, commonsense alternative to professionally chosen curriculum.

As the movement gained strength and confronted new legal obstacles, however, questions arose about the efficacy of local curricular authority in achieving conservative goals. As was the case with school funding, activists maintained support for local control in principle but in practice shifted their efforts toward individual and state-level curricular reforms by the mid-1980s.

REDEFINING PARENTS' RIGHTS

In the winter of 1981, two school board members from Montello, a small community in central Wisconsin, moved to ban Sol Stein's novel *The Magician* (1971) from a high school English class. They belonged to a local group called the Concerned Citizens, which opposed "smut, obscenities and sexual explicitness" in schoolbooks. When the rest of the board rejected their ban, the group simply marched into the school library and checked out thirty-three other books that they deemed offensive, vowing not to return them. Harriot Glover, one of the Concerned Citizen's supporters, exclaimed, "Filthy books are found in our school libraries where parents apparently have *no* control!" Referring to an overlapping complaint about sex education at the high school, she quipped that the Sex Information and Education Council of the United States, which held its national convention in Wisconsin the previous year, saw citizens like her as "representing the 'lunatic fringe,' waving flags and opposing any attempt to put sex education in the schools." Unsurprisingly, she continued, "our *educators* consider anyone with higher moral standards on the *lunatic fringe*. Are we going to let this continue until *all* parental rights are stripped away?" Faculty members retorted that parental rights did not permit the theft of publicly owned books. The board of education agreed, restricted adult access to the library, and threatened fines if the books were not returned.[1]

The little town drew widespread attention and it is easy to see why. School censorship had reached a pitch not seen in Wisconsin since the 1950s, with over three hundred cases a year cropping up in towns like Wauzeka, Adams, and Waukesha.[2] Hundreds of people offered financial support for the Concerned

Citizens, and several other right-wing organizations tried to exploit the publicity that the group generated. The *Wisconsin Report* newsletter criticized books in Montello's library for encouraging homosexuality. *Posse Comitatus*, a white-supremacist militia, staged a recruiting drive in the surrounding countryside, denouncing public schools as "'Government Centers for Indoctrination' [which] surreptitiously introduce drugs, sexual immorality, rebellion against parents, humanism, Marxism, and communism."[3] On the other side of the issue, professional and civil libertarian groups tried to use Montello as a stopgap against emboldened grassroots protests. Several of them held a conference in the state capital about the threat of religious fundamentalism, and the newly formed Freedom from Religion Foundation sent replacement copies of the confiscated books. Libraries around Wisconsin revised their borrowing policies to head off similar campaigns. Major newspapers editorialized against intolerance and censorship, while teachers' unions reaffirmed their defense of professional rights. When an angry parent accused Montello's biology teacher of promoting marijuana use, the Wisconsin Education Association Council's legal defense team filed a libel suit to use "as precedent for other Wisconsin teachers, and as a warning to individuals in [other] communities."[4]

For all the scrutiny that the Montello incident received, however, its significance was in some ways misunderstood. Contemporary news reports juxtaposed scenes of bigotry and book-banning with an otherwise tranquil heartland, giving the false impression that these attacks were new and externally inspired—that Montello and similar towns were "isolated communities" suddenly linked with "outside agents or agencies that supplied reviews of textbooks, tactical advice, and other information," rather than the products of longstanding local grievances.[5] In fact, while contemporaries described campaigns like the one in Montello as manifestations of a religiously energized "New Right," it is worth noting, from a historical perspective, how little was new about them. As one elderly resident remarked, locals had been "endeavoring to tear down the schools and create chaos . . . in the Westfield–Montello area for as long as I can remember." The same farmers who formed the Concerned Citizens had objected to the closure of the area's one-room schoolhouses two decades earlier, and their protests were motivated not only by religious fervor but because they felt they were "treated rudely" by administrators when they opposed a school renovation and higher tax rates.[6]

Campaigns for local control of curriculum surged nationwide in the late 1970s.[7] Sex education remained divisive; evolution became more so. Conservative groups denounced fairy tales as occult and stories with nonwhite characters as un-American. The specter of "secular humanism" especially incensed conservative parents, who regarded "Man: A Course of Study" and other values-clarification programs (which encouraged children to explore the social basis of morality) as relativistic attempts "to eliminate existing belief systems and replace them with new values and beliefs that will 'render the child susceptible to manipulation, coercion, control and corruption for the rest of his life.'"[8] These criticisms elicited the same sort of demagogy and confrontation seen in the textbook controversy in Kanawha County, West Virginia, now amplified by a new generation of educational activists and a growing network of Christian publishers and broadcasters. Although many other political forces led to the rise of the Religious Right, the polarizing, mobilizing effects of secular education occupied a central place in its agenda.

Yet the tide of school protest was as muddy as it was powerful. Conservatives often championed both the rights of school boards and those of individual parents, combining two seemingly contradictory interpretations of local control, one based on the principle of majority rule and the other on minority rights. These positions began to diverge during the late 1970s as courts limited the ability of local majorities to determine curriculum and strengthened the rights of individual parents, students, and teachers. The legal shift decoupled not only conflicting notions of democracy but the conservative movement's "radical" and "respectable" segments as well. "Radical" activists, those concerned with secularism and cultural issues, increasingly voiced explicitly Christian rhetoric and began to accept narrower conceptions of local control, invoking minority rights to secure equal treatment of their religious views. When that failed, they left public education altogether. By the 1980s, conservative Christians had convinced many local and state authorities, as well as federal courts, to honor exemptions from objectionable courses and to permit the spread of loosely regulated Christian academies and homeschools. Those concessions marked a sharp departure from the unitary system of educational oversight that had developed over the previous century, a system that "radical" activists had supported as long as they could control it.[9] Meanwhile, "respectable" conservatives, those primarily concerned with academic quality, started demanding a stronger state role in curricular standards and testing, leading to the bipartisan reforms of the 1990s and ultimately to federal initiatives such as No Child Left Behind.

As was the case with school finance, the conservative coalition began to dissolve and reform along new ideological lines, ensuring that the educational politics of the 1980s looked radically different from those a decade earlier. School boards retained the right to determine curriculum (and censorship campaigns continued), but debate moved away from the role of locally elected representatives to focus on the exercise of individual and state power. Thus, while opponents worried that the Montello incident represented a resurgent politics of censorship, in fact it was a high-water mark in the struggle for local control and the long battle over school district consolidation.

Courts and Curricular Authority

Implicit in conservative calls for parents' rights were the dual assumptions that local majorities—"silent," "moral," or otherwise—should govern public education without interference from teachers or policymakers, and also that individual parents should control their children's learning. These positions cohered as professional school administration expanded, so that when courts ruled in favor of either of them conservatives could act as if they supported both, as if the law protected school boards *and* parents from the overreach of unelected officials. Increasingly, however, as state and federal courts attended to the rights of minorities, they found in favor of individual parents, students, and teachers *against* local boards. When that happened, conservatives were forced to refine their message. The battle for traditional values narrowed from a defense of local authority to a defense of individual rights, and over the course of the 1970s, the adjudication of curricular disputes became increasingly entwined with the case law of religion in public schools.

Court rulings began to turn against local school boards in the early 1960s, when the Supreme Court banned state-sanctioned prayer and bible reading in public schools, arguing that government agencies could not impel a student to "profess a belief or disbelief in any religion."[10] Subsequent decisions established a strict test for religious activity in schools, prohibited school boards or administrators from stifling student speech, and enforced federal voting procedures in school board elections, particularly regarding civil rights enforcement and the "one man, one vote" doctrine, which had been flouted at the municipal level. Meanwhile, a wave of other cases (discussed in chapter 4) expanded professional protections for teachers. All of these rulings constrained the power of school boards, establishing new rights for teachers and students at the expense of traditional public oversight.[11]

The court's first and most significant foray into curriculum during this period followed the same pattern. *Epperson v. Arkansas* (1968) overturned prohibitions against teaching evolution, legislation that had persisted in Southern states since the Scopes "monkey trial" of the 1920s. *Epperson* invalidated antievolution laws by citing other precedents from that era, particularly *Meyer v. Nebraska* (1923) and *Pierce v. Society of Sisters* (1925).[12] *Meyer* and *Pierce* granted relief to parochial schools in Nebraska and Oregon, respectively, which had become targets of xenophobic legislation after World War I. *Meyer* prevented states from banning instruction in any language but English, and *Pierce* prevented them from outlawing private education altogether. Both cases used the Due Process Clause of the Fourteenth Amendment to bind state governments to federal freedoms of speech and religion. In these cases, however, the process played out in a strange way, with courts framing religious schooling largely as an economic freedom. For instance, while *Meyer* protected "the right of the individual . . . to worship God according to the dictates of his own conscience," it did so in the context of a teacher's right "to contract [and] engage in any of the common occupations of life." Arbitrarily banning private schools or the study of foreign languages was "materially to interfere with the calling of modern language teachers, with the opportunities of pupils to acquire knowledge, and with the power of parents to control the education of their own."[13] *Epperson* also cited *West Virginia Board of Education v. Barnette* (1943), a case filed by a group of Jehovah's Witnesses who refused to say the pledge of allegiance in school. *Barnette* restricted majority rule in education in ways similar to *Meyer* and *Pierce* but was decided on different grounds. The court found that the First Amendment prohibited school officials from "[prescribing] what shall be orthodox in politics, nationalism, religion, or other matters of opinion," where dictates of family and conscience took precedence.[14]

In 1968, Justice Abe Fortas combined this matrix of professional, student, and parental rights in the *Epperson* decision, arguing that the prohibition of scientific teaching unduly restricted both professional practice and the free exchange of ideas. "It is much too late," announced Fortas, "to argue that the State may impose upon the teachers in its schools any conditions that it chooses, however restrictive they may be of constitutional guarantees."[15] Although Fortas hoped that *Epperson* would settle the evolution issue in particular and (by outlining clearer boundaries for school boards) perhaps conflicts over curricular control in general, in at least two respects the case did not settle anything.

First, even as *Epperson* expanded the right of students and teachers to read what they chose, it also reiterated the right of state and local boards to select course content, making it difficult to say exactly when one impinged on the other.[16] That tension was evident in subsequent rulings, such as *Island Trees Independent School District v. Pico* (1982), which began when school board members in Levittown, New York, removed "objectionable" books from a junior high school library during the mid-1970s. Parents sued, claiming that the removal violated their children's rights to receive information, but appellate courts were unsympathetic to their argument, noting that "statutes, history, and precedent had vested local school boards with a broad discretion to formulate educational policy." "The board has restricted access only to certain books which [it] believed to be, in essence, vulgar," the courts explained. "While removal of such books from a school library may . . . reflect a misguided educational philosophy, it does not constitute a sharp and direct infringement of any first amendment right." If enough parents wanted to make the books available, they could simply elect new school board members.[17]

The U.S. Supreme Court saw the issue differently. Justice William Brennan wrote that "school officials cannot suppress expressions of feeling with which they do not wish to contend," a claim he based on students' rights on the one hand (citing *Epperson*) and on the other, teachers' rights against arbitrary dismissal and retribution.[18] Brennan repeatedly acknowledged the role of local boards in determining curriculum but insisted that "reliance upon that duty is misplaced . . . beyond the compulsory environment of the classroom, [particularly] into the school library and the regime of voluntary inquiry that there holds sway." Henceforth, school boards could not select or remove library books based on religious criteria or "in a narrowly partisan or political manner."[19]

Brennan felt that the distinction between mandatory classroom and voluntary library materials offered an acceptable limit on local prerogative, but the court's conservatives worried that the precedent would ease the way for further constraints.[20] After all, if school boards were prohibited from casting "a pall of orthodoxy over the classroom," as Brennan wrote, why should courts limit their scrutiny to the school library? Much as *Baker v. Carr* had led them into the "political thicket" of legislative redistricting, conservative jurists thought that *Epperson* and *Pico* would draw them into the jungle of curricular selection, leaving courts to determine what constituted unduly "political" motivations in an inherently political enterprise. Worse, the rulings imbued curricular decisions with a new, expansive logic: Once books got into a school they became much harder for boards to remove. *Epperson* and *Pico* typified a move away from unchecked local control of curriculum, but they hardly put the issue to rest. Debates about the limits and applications of the cases continue, as do political struggles for control of local and state boards of education, which retain significant influence in curricular choices.[21]

The *Epperson* ruling also failed to end curricular disputes because it prompted conservatives to adopt new tactics. Specifically, by citing precedents related to due process and the free exercise of religion, the decision encouraged right-wing activists to reposition themselves from a thwarted majority to an aggrieved minority, entitled to the same recognition and protections afforded other minority groups.[22] This was an easy shift to make under the nebulous rubric of "parents' rights," and continued themes of religious persecution and spiritual warfare sounded by Fred Schwartz, Billy James Hargis, and other evangelical activists in the 1960s. Soon, newcomers such as Jerry Falwell and Pat Robertson were voicing the same ideas in sermons, books, and radio and television appearances. Interspersed with their usual complaints about activist judges countermanding the majority's wishes was a new argument: that a secular majority was denying Christians' *individual* rights to religious freedom. Not only did the new approach simultaneously position Christians as both a majority and minority, by its logic it no longer mattered whether evangelical parents enjoyed popular support in their local districts. Evolution, sex education, and "dirty books" became matters of individual conscience rather than local consensus.[23]

Accompanying the adoption of minority rights rhetoric was a halfhearted embrace of moral relativism. Hoping to gain legal traction by blurring categories, conservative activists began to imbue religion with the trappings of science while framing science and secularism themselves as systems of religious belief. From this position, evangelicals could demand equal time for "creation science" or other quasi-theistic explanations of human origins—all in the name of tolerance and diversity—even as they challenged secular materials as impermissibly religious, as Alabama judge Brevard Hand did when he ordered the removal of forty-four "secular humanist" textbooks for violating the separation of church and state.[24] Despite its popularity, however, equating science and secularism as faith-based systems never succeeded as a legal strategy. An appeals court quickly reversed Hand's decision, while the Supreme Court, in *Edwards v. Aguillard* (1987), overturned a law requiring teachers to present creation science alongside evolution. Individual districts continue to vary widely in their handling of the subject, but subsequent legal challenges to evolutionary biology have yielded similar results.[25]

The campaign for minority rights was more successful when it came to withdrawing students from controversial classes, and once again a conflict over school consolidation in rural Wisconsin became the basis for a decisive legal precedent. The case that opened the door for student exemption policies was *Wisconsin v. Yoder* (1972), in which three Amish families sued the school district in New Glarus, Wisconsin, for religious discrimination.

Public education had long posed a quandary for Amish parents, who valued literacy and numeracy but worried that too much formal training would leave their children unfit for the sect's simple way of life. They accepted public elementary schools, but only because local control allowed Amish leaders to serve on boards and help determine the curriculum. The school consolidation movement posed a dual threat to that arrangement. First, it took children farther away from their homes and diluted parents' influence. Second, by subsuming elementary schools into high school districts, it opened the door for mandatory secondary education. Amish boys initially evaded attendance requirements by repeating eighth grade two or three times before getting their agricultural work permits. In 1955, uncomfortable with the prospect of churlish, bearded middle-schoolers, Pennsylvania became the first state to establish alternative vocational programs for Amish youth, allowing them to begin work after eighth grade provided that they kept a journal about their experiences. Other states established similar programs.[26]

Most of the Amish arrived in Wisconsin after 1965—from Ohio, where they fled suburban sprawl, or from Iowa, where school consolidation had incited a prolonged conflict with state administrators. When Iowa consolidated its school districts in 1962, state and county administrators rejected the Pennsylvania compromise. To the contrary, they enforced high school attendance, raised requirements for teacher certification (making it harder for Amish women to qualify), and mandated busing to central elementary schools. As in other states, Iowa's consolidation order yielded numerous cases of miscommunication and manipulation. The town of Olwein, for example, managed to annex a neighboring community only through Amish support, which it obtained with the promise that the Amish would continue to operate their local schools in the new district. When the superintendent who brokered the deal retired, however, Olwein not only retracted the agreement but thwarted the transfer of Amish neighborhoods to more accommodating districts. The result was a tense standoff, with Amish parents operating their own, unaccredited schools and children hiding from truancy officers in cornfields.[27]

The community relocated to Wisconsin hoping to find some reprieve. Shortly after arriving in New Glarus they built two one-room parochial schools staffed with young Amish women.[28] But district administrators proved no more accommodating on the high school issue than they had been in Iowa. The state mandated two years of schooling after eighth grade, as well as physical education, which required children to shower together and engage in aerobic dancing, both of which violated Amish notions of modesty. The New Glarus superintendent offered to let Amish children wear homemade gym uniforms but would make no broader concessions to parents' objections about the curriculum. Several parents began to hold their children out of school, a violation of attendance laws that led to arrests and fines. Eventually, an Amish minister named Jonas Yoder took the district to court. The case reached the U.S. Supreme Court, which found that the plaintiffs' right to religious freedom outweighed the state's interest in compulsory education and granted any sect with similar convictions an exemption from mandatory secondary education.[29]

Wisconsin v. Yoder may seem like an idiosyncratic case. Narrowly construed (as the court insisted it should be), it pertained only to Old Order Amish, Mennonites, and other religious minorities. But for many conservatives the court's ruling represented a far-reaching rejoinder to the government's "hydraulic insistence to conformity to majoritarian standards," a "[victory] for individualists and believers in freedom and family sovereignty."[30] Indeed, if one abridged specific references to Amish customs, the basis of the court's ruling spoke to the concerns of a wide swath of the public in the 1970s. "As long as compulsory education laws were confined to eight grades of elementary basic education imparted in a nearby rural schoolhouse," the justices wrote, parents "had little basis to fear that school attendance would expose their children to the worldly influence they reject." "But modern compulsory secondary education in rural areas is now largely carried on in a consolidated school," they continued, "often remote from the student's home and alien to his daily home life . . . [engendering] great concern and conflict."[31]

Wisconsin v. Yoder also offered opportunities for conservative activists in the suburbs. Legislators outside Milwaukee met repeatedly with Amish leaders, offering financial support and hoping to turn the case to their own ends. In 1967, Kenneth Merkel, an assemblyman from Brookfield, used the New Glarus standoff to propose a bill for religious exemptions from physical education classes. The bill failed when educators complained that the action, while aimed at the Amish, would "open the way to many other such bills . . . [and] make school administration difficult if not impossibly legal."[32] For Merkel, of course, complicating school administration was the whole idea: He also envisioned exemptions from biology classes discussing evolution, and for "any parent who wishes . . . to withdraw his child from any courses on health or sex education."[33] By 1971, Merkel was proposing an outright repeal of the state's compulsory education laws and fighting for specific guarantees of religious expression in schools.[34] While these bills never passed, they convinced many conservatives that the fight for the Amish was "a blow for all of us as parents . . . [whose] rights are being eroded," and encouraged them to support related causes, such as parental selection of textbooks and the preservation of union high schools.[35] Meanwhile, so many Wisconsinites stopped by to thank Jonas Yoder that he sold his farm and left the state to avoid the attention.[36]

Merkel and others like him were, at best, partial converts to the cause of minority rights. Most continued to support local censorship campaigns and to reject the agendas of any nonwhite, non-Christian minorities. Nevertheless, a rhetorical shift from community to individual control of education appealed to them, and the Amish became a useful symbol for reestablishing parental authority. Activists nationwide cited *Yoder* as the basis for new religious exemptions and opt out policies, which soon became widespread at the local level, defusing tensions in the Kanawha County conflict and scores of others. Educators worried that allowing parents to pick and choose the content of their children's learning would undermine professional prerogative and the uniformity of public education. In a reversal of emphasis, some teachers' unions began to insist that school boards, in consultation with teachers and librarians, had the responsibility to choose books and that all students should be compelled to read them. By the early 1980s, it fell to the judiciary to adjudicate the protections of parental freedom outlined in *Yoder*, and to determine how far those protections should extend.

The Supreme Court never ruled directly on opt out policies, and a series of contradictory lower court rulings underscores their uncertain legal status. In *Grove v. Mead School District* (1985), for instance, a family outside of Spokane, Washington, voiced religious objections to their daughter's literature textbook and demanded its removal. Much like Brevard Hand's ruling in Alabama, their petition invoked minority rights but sought to ban books for everyone. If upheld, it would have provided protesters with a new means to perpetuate the same old censorship campaigns, unconstrained even by the will of local majorities. The district court denied that possibility, noting that the plaintiffs' daughter had been offered alternative assignments as soon as she voiced her objections, so "the burden on [her] free exercise of religion was minimal." Religious sensitivity did not justify broad-based censorship and, in this case, opt out policies provided a way to sidestep thorny legal questions about state coercion.[37]

The same year that the *Mead* case was filed, a group of Christian fundamentalists in Hawkins County, Tennessee, also complained that their school's literature textbooks offended their religion. Administrators initially allowed their children to work from older textbooks in the office or library. When the school board eliminated that option, however, the parents sued. In *Mozert v. Hawkins County Board of Education* (1987), the district court initially found in favor of the parents, noting "that the defendants could accommodate the plaintiffs without material and substantial disruption to the educational process, by permitting the objecting students to 'opt out'" of the reading program. An appeals court overturned that decision on widely cited but fairly weak argumentative grounds, noting that simply because certain activities were in the teacher's manual did not mean that students actually performed them in the classroom. "Proof that an objecting student was required to participate beyond reading and discussing assigned materials, or was disciplined for disputing assigned materials, might well implicate the Free Exercise Clause," the judges conceded, but "the Director of Education for the State of Tennessee testified that most teachers do not adhere to the suggestions in the teachers' manuals ... but '[do their] own thing.'" Insofar as the plaintiffs did not want their children "to make critical judgments and exercise choices in areas where the Bible provides the answer," the court found "no evidence that any child in the Hawkins County schools was required to make such judgments." It did not say what would happen if teachers *did* follow the book or actually compelled their students to engage in critical thought, but ruled that mere exposure to offensive ideas did not require schools to excuse students from class.[38]

The latter point suggests that the real purpose of the decision was to limit conservatives' proliferating demands for religious exemptions by severing the connection between *Yoder* and *Mozert*. In addition to distinguishing between active compulsion in the former case (in which children actually had to engage in aerobics and bathing) and passive compulsion in the latter (which at most made them listen to other children read and discuss folk tales), the judges pointed out that while *Yoder* applied to an easily identifiable sect, the plaintiffs in *Mozert* had no particular affiliation other than being "born-again Christians" and that "other members of their churches, and even their pastors, do not agree with their position in this case." "The [Amish] parents in *Yoder* did not want their children to attend any high school or be exposed to any part of a high school curriculum," the decision continued, while "the parents in the present case want their children to acquire all the skills required to live in modern society [but] also want to have them excused from exposure to some ideas they find offensive." Courts were bound to respect religious freedom, but they could not practically accommodate individual beliefs on a case-by-case, book-by-book basis. If parents remained unsatisfied with the curriculum chosen by the local school board, they would have to "send their children to church schools or private schools, as many of them have done, or teach them at home." Many school districts continued to offer opt out policies for controversial classes, but decisions like *Mozert* underscored that the practice was not mandatory and certainly would not reverse the broader trend toward secular public education. Over the course of the 1980s, tens of thousands of Christian parents took the court's advice and turned to private education or homeschooling, the only sure opt outs left to them.[39]

Christian Education and the Rise of Homeschooling

On average, two Christian academies opened every day between 1960 and 1990. Although many closed due to fluctuating enrollments or religious schisms, by the end of that period the two largest Christian school associations supervised an enrollment of over 500,000 pupils, with thousands more in unaccredited schools.[40] Independent Christian schools had first gained popularity in the South as a means to avoid racial integration, but they were present in other regions and for other reasons as well.[41] As a Harvard researcher warned, liberals' tendency "to reduce [revived] conservatism—and the Christian schools that have emerged from it—to racism is simply to ignore two decades of social and cultural upheaval." A variety of back-to-basics reformers, including William Smeeth in Wisconsin and the parents in Kanawha County, West Virginia, saw Christian schools as a means of reinforcing traditional curriculum and cultural values. Many preferred their small class sizes, strict discipline, and dress codes to public schools that they perceived as increasingly permissive.[42]

Regardless of whether parents chose Christian academies for their racial exclusivity or their religious content, efforts to sidestep government regulation ensured that these institutions would inevitably clash with local, state, and federal officials. Federal courts had prohibited the diversion of public funds (through vouchers) to Southern "segregation academies" since the 1960s, and in 1970 the Internal Revenue Service (IRS) denied tax exemptions to any school with discriminatory admission policies. It strengthened that position in 1978, requiring that Southern private schools enroll demonstrably integrated student bodies. Evangelicals, perceiving a threat to their religious liberty, mounted grassroots protests. They complained that unelected officials were not only exceeding the law but holding Christians to a higher standard than other groups.[43] The IRS eventually scaled back its requirements. Congressional Republicans passed amendments prohibiting the agency from acting on the guidelines, and the Reagan administration showed little interest in pursuing violators. Many Christian schools had already begun to accept students of color anyway, but activist Paul Weyrich remembers the IRS showdown "[shattering] the Christian community's notion that Christians could isolate themselves inside their own institutions and teach what they pleased." As a result, even as explicitly racist Christian schools disappeared, the threat of government intervention encouraged those using unlicensed teachers or unscientific or historically stilted textbooks to sharpen the legal defense of their curriculum.[44]

Most of them cited the right to a private education outlined in *Pierce* and the religious objections sanctioned in *Yoder* to claim that the state had no business regulating their programs, but those were problematic interpretations. *Pierce* had established private schools' right to prayer and religious exercises only by conceding state supervision over all other areas of curriculum and administration—that is, the case was *predicated* on regulation, to which Catholic schools had willingly submitted in the 1920s—and serious questions remained about *Yoder's* applicability to mainstream religious groups.[45]

State courts were far from uniform in their adjudication of these issues, but they proved more willing to recognize religious exemptions for entire private schools than for individuals in public school. For example, several extended the *Yoder* decision to evangelical schools and ruled that teacher certification requirements were unnecessarily burdensome to religious groups. In *State v. Whisner* (1976), the Ohio Supreme Court wrote, "It is difficult to imagine a state interest of sufficient magnitude to override . . . the free exercise clause," and promised that it would not "attempt to conjure up such an interest, in order to sustain application of the 'minimum [teacher certification] standards'" to Christian schools. "So pervasive and all-encompassing [would] total compliance with each and every standard" be for a private school, the decision continued, that it "would effectively eradicate the distinction between public and nonpublic education, and thereby deprive these appellants of their traditional interest as parents to direct the upbringing and education of their children." The Kentucky Supreme Court came to the same conclusion in *State Board of Education v. Rudasill* (1976). When plaintiffs in Nebraska and North Dakota tried to apply the rulings to their schools, however, courts in those states demurred, citing the narrow basis of the *Yoder* decision and the long tradition of state regulation of private education.[46]

Debates about the regulation of teachers, curriculum, and facilities became more complicated the fewer students a school enrolled. By the 1970s, some Christian schools rivaled their public counterparts in size and structure, but most were smaller affairs, taught by pastors, parents, or retirees in church basements and private homes.[47] One of the largest publishers of Christian materials designed "teacherless" lesson plans, with self-guided workbooks and training manuals for parents.[48] It was not much of a leap from teacherless schools operated in one's living room to single-family homeschooling, which met minimal content regulations but allowed parents to avoid discussions of evolution or, like one mother in Massachusetts, to use older books "in which there [was] respect for government and historical figures."[49]

The homeschool movement was never a uniquely conservative phenomenon but one of several points of overlap between the antistatism of the postwar Right and Left. Hippies and other back-to-the-land activists were some of the first practitioners in rural areas, and in cities some African Americans saw it as the only way to protect their children from peer violence and racist teachers.[50] Nevertheless, as the historian Milton Gaither notes, white evangelicals comprised the bulk of the movement's membership from the outset, and most of its growth occurred in suburban and rural areas, which became "a breeding ground for libertarian sentiment and antigovernment activism."[51]

The question facing conservative parents was how to teach their children at home without running afoul of truancy laws. Gaither argues that the most effective recourse was to characterize their efforts as a form of private schooling, in which the law permitted a degree of flexibility, and either describe the home itself as a private school—a plausible claim if one of the parents was a certified teacher—or enroll their children in correspondence programs with an established private school. Courts had specifically rejected such claims over the previous fifty years on the grounds that socialization required a proper school setting, but increasing rights consciousness left many judges uncomfortable dictating children's social needs to parents.[52] Likewise, the tendency to twist placement and attendance policies against minority groups had heightened judicial scrutiny of school administration during this period and, if it did not lead courts to invalidate compulsory education outright (as some conservatives hoped), it at least encouraged them to clarify and liberalize the application of attendance laws.

Once again, a widely cited precedent came from rural Wisconsin. In 1983, school administrators in Avoca, a town in the southwest corner of the state, fined Laurence Popanz for operating a private school out of his home. They complained that Popanz had not provided them with descriptions of the school's enrollment or curriculum and that he was not listed in the state's nonpublic school directory. Popanz countered that his teaching met all the relevant requirements, that administrators had never visited his home for further information, and that it was immaterial whether he was listed in an unofficial directory. The Wisconsin Supreme Court agreed with him. In a strongly worded opinion, the court demanded that the legislature "define the phrase 'private school'; citizens or the courts should not have to guess at its meaning," and warned that "leaving the determination of whether or not children are attending a private school to local school officials whose decisions may rest on *ad hoc* and subjective standards . . . poses the danger of arbitrary and discriminatory enforcement."[53] Lawmakers responded with legislation requiring private schools to provide "education and instruction substantially equivalent to that offered in public schools," offer a requisite number of school days, and provide sequential programs in the core subjects. Without mandating certification, they also reserved the DPI's right to check teachers' qualifications. But, for the first time, they specifically approved (and regulated) homeschooling in Wisconsin.[54]

Since most other state courts continued to reject the right to homeschool—particularly when plaintiffs tried to use *Yoder* as the basis of broad-based exemptions from compulsory attendance—*State v. Popanz* provided a way forward for conservative activists across the country.[55] One merely had to accept the principle of state regulation while arguing that existing statutes were overly vague in their definition of private schools, and from there that homeschooling qualified as a form of private education. By 1990 most states were willing to accept that logic and evaluate "schools" by academic rather than social standards. Nor did regulators push very hard for those standards. Perhaps afraid of more sweeping court rulings, most required only a general adherence to public school curriculum and rarely challenged a parent's qualifications or compliance with specific course content. The result was an ambiguous accommodation that allowed courts to preserve state curricular authority in principle, and in practice allowed conservatives to teach children in their churches and homes, withdrawn from public schools that they no longer controlled.

The Excellence Movement

Just as conservative Christians were narrowing their conceptions of local control, other members of the Right began to call for broader state and federal influence in school curriculum. This was an unexpected shift. Ronald Reagan staked much of his 1980 presidential campaign on local control of education, promising to restore school prayer, limit race-based busing, institute tax credits for students in private schools, convert federal funding to block grants, and, ultimately, abolish the federal Department of Education, which he referred to as a "bureaucratic boondoggle." Echoing widespread conservative sentiments, he insisted that "local needs and preferences, rather than the wishes of Washington, determine the education of our children," and promised, upon taking office, to appoint a task force "to look at the appropriate role of the Federal Government in education, if there is one, and to report back." Presidential advisers hinted that incoming secretary of education Terrell Bell should not get too comfortable in his office.[56]

Bell was not the administration's first choice for the position but was appointed as a favor to Senator Orrin Hatch and because staffers could find few other conservatives with experience in federal education policy. Bell had been a teacher and superintendent, Utah's state commissioner of education, and the national commissioner of education in the Ford administration's Department of Health, Education, and Welfare. Thus, while amenable to many of Reagan's initiatives, he was nonetheless a product and supporter of the same bureaucratic structures that the administration hoped to dismantle. Bell saw his challenge as revitalizing the nation's school system without allowing right-wing ideologues to defund or discredit the federal government's role in education altogether. He did so with a genius stroke of insubordination. After taking office, Bell quietly convened the National Commission on Excellence in Education to assess curriculum and achievement in the nation's schools. In 1983, he released its findings in a report entitled *A Nation at Risk*.[57]

The brief and readable report redirected conservative calls for academic "excellence" into support for greater state and federal oversight of schools. Exploiting fears of international economic competition, it declared, "If an unfriendly foreign power had attempted to impose on America the mediocre educational performance that exists today, we might well have viewed it as an act of war. As it stands, we have allowed this to happen to ourselves." A sense of urgency pervaded the report, which argued that falling SAT scores, poor performance on international tests, and a general drift in secondary coursework had led to "a rising tide of mediocrity" in the schools, with "more and more young people [emerging] from high school ready neither for college nor for work." Progressive educators had served up a "curricular smorgasbord, combined with extensive student choice," allowing students to avoid rigorous coursework, while back-to-basics reformers and the Elementary and Secondary Education Act had prioritized lower-order skills instead of the critical thinking necessary for a technologically advanced economy. Teacher salaries were too low, and teachers and administrators lacked access to the aggregated information necessary for effective policy-making. The report called for immediate action, insisting "that the Federal Government should supplement State, local, and other resources to foster key national educational goals."[58]

A Nation at Risk caused a sensation, selling out its first run and going through several more, but its significance was not immediately clear. President Reagan used the publication ceremony to repeat talking points about tuition tax credits, vouchers, school prayer, and abolishing the Department of Education. Appearing at a conservative educational forum, Bell still received the loudest applause when he said, "Education is a family matter. The parent is the foremost teacher, the home is the most influential classroom, and schools should exist to support the home." Subsequent presenters at the forum spoke about "returning education of children to parental and local control," and "parents [acting] to eliminate obscene or inaccurate textbooks from reading lists."[59] Several other commission members expressed disappointment at what they perceived as partisan attempts to twist the report's message. Gerald Holton, the Harvard professor who had coined the phrase "rising tide of mediocrity," grumbled, "We've been had."[60]

Contrary to Holton's assumptions, however, it was Reagan who had been had. The report's popularity forced him to appear with Bell at over a dozen events and to voice full-throated support for the commission's findings. In a situation "replete with irony," wrote an analyst at the American Enterprise Institute, "the most anti-education President in our history has succeeded in making education an issue," to the point that he soon positioned himself "as the leading advocate of education reform." Reagan continued to argue that the federal government spent too much on categorical funding of education, and the Department of Education's staff fell dramatically during his presidency, but given the gravity of the threat, he could hardly persist in calls for the department's abolition. The public increasingly demanded to know what state and federal agencies were doing to improve the schools.[61]

The criticisms in A Nation at Risk aligned with efforts already underway in several states, including the establishment of uniform content standards, stricter graduation requirements, better pre- and in-service training for teachers, higher salaries, and statewide tests of elementary, middle, and high school students.[62] Within two years of the report's release, over forty states had implemented some version of these reforms; several even tied state funding to minimum levels of achievement on standardized tests.[63] Essentially, researchers argued, "state legis-latures [began] acting as super-school boards, and telling the school districts and administrators how to manage the schools," a shift they ascribed to the changes outlined in previous chapters—the consolidation of school districts, expanded collective bargaining, and increased educational funding—as well as the im-proved capacity of state departments of education to collect and analyze data.[64]

Comparatively high levels of achievement and stronger traditions of local control slowed curricular reform in many Northern states. Wisconsin, for in-stance, accepted federal grants to assess effective teaching and administration and instituted a competency-based testing program in 1982, but for several years it allowed districts to design their own tests or choose items from a statewide data bank. Only in 1988 did it require a statewide reading comprehension test (and then only for third graders) or require that districts sequence their course offerings.[65] Strongest support for statewide standardization came from Southern governors, most prominently Tennessee's Lamar Alexander, South Carolina's Richard Riley, and Arkansas's Bill Clinton. These leaders worried about the gap between their rapidly growing economies and comparatively weak school sys-tems. Because of the region's unique educational history—with comparatively late adoption of public schools and strong traditions of county administration—Southern reform efforts also faced less opposition from teachers' unions or local-control conservatives than did their counterparts elsewhere. Thus, while the Reagan and Bush administrations struggled to move school reform through a Congress dominated by traditional partisan interests, Southern leaders appeared appealingly pragmatic in their calls for reform. They seized the initiative at the Charlottesville Summit, in 1989, a meeting of governors that led to the first, non-binding push for national testing and curricular standards.[66]

It was not only state-level politicians that found excellence to be a winning issue. As had been the case with vouchers, a variety of national interest groups recognized in the ferment of the 1980s a once-in-a-lifetime opportunity for meaningful school reform. From the Right, neoconservatives like Chester Finn and Diane Ravitch supported state and federal intervention in education, pro-vided that it actually improved student achievement.[67] Standards reform also began attracting liberal support, from civil rights advocates like Senator Edward Kennedy—frustrated by persistently low academic outcomes for poor and mi-nority students twenty years after federal spending had targeted the problem—as well as teachers' unions who sought increased school funding.[68] Thus, by the 1990s, a new, bipartisan coalition had emerged, advocating traditionally liberal goals of racial equality, increased funding, and centralized governance through traditionally conservative means of academic outcomes, market discipline, and parental choice. The long-term viability of this regime remains to be seen but its short-term effect could not be clearer: Political compromise decisively shifted curricular debates away from the issue of local control.[69]

Conclusion

Five years after its release, the conservative columnist Russell Kirk cited *A Nation at Risk* as justification for the growing number of private Christian schools. In an article called "The End of Learning"—a reference to the ultimate purpose of schooling as well as a complaint about its decline—he declared: "Our first necessity, if we mean to restore the 'life-long learning' which the National Commission on Excellence in Education seeks after, is to return that learning to its original end of orientation toward the divine. . . . Certain judges in this land—not to mention the National Education Association—do what they can to impede such a restoration of the end of learning. Yet even such powers and dominations cannot interfere with private and familial pursuit of wisdom."[70] Kirk had spent his life emulating Edmund Burke. He was always proud to stand against the tide of public opinion and the corrupting influences of modernity, and this prescription for religious school reform, written only a few years before his death, struck a particularly contrarian note. The field of public education had been lost, he felt, legally, politically, and morally. The best course left was to abandon its faddish secularism for the nurture and piety of the family. Rather than defend the primacy of local school boards, as they once had, or exercise the political power they had accrued with *A Nation at Risk*, he recommended that conservatives retreat to the principles of privacy and parents' rights.

Thousands of families followed that advice, forgoing public schools to ensure religious orthodoxy for their children; indeed, it became commonplace for conservative Christians to teach their children at home. Yet the fact that Kirk spoke for a large segment of the population should not inure us to the strangeness of his remarks or the profound historical flux in which he wrote.

Twenty-five years earlier, the notion that courts or the NEA could restrict religious exercises in school would have been unthinkable, as would the idea that local majorities might be unable to determine the content of their schools' curricula. Before the 1960s, community control seemed a natural extension of parental authority. Only as courts sought to protect minority viewpoints and free expression, threatening existing systems of school governance, were writers like Kirk forced to take a new, individualistic interpretation of parents' rights. In the conservative imagination, the subordination of local control to professional and judicial oversight transformed public schools: Institutions that had once reinforced family values now seemed intent on destroying them. Little surprise, then, that the dissenters began to perceive themselves as a minority, with religious beliefs incompatible with mainstream education, and sought their schooling elsewhere.

Kirk's remarks also sound strange twenty-five years later, though for different reasons. From a policy standpoint, the greatest impact of *A Nation at Risk* was the imposition of tougher curricular standards and uniform expectations for student learning, initially within states but eventually between them as well. In hindsight, one can recognize the 1980s as the origin of most of today's accountability reforms. Kirk was unable to foresee the speed and breadth of these developments and made no mention of them. Rather, he interpreted *A Nation at Risk* as an indictment of government regulation and professionalism run amok, a reason to turn away from public education. It is a testament to the pace of school reform in the past few decades that Kirk's position could be at once radically new and partially obsolete.

A PAST LOST

In 1955, the political scientist William Anderson called attention to a profound change in U.S. government. In rural areas, he noted, "townships and the smallest school districts have . . . been losing functions to larger governmental units above them . . . and many of the little units have passed from the scene." He was quick to point out that their disappearance did not mean fewer public services in those communities. "Quite the contrary," he wrote, "people are now simply acting in and through larger local units of government, and these units are actually doing more than the . . . small units ever did. The educational programs of the consolidated school [for instance] are more complete than the one-room ungraded schools could provide." Anderson conceded that traces of localism persisted, particularly in the " 'small-town attitudes' of legislators . . . [and] displaced ruralites and villagers who found themselves living in big cities," and he worried that these attitudes could impede "a frank confrontation of the problems of the large urban place." Overall, however, he was optimistic that government agencies would continue to grow, allowing Americans to enjoy more comprehensive public services and more efficient administration.[1]

Anderson's confidence belied the numerous challenges facing educational policymakers at the time. Racial segregation remained entrenched, and it would be years before state and federal agencies made any real effort to enforce *Brown v. Board of Education*. Conservative activists had thousands of teachers fired for their political leanings and harangued thousands more for poor instructional quality. Worst of all, despite booming enrollments and districts' desperate calls for more buildings, staff, and equipment, state aid to education remained inadequate and federal support negligible. Whatever changes had come to rural areas, "small-town attitudes" about the local control of schools had created a logjam in the education system as a whole. With questions of race, communism, and taxes dominating domestic politics in the 1950s, the prospect of further centralization in school governance was far more precarious than Anderson let on.

But local control could not hold change back forever. Cold War fears about international competition and domestic inequality soon opened the door to increased state and federal spending, a source of funds that eased the burden on local taxpayers but also installed new administrative regimes. Courts and regulatory agencies used government subsidies as an incentive to implement district-wide desegregation programs. They also introduced new civil rights requirements for women, English language learners, and the disabled. Regulators demanded more oversight of school district quality, measured by faculty pay and credentials, school programming, expenditures, and facilities, as well as by students' performance on a battery of standardized tests.

Liberal policymakers tended to support these developments, having advocated stronger state and federal roles for decades. The conservative response was more nuanced. Arresting or reversing the federal role in education was a top priority for conservative activists and judges during the 1970s, and although they were unable to reject government oversight outright they managed to reaffirm certain aspects of local control within the new political order. They did so by reviving an earlier, almost forgotten tradition of resistance: the defense of one-room schoolhouses, which began in response to district consolidation in the 1890s but remained unresolved seventy-five years later. Just as one cannot understand U.S. public education apart from local control, one cannot understand local control without the one-room schoolhouse, which became both an object of nostalgia and a legal bulwark in the postwar era. In the midst of profound change, the small-town school district became a liminal space, a site of political, cultural, and legal experimentation, and a crucible for new forms of conservative activism. As conservatives selectively incorporated elements of the rural past into a new defense of district boundaries, calls for community governance migrated from the suburban fringe back toward the city, and from there into constitutional law. Supreme Court rulings like *San Antonio v. Rodriguez* and *Milliken v. Bradley* relied on memories of the one-room schoolhouse to halt interdistrict funding and busing reforms, creating a right to school district autonomy that had not existed before. These decisions cited traditions of rural democracy but in effect created islands of economic and racial exclusion in the suburbs, reinforcing the powerful nexus of home values, attendance zones, and school funding that continues to dictate students' educational opportunities to the present. Persistent disparities between urban and suburban school districts are the result of a legal doctrine that was more or less invented in the 1970s.

State and federal courts used rural precedents to grant school boards power over personnel and curriculum decisions as well, but in these areas localism proved less durable. For even as court rulings acknowledged school boards' authority, they constrained it with new protections for teachers and students, giving statewide interest groups (particularly teachers' unions) greater leverage over budgeting, hiring, and classroom instruction. On these issues, the impregnable wall of local control had by the late 1970s become a Maginot Line, easily outflanked by supporters of higher spending, professional administration, and modern, secular curriculum. If conservative groups hoped to reestablish fiscal discipline and the place of religion in schools they needed a new point of counterattack.

They found two. The first was to co-opt the push for state and federal oversight, which during the 1980s shifted from civil rights enforcement to a new focus on academic standards. With conservative support, state legislatures began to standardize curricular tracks, raise graduation requirements, and expand high-stakes testing, even as they limited the tax revenues with which districts could meet the new requirements. By the end of the decade, school boards and local administrators were complaining that top-down reforms prevented them from determining their own policies, a sharp departure from times past.[2] The second point of counterattack was to reconceive of local control and parents' rights as matters of individual choice, best secured through the free market, with an attendant expansion of open-enrollment programs, vouchers, and home-schooling. When George W. Bush signed No Child Left Behind into law, in 2001, it was a watershed moment because it incorporated both branches of reform, holding districts to stricter accountability standards and forcing those that failed to meet them to provide more opportunities for parental choice. In both respects, the law abandoned conservatives' traditional commitments to small government and local representation.

Liberals and conservatives could each find fault with the fusion of their educational politics in today's "neoliberal" or "neoconservative" reform movements. Many liberals are disappointed that federal intervention has not fulfilled the goal of equal educational opportunity, while conservatives complain that it has limited free-market competition. In either case, one could argue that what has undermined democracy is the imposition of federal regulation and parental choice within existing school district boundaries. The question facing voters now is what to do about it. Unfortunately, the primary options seem to be more of the same.

One option is to strengthen state and federal roles further, overcoming disparities between local schools with intervention from above. Although most courts remain unwilling to address issues of funding or segregation between districts, some scholars are pushing them to ensure a degree of academic adequacy within them. Schools have generated large amounts of data on student performance and teacher impact under No Child Left Behind, allowing more targeted instruction and closer alignment between local, state, and federal curricular standards. That data has also opened new opportunities for civil rights litigation. For instance, insofar as "value-added" assessments demonstrate the quality of a child's education, courts could now hold districts liable for shuttling around or shielding ineffective teachers, essentially finding them guilty of educational malpractice.[3] Supporters discuss this sort of lawsuit as an attainable way to improve school quality, bringing government leadership to bear without stripping school districts of their administrative responsibilities. Yet even this moderate approach faces likely impediments. Stalled campaigns for adequate funding raise serious questions about the judiciary's ability to craft nuanced educational policy independent of legislatures, to say nothing of whether academic efficacy falls under the courts' purview in the first place. Moreover, while it is true that implementing any educational policy depends on cooperation from "local stakeholders"—a point that proponents underscore—academic standards can carry very different meanings for teachers and administrators than for taxpayers, businesses, or parents, producing a passel of "local" actors with distinct, sometimes contradictory interests in the definition and assessment of adequacy. State and federal mandates have forced these groups to engage less with locally elected school boards and instead pursue their agendas at higher levels of government, for significantly higher stakes. Yet, at the same time, many interest groups continue to invoke local control as a hedge against political rivals. For example, there has been a groundswell of objections to the Common Core standards, a set of rigorous learning targets pegged to federal funding and applicable across states. Parents have started to exempt their children from taking Common Core tests, unions have voiced criticism, and politicians from both parties have pilloried the standards as unfair and unreliable snapshots of student learning. It is difficult to know whether opposition to the Common Core is a short-term political gambit or the beginning of a larger turn against centralized planning and coercive funding, but it signifies the sort of widespread resistance that state curricular oversight will face for the foreseeable future.

A second avenue of reform points in the opposite direction, claiming that an expansion of school choice will burst through district boundaries, like new wine in old skins, and eliminate the inequality that local control perpetuates. Some scholars are particularly interested in the possibility that suburban conservatives, in the name of market-driven reform, might let vouchers or charter schools erase the lines that "forced busing" could not. If so, decentralized decision-making might rend districts apart, providing a more individualized and, paradoxically, more uniform standard of education.[4] Yet that scenario, too, faces some predictable obstacles. Critics have identified many factors preventing truly equal school choice—including high transportation costs, limited openings at top schools, and a lack of data for informed decision-making—and have questioned whether there is sufficient oversight to guarantee quality instruction. As proponents of vouchers discovered in the 1970s, the imposition of meaningful oversight often suppresses the dynamism that makes choice-based policies attractive in the first place, diminishing the distinctions between public, private, and charter schools. Even more problematic are the powerful interests maintaining the connections between community wealth and school quality, most of all the real estate industry and homeowners themselves. Indeed, rather than accommodating larger and more diverse populations within current systems of school administration, suburban communities have lately begun carving out new, smaller districts to serve their children, reversing a century of consolidation and centralized governance. The trend has been most pronounced in the sprawling districts around Southern cities, where wealthier and whiter areas have petitioned to end district-wide busing programs and even seceded to form their own school districts. If it once seemed remarkable that Southern school districts should have the most integrated schools in the country, they now seem to be regressing, becoming more like the small, hypersegregated districts of the North.[5]

All of this should underscore that, despite the allure of increased standardization and individual choice, Americans retain a widespread commitment to local education. The defense of school district autonomy can be as destructive now as it ever was, an obstacle to coherent reform and a mask for racial and class bias, but it also remains true that this sort of political opportunism only succeeds when aligned with deeper, more defensible ideals. Local control is an effective slogan not because it protects the wealthy but because a much larger group of citizens find value in democratic oversight. Thousands welcome the opportunity to serve on local school boards and take seriously the responsibility of community deliberations. Voices from across the political spectrum continue to question the value of standardized curriculum, the characterization of students as consumers, and the increase of both privatization and bureaucratization in educational policy. Indeed, the same demands voiced by rural and suburban parents have also come from inner-city minority groups, whose support for decentralized "community schools" speaks to a desire for empowerment and self-determination; and from some teachers, for whom parental involvement, small class sizes, and local knowledge have become pillars of "place-based education" and the "small schools" movement. These are all legitimate goals, despite the fact that they do little to improve equality or uniformity between districts. Is it fair to condemn the shortcomings of localism in some cases while celebrating its bene- fits in others, or to judge voters' motives based on shifting, selective notions of virtue? Answering yes forces one to thread a fine needle of justification. Answer- ing no leads either to a rejection of localism's benefits or a tacit acceptance of its flaws. The ambiguity and discomfort of that choice, encompassing at once both the best and basest elements of American politics, explains the endurance of school district boundaries and the political power of local control.[6]

A primary goal of this book has been to elucidate a set of values that have been lost and the history through which they might be found again. Its attach- ment is not to small schools per se, nor to a romanticized view of local wisdom or virtue. To the contrary, the preceding chapters outline profound limitations of community-based schooling, and some readers may conclude that state inter- vention remains a vital necessity in public education. Others may question whether memories of the one-room schoolhouse could have any significant ef- fect on the current trajectory of school governance, especially with the massive amount of money and political capital invested in recent years. The fact is they might. It is during moments of social and political change that Americans look to the past for models of community organization, democratic deliberation, and direct action. And as conservatives discovered in the 1970s, while rural schools may seem outdated, the values they embody are not.

To appreciate the lingering influence and potential relevance of rural school consolidation, one need only return to the state where this book started. Wis- consin has once again become a front line in battles over teacher unionization and school funding. Thousands of people occupied the state capitol in the spring of 2011, hoping to prevent the passage of Act 10, a controversial measure weak- ening collective bargaining rights for the state's public workers. The stand-off between protesters, counterprotesters, and legislators broke not only along po- litical lines, with Democrats rallying behind organized labor and Republicans behind governor Scott Walker, but along geographical lines as well, with affluent suburbs in the southeastern part of the state overwhelmingly supporting Act 10, and Madison and Milwaukee, the state's largest urban centers, flatly rejecting it. Whatever swing votes there were came from rural areas, presenting small-town voters with essentially the same choice they faced fifty years earlier. Would they support teachers' professional rights?

As the capital settled in for a prolonged struggle, Katherine Cramer, a politi- cal scientist and professor at the University of Wisconsin-Madison, ventured into the countryside to find out. She interview hundreds of rural, working-class voters and found, in many communities, that public school teachers were the highest-paid workers and the only ones with reliable access to health care and pensions. For the small-town residents that Cramer met, the benefits of unionization seemed remote; its costs, in the form of higher taxes and less control of school administration, were much clearer. While others were compelled to sacrifice, there was a perception that teachers were living high on public expense. Thus, while busloads of teachers from rural areas drove to the capital to protest the attack on collective bargaining, voters back home generally broke in the other direction. Despite some initial reservations, rural legislators remained unified in support of the Walker administration.[7] It is important to underscore that this outcome was never preordained, that rural voters and their representatives did not act with reflexive hostility to unions or an unshakable loyalty to the Republican Party. Support for Act 10 sprang in part from a commitment to community welfare and local democracy that unions were unable to articulate.[8]

Yet one could imagine a different outcome, one in which Wisconsin teachers protested less for their health benefits than for the fate of public education itself, and perhaps in which they could subordinate conflicts between local and professional prerogative. Almost unmentioned during the events of 2011 was the meaningless "flexibility" that Act 10 promised local school boards. In addition to its antiunion measures, the Walker administration introduced a raft of laws that constrained school funding, including new property tax limits, drastic cuts to state subsidies, and the diversion of millions of dollars to an expanded school voucher program. Essentially, Republicans were robbing Peter to pay Paul. Although targeted at profligate urban districts, the real victims of these policies have been rural schools, which "lack the resources to provide students with educational opportunities anywhere near those of . . . wealthier, suburban districts" and have been forced to rely on public referendums at rates significantly higher than elsewhere in the state.[9] Funding cuts have made the threat of district consolidation as palpable as it was a century ago, and just as divisive. In 2010, the town of Montello, whose library books caused such a stir in the 1980s, considered consolidating its schools with the neighboring Westfield school district. Combining the two would have ended budget shortfalls and eased local property taxes, but voters rejected the proposal. "Montello folks are extremely proud people," noted the school superintendent. "They've had a school here for 130 years and it was extremely difficult for people to give up their high school."[10]

The misfortune of rural schools speaks to the declining population and political influence of rural communities in general, but it also suggests new possibilities for a usable past. For as conservatives shift their attention from local control to school choice—and as suburbanites ignore the outlying communities with whom they once identified—they discard a valuable legacy of democratic participation, a cause with the potential to unite rural and urban areas as well as teachers and taxpayers. Rural teachers may have an important role to play in contemporary politics, not because their concerns are distinct from those of urban teachers but because conservative policies have hurt the communities in which both groups work. Indeed, rural teachers' lack of political power could actually make them stronger, less compromised spokesmen for the public good than their urban counterparts. But the change must begin in their home districts, where the antagonism between teachers and community members often runs deep, drawing from the same disagreements about professionalization that have dogged unions since their inception. The best way to overcome such hostility is to reaffirm teachers' commitment to cooperative school governance. Small-town voters are never likely to accept teachers' unions outright, but insofar as the groups are both committed to educational quality, they should rally around the traditions of local pride and participation that lead to meaningful public oversight. Indeed, we would all do well to recognize those traditions, those towns, which within them hold deep wells of experience.

Bibliographic Note

This book builds on extensive archival research, outlined below for interested scholars.

Featured throughout the book is material from the Wisconsin Historical Society, which (outside of the Library of Congress) has perhaps the best public archive in the nation. The strength of its collection is borne out by the diversity of sources woven through each chapter, which allow the reader to understand school politics in a variety of contexts and from different ideological perspectives. The chapter on school consolidation, for instance, not only relies on reports of the Department of Public Instruction and other public agencies, but on oral history interviews with state politicians, the publications of anticonsolidation groups like the Wisconsin Rural Schools Association, and the correspondence of local activists. Other chapters benefit from the society's extensive holdings on right-wing politics, both in Wisconsin and nationwide. Especially helpful are the records of Verne Kaub and his American Council of Christian Laymen; the papers of William Grede, H. S. Tuttle, and other members of the John Birch Society; the correspondence of state representatives George Klicka, Delmar DeLong, and Kenneth Merkel; and the investigative records of Wisconsin Interchange and various civil liberties groups. Finally, the chapters on unionization and funding draw heavily from the records of the Wisconsin Education Association Council—which preserved dozens of oral history interviews about the Hortonville strike—and the Wisconsin Federation of Teachers.

Another valuable repository is the Iowa State University archive, whose holdings include the papers of anticonsolidation organizations like the Iowa School Organization and People United for Rural Education, both of which preserved innumerable studies, clippings, and written exchanges about the closure of rural schools. The University of Vermont has bound copies of the bulletin of the Committee for Home Rule in Vermont Towns, another anticonsolidation group, while the University of Central Arkansas has a large file on the Arkansas Rural Education Association. Given how few anticonsolidation groups preserved their records, these resources are vital for future studies of rural education in the twentieth century.

The chapter on teacher unionization obviously depends on the records of the unions themselves. While local chapters have donated their papers to a number of state and university repositories, the most comprehensive materials can be found in the National Education Association archives, housed at George Washington University's Gelman Library, and the American Federation of Teachers archives, at Wayne State University's Reuther Library. These organizations not only preserved records pertaining to collective bargaining and strikes, but also to school governance, public finance, academic freedom, and corporal punishment. It is unfortunate that historians of education have (to date) made so little use of them for broader studies of the field.

Lastly, while the chapters on curricular disputes draw heavily from the Wisconsin Historical Society, they would not have been possible without the papers of Mortimer Smith and the Council for Basic Education, housed at the University of Illinois. Both collections offer detailed insights into the mobilization of conservative curricular reform during the 1950s and 1960s.

A few other minor archives are mentioned in the endnotes. Abbreviations for the archival collections described here are as follows:

GWU	George Washington University, Gelman Library
ISU	Iowa State University Archives
UCA	University of Central Arkansas Archives
UI	University of Illinois Archives
UVM	University of Vermont Archives
WHS	Wisconsin Historical Society Archives
WSU	Wayne State University, Reuther Library

Notes

INTRODUCTION. A PAST FOUND

1. Arthur F. Wileden, Oral History Interview, tape 10, side 2, part 2; tape 11, side 1, part 1, both in Wisconsin Historical Society (WHS) Archives.

2. "Optimists Accept Challenge to Aid French Island Youths," *La Crosse Tribune*, January 27, 1949, 8; Wileden, Oral History Interview, tape 10, side 2, part 2.

3. "Expect Formal Hearing on Isle School Issues," *La Crosse Tribune*, December 8, 1948, 2; "Reveal Lower French Island Has Difficult School Problem," *La Crosse Tribune*, December 5, 1948, 26.

4. Arthur Wileden, *French Island: Modern Magic in the Suburbs* (Madison: University of Wisconsin, 1961), 10–15.

5. Ibid., 9–10; Marybeth Clark, "Campbell Attorney Vexed as Incorporation Fails," *La Crosse Tribune*, December 29, 1977, 1.

6. Bernard Bailyn, *Education in the Forming of American Society: Needs and Opportunities for Study* (Chapel Hill: University of North Carolina Press, 1960); Merle Curti, *The Growth of American Thought* (New York: Harper & Row, 1964); and Richard Hofstadter, *Anti-intellectualism in American Life* (New York: Knopf, 1963).

7. Examples include Thomas Sugrue, *Sweet Land of Liberty: The Forgotten Struggle for Civil Rights in the North* (New York: Random House, 2009); and Nancy Beadie, *Education and the Creation of Capital in the Early Republic* (New York: Cambridge University Press, 2010).

8. For an example of other uses of localism, see Benjamin Michael Superfine, *Equality in Education Law and Policy, 1954–2010* (New York: Cambridge University Press, 2013).

9. An explanation of the Bureau's methodology can be found at http://www.census.gov/geo/reference/ua/uafaq.html.

10. Southern states with county systems and few one-room schools that will *not* appear here include Alabama, Delaware, Florida, Georgia, Louisiana, Maryland, North Carolina, Virginia, and, by the mid-1950s, Mississippi and South Carolina. Only Texas and Arkansas retained small districts through the 1960s—although, as noted above, areas of Kentucky, Tennessee, and West Virginia preserved one-room schools within the county structure and will be included in this study. In the West, Nevada, New Mexico, and Utah adopted county districts by the mid-1950s, while the unique traditions of public education in Hawaii, which has a single, statewide school district, and Alaska, which still maintains hundreds of remote rural schools, exclude them from consideration.

11. Foundational texts include Lisa McGirr, *Suburban Warriors: The Origins of the New American Right* (Princeton, NJ: Princeton University Press, 2001); Matthew Lassiter, *The Silent Majority: Suburban Politics in the Sunbelt South* (Princeton, NJ: Princeton University Press, 2006); and Michelle M. Nickerson, *Mothers of Conservatism: Women and the Postwar Right* (Princeton, NJ: Princeton University Press, 2012).

12. Lassiter, *Silent Majority*, 1–3.

13. For the best overview of Wisconsin politics during this period, see William Fletcher Thompson, ed., *The History of Wisconsin*, vol. 6 (Madison: State Historical Society of Wisconsin, 1998); or James R. Donoghue, *The Local Government System of Wisconsin* (Madison: Wisconsin Blue Book, 1968).

14. Christopher Lasch, *The True and Only Heaven: Progress and Its Critics* (New York: W. W. Norton, 1991), 117–18.

15. On the culture wars in twentieth-century education, see Jonathan Zimmerman, *Whose America? Culture Wars in the Public Schools* (Cambridge, MA: Harvard University Press, 2002); and Andrew Hartman, *A War for the Soul of America: A History of the Culture Wars, from the 1960s to the Present* (Chicago: University of Chicago Press, 2015). For a criticism of the term's accuracy in educational debates, see Keith Barton, "Wars and Rumors of War: Making Sense of History Education in the United States," in *History Wars and the Classroom*, ed. Tony Taylor and Robert Guyver (Charlotte, NC: Information Age Publishing, 2011), 187–202.

1. THE MEANING OF LOCAL CONTROL

1. Richard Hofstadter, *The Age of Reform: From Bryan to F. D. R.* (New York: Knopf, 1955), 23, 303–4.

2. Critics often emphasize the "myth" of local control. For example, "On Public Education, a Myth of Local Control," *New Hampshire Union Leader*, June 4, 2012, http://www .unionleader.com/article/20120605/OPINION01/706059977/0/opinion. See also, Miles Orvell, *The Death and Life of Main Street: Small Towns in American Memory, Space, and Community* (Chapel Hill: University of North Carolina Press, 2012).

3. Walter Lippman, *Drift and Mastery: An Attempt to Diagnose the Current Unrest* (New York: Henry Holt, 1917), 153, 158.

4. Casey Nelson Blake, *Beloved Community: The Cultural Criticism of Randolph Bourne, Van Wyck Brooks, Waldo Frank, and Lewis Mumford* (Chapel Hill: University of North Carolina Press, 1990); Robert B. Westbrook, *John Dewey and American Democracy* (Ithaca, NY: Cornell University Press, 1993); and Robert S. Lynd and Helen Merrell Lynd, *Middletown: A Study in Modern American Culture* (New York: Harcourt Brace, 1959).

5. Historians have thoroughly documented the connection between local, state, and federal policies and suburban inequality. Several books point out that federally subsidized mortgages and highways provided a welfare program for middle- and working-class whites while systematically denying benefits to minorities and the poor. As the latter groups demanded equal treatment, the original beneficiaries of government support began to reject taxation for unearned "handouts." See Ira Katznelson, *When Affirmative Action Was White: An Untold History of Racial Inequality in Twentieth Century America* (New York: W. W. Norton, 2005); Thomas Sugrue, *The Origins of the Urban Crisis: Race and Inequality in Postwar Detroit* (Princeton, NJ: Princeton University Press, 1996); Robert O. Self, *American Babylon: Race and the Struggle for Postwar Oakland* (Princeton, NJ: Princeton University Press, 2003); David Farber and Jeff Roche, eds., *The Conservative Sixties* (New York: Peter Lang, 2003); Joseph Lowndes, *From the New Deal to the New Right: Race and the Southern Origins of Modern Conservatism* (New Haven, CT: Yale University Press, 2008); Joseph Crespino, *In Search of Another Country: Mississippi and the Conservative Counterrevolution* (Princeton, NJ: Princeton University Press, 2007); and Kevin M. Kruse, *White Flight: Atlanta and the Making of Modern Conservatism* (Princeton, NJ: Princeton University Press, 2005).

6. This legal interpretation, commonly referred to as "Dillon's Rule," holds that state legislatures must explicitly grant rights of municipal autonomy, and that courts should construe those rights narrowly.

7. David Barron, "Reclaiming Home Rule," *Harvard Law Review* 116, no. 8 (June 2003): 2280–86.

8. Charles W. Eagles, *Democracy Delayed: Congressional Reapportionment and Urban-Rural Conflict in the 1920s* (Athens: University of Georgia Press, 1990), 55; Margo J.

Anderson and Stephen E. Fienberg, *Who Counts? The Politics of Census-Taking in Contemporary America* (New York: Russell Sage Foundation, 2001), 26–27.

9. Gordon Baker, *The Reapportionment Revolution: Representation, Political Power, and the Supreme Court* (New York: Random House, 1967), 32–33. Even some urban business interests favored rural apportionment "as a means of keeping taxes low, regulations to a minimum, and labor unions politically weak." Furthermore, notes historian Douglas Smith, because corporations often controlled large swaths of land and jobs in rural areas, by the midcentury many of these "farmers and businessmen were not only friends but 'often the same person.'" Douglas Smith, "Into the Political Thicket: Reapportionment and the Rise of Suburban Power," in *The Myth of Southern Exceptionalism*, ed. Matthew Lassiter and Joseph Crespino (New York: Oxford University Press, 2009), 263–85, esp. 268.

10. Robert H. Wiebe, "Crisis in the Communities," in *The Search for Order, 1877–1920* (New York: Hill and Wang, 1967), 44–75.

11. These measures combined with internal reforms, such as shifting from ward- to citywide elections and instituting civil services exams.

12. In addition to Barron, "Reclaiming Home Rule," see Kenneth E. Vanlandingham, "Municipal Home Rule in the United States," *William and Mary Law Review* 10, no. 2 (1968): 271–78.

13. Barron, "Reclaiming Home Rule," 2294–96.

14. For an example from the period, see Howard W. Hamilton, *Small and Large Together: Governing the Metropolis* (Beverly Hills, CA: Sage Publications, 1977). For more contemporary analysis, see Andrew E. G. Jonas, "Local Territories of Government: From Ideals to Politics of Place and Scale," in *American Space/American Place*, ed. John A. Agnew and Jonathan M. Smith (New York: Routledge, 2002), 108–49.

15. Daniel Bell, "The Dispossessed," in *The Radical Right*, ed. Daniel Bell (New York: Anchor Books, 1964), 1–38, esp. 16.

16. Baker v. Carr, 369 U.S. 186 (1962); Reynolds v. Sims, 377 U.S. 533 (1964). It should be pointed out that this ruling did nothing to change the unequal representation built into the U.S. Senate and Electoral College, nor did it prevent the practice of gerrymandering, which promises voters equal weight but, by separating them into largely homogenous districts, minimizes the number of "swing" votes in play.

17. The dilution of Democratic strongholds in the rural South and West promised a net gain for Republicans, who in turn stood to lose ground in the rural North and Midwest. It is important to note that neither party welcomed the reapportionment rulings, and by 1970, thirty-three states supported a constitutional amendment to overturn them. Gary W. Cox and Jonathan N. Katz, *Elbridge Gerry's Salamander: The Electoral Consequences of the Reapportionment Revolution* (New York: Cambridge University Press, 2002), 15–18; Smith, "Into the Political Thicket," 263.

18. Cox and Katz, *Elbridge Gerry's Salamander*, 14.

19. Richardson Dilworth, *The Urban Origins of Suburban Autonomy* (Cambridge, MA: Harvard University Press, 2005), 2, 27–32.

20. David M. P. Freund, *Colored Property: State Policy and White Racial Politics in Suburban America* (Chicago: University of Chicago Press, 2007), 45–50.

21. Ibid., 217–18.

22. This approach laid the foundation for subsequent redlining practices, whereby banks (and later, the Federal Housing Administration and Veterans Administration) would qualify home loans based on a neighborhood's proximity to commercial properties, the age of its housing stock, and, crucially, its racial homogeneity.

23. Rulings by the federal judiciary and executive branches only gradually overturned explicitly racist housing segregation. The Supreme Court outlawed the passage of racially

restrictive zoning ordinances with *Buchanan v. Warley* (1927), but it was not until *Shelley v. Kramer* (1948) that it declared private housing covenants unenforceable. Even then, discriminatory practices remained largely untouched until Title VII of the Civil Rights Act (1968) increased the level of federal oversight.

24. Freund, *Colored Property*, 219.

25. The foundational text is Kenneth Jackson, *Crabgrass Frontier: The Suburbanization of the United States* (New York: Oxford University Press, 1985). Others include Robert Fishman, *Bourgeois Utopias* (New York: Basic Books, 1987); John Teaford, *The Metropolitan Revolution* (New York: Columbia University Press, 2006); Roslyn Baxandall, *Picture Windows: How the Suburbs Happened* (New York: Basic Books, 2000); Robert Bruegmann, *Sprawl: A Compact History* (Chicago: University of Chicago Press, 2006); and Richard Harris, *Building a Market: The Rise of the Home Improvement Industry, 1914–1960* (Chicago: University of Chicago Press, 2012).

26. There are notable exceptions, of course. William Cronon's *Nature's Metropolis: Chicago and the Great West* (New York: W. W. Norton, 1991); Mark Zaltman's *Suburban/Rural Conflicts in Late 19th Century Chicago* (San Francisco: International Scholars Publications, 1998); and John Stilgoe's *Borderland: Origins of the American Suburb, 1820–1939* (New Haven, CT: Yale University Press, 1988) all creatively conceptualize the borders between urban, suburban, and rural areas. Yet they also end their studies in the nineteenth century, leaving unexplored how mass suburbanization in the 1950s affected rural America.

27. See David B. Danbom, *Born in the Country: A History of Rural America*, 2nd ed. (Baltimore: Johns Hopkins University Press, 2006); or Richard E. Wood, *Survival of Rural America: Small Victories and Bitter Harvests* (Lawrence: University Press of Kansas, 2008). There is much popular and social science literature on rural decline. See, for example, Osha Gray Davidson, *Broken Heartland: The Rise of America's Rural Ghetto* (Iowa City: University of Iowa Press, 1996); or Noel Perrin, *Best Person Rural: Essays of a Sometime Farmer* (Boston: David Godine, 2006).

28. Andrew Needham and Allen Dietrich-Ward, "Beyond the Metropolis: Metropolitan Growth and Regional Transformation in Postwar America," *Journal of Urban History* 35, no. 7 (2009): 944. For more on a metropolitan perspective on urban history, see Raymond A. Mohl, "City and Region: The Missing Dimension in U.S. Urban History," *Journal of Urban History* 25, no. 1 (November 1998): 3–21.

29. Smith, "Into the Political Thicket," 264, 280.

30. *Wisconsin Towns Association History, 1947–1977* (Shawano: Wisconsin Towns Association, 1977); Ben A. Hanneman, *Wisconsin Towns Association: The Only Cooperative Enterprise for Better Rural Government,* (Wisconsin Rapids: Wisconsin Towns Association, 1967), i–iii.

31. Lionel Trilling, *The Liberal Imagination: Essays on Literature and Society* (New York: New York Review of Books, 2008), xv; Richard Hofstadter, "The Pseudo-Conservative Revolt," in *The New American Right,* ed. Daniel Bell (New York: Criterion Books, 1955), 33–55.

32. Leo P. Ribuffo, "Twenty Suggestions for Studying the Right, Now That Studying the Right is Trendy," *Historically Speaking* 12, no. 1 (January 2011): 2–6.

33. For a trenchant discussion of this issue, see Alan Brinkley, "The Problem of American Conservatism," *American Historical Review* 99, no. 2 (April 1994): 409–29; and George Scialabba, "Privilege and Its Discontents," *What are Intellectuals Good For?* (Boston: Pressed Wafer, 2009), 137–44.

34. The fracture of the diverse New Deal coalition has been the subject of several books, including Allen J. Matusow, *The Unraveling of America: A History of Liberalism in the 1960s* (New York: Perennial, 1985); Alan Brinkley, *The End of Reform: New Deal Liberalism in Recession and War* (New York: Knopf, 1995); Lizabeth Cohen, *A Consumers'*

Republic: The Politics of Mass Consumption in Postwar America (New York: Vintage Books, 2003); and Daniel Rodgers, *Age of Fracture* (Cambridge, MA: Harvard University Press, 2011).

35. George Nash, *The Conservative Intellectual Movement in America Since 1945* (Wilmington, DE: International Scholastic Institute, 2008), 35, 165.

36. Emphasizing conservatism's European origins buoyed Nash's notion of a principled elite, but at the same time tacitly accepted the notion of a liberal American consensus. As Jennifer Burns observes, "if conservatives were not so exceptional, but rather inherited a series of longestablished American beliefs and shared with the broader populace certain fundamental attitudes and opinions about communism, government, religion, and so forth, the embattled remnant Nash valorizes loses much of its luster." Jennifer Burns, "In Retrospect: George Nash's 'The Conservative Intellectual Movement in America Since 1945,'" *Reviews in American History* 32, no. 3 (September 2004): 457.

37. As Nash himself notes, "Whereas the traditionalists of the 1940s and 1950s had largely been academics in revolt *against* secularized, mass society, the New Right was a revolt *by* the 'masses.'" Nash, *Conservative Intellectual Movement*, 35, 165, 174, 193, 276, 365, 558. For similar sentiments, see Susan Jacoby, *The Age of American Unreason* (New York: Pantheon, 2008), xv–xvii, 24–29, 52.

38. As subsequent chapters will point out, these were far from natural political alignments: local voters could often violate individual rights in ways that offended libertarians, for instance.

39. The quote is from Jonathan Zimmerman, *Whose America? Culture Wars in the Public Schools* (Cambridge, MA: Harvard University Press, 2002), 215. For more on local resistance to desegregation and secularization, respectively, see James Patterson, *Brown v. Board of Education: A Civil Rights Milestone and Its Troubled Legacy* (New York: Oxford University Press, 2001); and Bruce J. Dierenfield, *The Battle over School Prayer: How Engel v. Vitale Changed America* (Lawrence: University Press of Kansas, 2007).

40. Jonathan M. Schoenwald, "We Are an Action Group: The John Birch Society and the Conservative Movement in the 1960s," in Farber and Roche, *The Conservative Sixties*, 21–36.

41. Nixon's appointees were Warren Burger, Harry Blackmun, Lewis Powell, and William Rehnquist. Both Burger and Blackmun softened their conservative views early in their tenures. For a discussion of the Burger court, see Bernard Schwartz, ed., *The Burger Court: CounterRevolution or Confirmation* (New York: Oxford University Press, 1998).

42. Rodgers, *Age of Fracture*, 195.

43. To understand Americans' gradual acceptance of a republican education system, see Carl F. Kaestle, *Pillars of the Republic: Common Schools and American Society, 1780–1860* (New York: Hill and Wang, 1983).

44. Richard Briefault, "The Local School District in American Law," in *Besieged: School Boards and the Future of Education Politics*, ed. William Howell (Washington, DC: Brookings Institution, 2005), 24–55; David Gamson, "Democracy Undone: Reforming and Reinventing the American School District, 1945–2000," in *Clio at the Table: Using History to Inform and Improve Education Policy*, ed. Kenneth K. Wong and Robert Rothman (New York: Peter Lang, 2008), 79–90.

45. Carl F. Kaestle and Alyssa E. Lodewick, *To Educate a Nation: Federal and National Strategies of School Reform* (Lawrence: University Press of Kansas, 2007); Adam R. Nelson, *The Elusive Ideal: Equal Educational Opportunity and the Federal Role in Boston's Public Schools, 1950–1985* (Chicago: Chicago University Press, 2005); and David K. Cohen and Susan L. Moffitt, *The Ordeal of Equality: Did Federal Regulation Fix the Schools?* (Cambridge, MA: Harvard University Press, 2009).

46. James Coleman, *Community Conflict* (Glencoe, IL: Free Press, 1957), 17; Robert Bendiner, *The Politics of Schools: A Crisis in Self-Government* (New York: Harper & Row, 1969), 3.

47. David Tyack, *The One Best System: A History of American Urban Education* (Cambridge, MA: Harvard University Press, 1974).

48. One exception is Arthur Zilversmit, *Changing Schools: Progressive Education Theory and Practice, 1930–1960* (Chicago: University of Chicago Press, 1993), which analyzes four rural and suburban districts north of Chicago.

49. For a list of histories of rural education, see chapter 2, note 2.

50. Tracy L. Steffes, "Solving the 'Rural School Problem': New State Aid, Standards, and Supervision of Local Schools, 1900–1933," *History of Education Quarterly* 48, no. 2 (May 2008): 181–220.

51. William Fischel, *Making the Grade: The Economic Evolution of American School Districts* (Chicago: University of Chicago Press, 2009); Jonathan Zimmerman, *Small Wonder: The Little Red Schoolhouse in History and Memory* (New Haven, CT: Yale University Press, 2009).

52. Dougherty's article includes a suburb of Hartford, Connecticut, Avon, where one-room schools and tuition-based high school attendance persisted into the 1950s and became a point of contention in the campaign to attract wealthy suburbanites. Jack Dougherty, "Shopping for Schools: How Public Education and Private Housing Shaped Suburban Connecticut"; Karen Benjamin, "Suburbanizing Jim Crow: The Impact of School Policy on Residential Segregation in Raleigh"; and Ainsley Erickson, "Building Inequality: The Spatial Organization of Schooling in Nashville, Tennessee, after *Brown*," all in *Journal of Urban History* 38, no. 2 (March 2012): 205–70.

53. John Rury and Donna Gardner, "Suburban Opposition to District Reorganization: The 1968 Spainhower Commission and Metropolitan Kansas City and St. Louis," *Urban Review* 46 (2014): 125–45; John Rury, "Trouble in Suburbia: Localism, Schools and Conflict in Postwar Johnson County, Kansas," *History of Education Quarterly* 55, no. 2 (May 2015): 133–63.

54. Suleiman Osman, "The Decade of the Neighborhood," in *Rightward Bound: Making America Conservative in the 1970s*, ed. Bruce J. Schulman and Julian E. Zelizer (Cambridge, MA: Harvard University Press, 2008), 106–27, esp. 114.

55. Osman, "Decade of the Neighborhood," 110.

56. Shane Hamilton, *Trucking Country: The Road to America's Wal-Mart Economy* (Princeton, NJ: Princeton University Press, 2008); Bethany Moreton, *To Serve God and Wal-Mart: The Making of Christian Free Enterprise* (Cambridge, MA: Harvard University Press, 2009).

57. Christopher Lasch, *The True and Only Heaven: Progress and Its Critics* (New York: W. W. Norton, 1991), 116–17.

2. THE LONG HISTORY OF SCHOOL DISTRICT CONSOLIDATION

1. *Historical Statistics of the United States: Earliest Times to Present*, vol. 2 (New York: Cambridge University Press, 2006), 398. Other relevant statistics for this chapter can be found in the *Biennial Survey of Education in the United States* (Washington, DC: Office of Education, 1946–60); *Digest of Educational Statistics* (Washington, DC: U.S. Department of Health, Education, and Welfare, 1962–70); and *Statistics of State School Systems* (Washington, DC: Office of Education, 1956–70).

2. Again, the clearest example of this type of history is David Tyack, *The One Best System: A History of American Urban Education* (Cambridge, MA: Harvard University Press, 1974). Other books that focus on or end at the Progressive Era include Wayne Fuller, *The*

Old Country School: The Story of Rural Education in the Middle West (Chicago: University of Chicago Press, 1982); Andrew Gulliford, *America's Country Schools* (Washington, DC: Preservation Press, 1984); Paul Theobald, *Call School: Rural Education in the Midwest to 1918* (Carbondale: Southern Illinois University Press, 1995); David R. Reynolds, *There Goes the Neighborhood: Rural School Consolidation at the Grass Roots in Early Twentieth-Century Iowa* (Iowa City: University of Iowa Press, 1999); William A. Link, *The Paradox of Southern Progressivism, 1880–1930* (Chapel Hill: University of North Carolina Press); Hal S. Barron, "Teach No More His Neighbor: Localism and Rural Opposition to Educational Reform," in *Mixed Harvest: The Second Great Transformation of the Rural North, 1870–1930* (Chapel Hill: University of North Carolina Press, 1997), 43–80; and Charles Postel, "Knowledge and Power: Machinery of Modern Education," in *The Populist Vision* (New York: Oxford University Press, 2009), 45–68.

3. David Strang makes a similar observation in "The Administrative Transformation of American Education: School District Consolidation, 1938–1980," *Administrative Science Quarterly* 32, no. 3 (September 1987): 356.

4. In 1890, there were only 129 state education officials in the entire country and the median number of employees in a state department of education was two. Strang, "Administrative Transformation," 352–55; Tracy Steffes, *School, Society, and State: A New Education for Modern America, 1890–1940* (Chicago: University of Chicago Press, 2012), 207.

5. For the history of schools as community centers, see William J. Reese, *Power and the Promise of School Reform: Grassroots Movements during the Progressive Era* (New York: Teachers College Press, 2002); and Michael C. Johanek and John L. Puckett, *Leonard Covello and the Making of Benjamin Franklin High School: Education as if Citizenship Mattered* (Philadelphia: Temple University Press, 2007).

6. Paul Theobald, "Country School Curriculum and Governance: The One-Room School Experience in the Nineteenth-Century Midwest," *American Journal of Education* 101, no. 2 (February 1993): 116–39.

7. Fuller, *Old Country School*, 57.

8. For a detailed discussion of high school reform in the early twentieth century, as well as the disparities between urban and rural capacities, see Claudia Goldin and Lawrence F. Katz, "Economic Foundations of the High School Movement," in *The Race between Education and Technology* (Cambridge, MA: Harvard University Press, 2008), 163–93.

9. These ideas had been in circulation since the turn of the century but usually but are usually associated with James Conant, *The American High School Today* (New York: McGraw Hill, 1959).

10. See James Leloudis, *Schooling the New South: Pedagogy, Self, and Society in North Carolina, 1880–1920* (Chapel Hill: University of North Carolina Press, 1996), as well as James Anderson, *The Education of Blacks in the South* (Chapel Hill: University of North Carolina Press, 1988).

11. Tracy Steffes, "Solving the 'Rural School Problem': New State Aid, Standards, and Supervision of Local Schools, 1900–1933," *History of Education Quarterly* 48, no. 2 (May 2008): 181–220; Postel, *Populist Vision*, 45–68; Clayton Ellsworth, "Theodore Roosevelt's Country Life Commission," *Agricultural History* 34, no. 4 (October 1960): 155–72; David Danbom, "Rural Education Reform and the Country Life Movement, 1900–1920," *Agricultural History* 53, no. 2 (April 1979): 462–74.

12. *A Study of Education in Vermont* (New York: Carnegie Foundation, 1914); and John C. Huden, *Development of State School Administration in Vermont* (Burlington: Vermont Historical Society, 1944), 85–94.

13. Institute of Government Research of the Brookings Institution, *Report on a Survey of Administration in Iowa* (Des Moines: State of Iowa, 1933), 142.

14. Ellwood Cubberley, *Rural Life and Education: A Study of the Rural-School Problem as a Phase of the Rural-Life Problem* (1914), quoted in Kathleen Weiler, "Women and Social Reform: California, 1900–1940," *History of Education Quarterly* 34, no. 1 (Spring 1994): 31. For the NEA's positions on rural education, see Committee of Twelve on Rural Schools, 1897, box 1236, folder 7; Committee of One Hundred on Rural Teacher's Problems, 1926, box 1236, folder 3; "Educational Policies for Rural America," 1939, box 1049, folder 3; "Rural Education," 1959–1968, box 2922, folder 18, all in NEA Records, GWU.

15. Stuart Rosenfeld and Jonathan Sher, "The Urbanization of Rural Schools, 1840–1970," in *Education in Rural America: A Reassessment of Conventional Wisdom*, ed. Jonathan Sher (Boulder, CO: Westview Press, 1977), 11–42, esp. 27. See also David Leverich, "Consolidation for Democracy: Rural School Reform in the Midwest, 1910–1930" (PhD diss., University of Wisconsin, 2004).

16. Rosenfeld and Sher, "Urbanization," 32; Stuart Rosenfeld, "Centralization versus Decentralization: A Case Study of Rural Education in Vermont," in Sher, *Education in Rural America*, 210.

17. Debates about the consensual nature of school consolidation go back to the 1960s. See Michael B. Katz, *The Irony of Early School Reform: Educational Innovation in Mid-Nineteenth-Century Massachusetts* (Cambridge, MA: Harvard University Press, 1968); and Michael B. Katz, Edward Stevens, and Maris Vinovskis, "The Origins of Public High Schools," *History of Education Quarterly* 27, no. 2 (Summer 1987): 241–58. In the latest round, the economist William A. Fischel argues that consolidation "was almost entirely consensual," driven by rural demands for high school. At the same time, however, he relies more on deductive speculation than historical evidence and concedes that "without some organized campaign, one-room schools and their districts tended to persist." William Fischel, *Making the Grade: The Economic Evolution of American School Districts* (Chicago: University of Chicago Press, 2009), 67–70, 92, 97–98.

18. Both methods were legalized in the 1910s. Steffes, "The Rural School Problem," 189.

19. Karen Schlenker, "'Let Us Go a Little Slow': Rural School Consolidation in Mille Lacs County," *Minnesota History Quarterly* 59, no. 3 (Fall 2004): 123.

20. Monty J. Ellsworth, *The Bath School Disaster* (Bath, MI: Bath School Museum Committee, 1927). Also see David Benac, *Conflict in the Ozarks: Hill Folk, Industrialists, and Government in Missouri's Courtois Hills* (Kirksville, MO: Truman State University Press, 2010), 67.

21. The validity of these beliefs was a point of debate among contemporary sociologists and remains unresolved. Later chapters suggest that reformers promised tax savings while privately hoping that consolidation would increase expenditures. See interview with Burton Kreitlow, tape 2, side 2, Oral History Interview: Burton W. Kreitlow, University of Wisconsin Archives.

22. Richard N. Smith, *Development of the Iowa Department of Public Instruction, 1900–1965* (Des Moines: Iowa Department of Public Instruction, 1969), 107–8.

23. For a pseudonymous case study, see Arthur J. Vidich and Joseph Bensman, "The Clash of Class Interests in School Politics," in *Small Town in Mass Society: Class, Power, and Religion in a Rural Community* (Princeton, NJ: Princeton University Press, 2000), 171–97.

24. Charles O. Fitzwater, *Selected Characteristics of Reorganized School Districts* (Washington, DC: U.S. Government Printing Office, 1953), 18; "Committee on Policies and Programs for Rural Education," box 1881, folder 03, pp. 12, 16, NEA Archives, GWU; Editorial, *The American School Board Journal* 116, no. 5 (May 1948): 100; Strang, "The Administrative Transformation," 355.

25. Roy Hall, Frank Leathers, and Charles Roberts, "Organization of School and Administrative Units," *Review of Educational Research* 25, no. 4 (October 1955): 335;

Conant, *The American High School Today*, 40; Arthur Summers, *Effective Legislation for District Reorganization*, (Lincoln, NE: Great Plains School District Organization Project, 1968), 47.

26. See, for example, "Rural Schools Suggest Limits on Standards," *Arkansas Gazette*, January 8, 1969, 1. Many legislatures passed consolidation measures on the understanding that they would grant individual waivers, which offered the state more discretion over which districts to close.

27. "Why So Much in Home Rule about Schools and Especially about Smaller Schools?" *Home Rule in Vermont Towns* 1, no. 13 (December 8, 1956): 1, UVM.

28. Thompson, *The History of Wisconsin* (Madison: State Historical Society of Wisconsin: 1998), 495–97.

29. Ibid., 503.

30. G. E. Watson, "Directions for Preparing and Filing Master Plan for School District Reorganization," January 1951, box 5, folder 3, Wisconsin Cooperative Educational Service Agency (CESA) No. 9 Records, WHS.

31. "What Shall We Do About Our School?" University of Wisconsin Extension, box 5, folder 3, CESA No. 9 Records, WHS; Thompson, *History of Wisconsin*, 499; *Good Old Golden Rule Days: A History of Sauk County Wisconsin Country Schools* (Baraboo, WI: Sauk County Historical Society, 1994).

32. Thompson, *History of Wisconsin*, 506.

33. Ibid., 495, 502.

34. David Bogue, "Origin of Our Organization," *Rural School Messenger*, July 1, 1944: 53, 65, Wisconsin Rural School Association (WRSA) Records, WHS.

35. Minutes, July 16 and August 28, 1953; Minutes, August 27, 1954, both in WRSA Records, WHS.

36. "A Dictatorship by Bureaucracy," *Rural School Messenger*, May/June 1954; "A Dictator in Action" and "Betrayal," *Rural School Messenger*, March/April 1956; "Editorial," *Rural School Messenger*, May/June 1954, all in WRSA Records, WHS.

37. Angus B. Rothwell, *Forty-First Biennial Report* (Madison: Wisconsin Department of Public Instruction, 1961–63), 69; *Forty-Second Biennial Report* (Madison: Wisconsin Department of Public Instruction, 1963–65), 180, 190.

38. Oral History Interview with Roy R. Meier, 1979, tape 5, side 2, WHS; "Allouez Residents Told Town Needs Own High School; Concern Voiced," *Green Bay Press-Gazette*, January 20, 1960, 1.

39. Oral History Interview with Melvin Sprecher, 1976, tape 6, WHS; William Harrington to the Board of Education, Twin Lakes, October 16, 1961; F. W. Johnson to Angus Rothwell, January 16, 1962, General correspondence of the State Superintendent, State Department of Public Instruction (DPI) Correspondence, all in WHS.

40. Smith, *Development of the Iowa Department of Public Instruction*, 111–12; "What is Going On in the Educational Picture in Iowa," n.d., box 1, folder 29, Iowa Schools Organization (ISO) Records, ISU.

41. Smith, *Origins of the Iowa DPI*, 117; Lewis Consolidated School District of Cass County v. Paul F. Johnston, box 1, folder 11, ISO Records, ISU; George Mills, "2 Call State School Chief a 'Dictator,'" *Des Moines Register*, Feburary 13, 1965, 1.

42. J. Henry Lucken, "Abolish State School Control, Says Sen. Lucken," *Le Mars (IA) Daily Sentinel*, January 8, 1969, box 1, folder 21, ISO Records, ISU.

43. Barron, *Mixed Harvest*, 75.

44. "School Reorganization Law," *Pennsylvania Township News* 15, no. 5 (May 1962): 6; "How the Vote Was Cast in the House on the Repeal of Act 561," *Pennsylvania Township News* 16, no. 8 (August 1963): 25. For more on the history of consolidation in Pennsylvania, see Summers, *Effective Legislation*, 16–17.

45. "Withdraw from School Union?" *Home Rule in Vermont Towns* 2, no. 5 (March 6, 1957): UVM; Rob Woolmington, "School-District Secession Moves Spread," *Bennington Banner*, December 1, 1976, 20.

46. Terry Neal Bishop, *Small Schools: A History of the Texas Small Schools Association and the Texas Small Schools Project* (Austin: University of Texas Press, 1970), 27, 40. In addition to the cases listed in later chapters, see Robert Bartlett et al., vs. Board of Trustees of the White Pine County School District, 550 P.2d 416 (1976).

47. "Small Schools Committee Report, 1974–75," box 1900, folder 5, NEA Archives, GWU.

48. Oral History Interview with Harold L. Tomter, 1978, tape 4, side 2, WHS; Kathy Wendling, *From One Room School to Union High School: The History of Windsor Central Supervisory Union* (Woodstock, VT: Windsor Supervisory Union, 1989), 20, 38. For other examples, see "Rural Education Committee," box 1887, folder 10, NEA Archives, GWU.

49. Alan Peshkin, *The Imperfect Union: School Consolidation and Community Conflict* (Chicago: University of Chicago Press, 1982), 9–10, 48, 90–91.

50. Phillip Hoffman, "School District Reorganization in Upstate New York: Case Studies from Homer and Truxton," (PhD diss., Syracuse University, 1977), 22, 27–29, 31, 34–35.

51. "When we realized just how much time and energy we were spending on a cumbersome system that wasn't saving us a dime," recalled a Vermont administrator about his district's supervisory union, "we scrapped the whole joint purchasing idea." Jonathan Sher and Rachel B. Tompkins, "Economy, Efficiency, and Equality: The Myths of Rural School and District Consolidation," in Sher, *Education in Rural America*, 47–48.

52. J. Black to Superintendent of Schools, Brown County, April 7, 1964, box 3, folder 7, CESA No. 9 Records, WHS.

53. Kathy Wendling, *From One Room School to Union High School: The History of Windsor Central Supervisory Union* (Woodstock, VT: Windsor Supervisory Union, 1989), 20, 38.

54. Fischel, *Making the Grade*, 78.

55. In addition to Sher, *Education in Rural America*, which features several of these authors, a good example of this research is Alan J. DeYoung and Craig B. Howley, "The Political Economy of Rural School Consolidation," *Peabody Journal of Education* 67, no. 4 (Summer 1990): 63–89.

56. "Rural Education Committee," box 1887, folders 10, 12, NEA Archives, GWU.

57. Timothy Weaver, "Community Schools versus Consolidation for the 1980s," box 34, folder 2, People United for Rural Education (PURE) Records, ISU.

58. Association of Retired Teachers of Vermont, *School Bells among Green Hills* (Essex Junction, VT: Essex Publishing Company, 1975), 17.

59. "School's Out for Good in District 34: Rural Consolidation Continues," *Nebraska's New Land Review* 1, no. 3 (Summer 1975): 10. I do not mean to suggest that the new perspectives had no effect. Rural districts continue to experiment with new technologies, programs, and structures to this day, and the scholarly consensus remains much more skeptical of consolidation than it had been at midcentury, often including warnings for states to *avoid* setting minimum sizes for either schools or districts. Nonetheless, consolidation remains the dominant mode of reform in most rural areas. See Craig Howley, Jerry Johnson, and Jennifer Petrie, "Consolidation of Schools and Districts: What the Research Says and What It Means," *National Education Policy Center*, February 2011. Available online at http://nepc.colorado.edu/publication/consolidation-schools-districts.

60. Ida Lieszkovszky, "Why It's So Hard for Rural Schools to Pass Levies," *State Impact Ohio* Ohio Public Radio, April 22, 2013, http://stateimpact.npr.org/ohio/2013/04/22/why-its-so-hard-for-rural-schools-to-pass-levies/.

3. THE EXURBAN EXCHANGE

1. "The Confrontation," *Green Acres*, season 5, episode 20, (CBS Television, 1970). Most of the period's television shows remained silent on current events. *The Andy Griffith Show* has drawn particular scrutiny for its omission of civil rights issues. See Allison Graham, *Framing the South: Hollywood, Television, and Race During the Civil Rights Struggle* (Baltimore: Johns Hopkins University Press, 2001), 159–60.

2. Other casualties included *Petticoat Junction, Mayberry RFD, The Beverly Hillbillies, Lassie*, and *Hee-Haw*. See Anthony Harkins, *Hillbilly: A Cultural History of an American Icon* (New York: Oxford University Press, 2005), 203.

3. At least twelve percent of the population within metropolitan boundaries remained nominally rural. Mark B. Lapping and Owen J. Furuseth, eds., *Contested Countryside: The Rural-Urban Fringe in North America* (Aldershot, UK: Ashgate, 1999), 18; Robert Healy and James Short, "Changing Markets for Rural Lands: Patterns and Issues," in *Beyond the Urban Fringe: Land Use Issues of Nonmetropolitan America*, ed. George Macinko and Rutherford H. Platt (Minneapolis: University of Minnesota Press, 1983), 109–34, esp. 118; David K. Hamilton, *Governing Metropolitan Areas: Response to Growth and Change* (New York: Garland, 1999), 8; Ronald Briggs, "The Impact of the Interstate Highway System on Nonmetropolitan Development," in Macinko and Platt, *Beyond the Urban Fringe*, 83–108, esp. 93, 160.

4. On the origins of interstate highways, see Earl Swift, *The Big Roads: The Untold Story of the Engineers, Visionaries, and Trailblazers Who Created the American Superhighways* (Boston: Houghton Mifflin Harcourt, 2011).

5. Briggs, "The Impact of the Interstate Highway System," in Macinko and Platt, *Beyond the Urban Fringe*, 93; Wood, *Survival of Rural America*, 13; Hamilton, *Trucking Country*; Moreton, *To Serve God and Wal-Mart*; Emil A. Jirik, "Marketing in the Exurbs: Selling a Small Town," (PhD diss., Minnesota State University, 1988).

6. See, for instance, the discussion in Milton D. Rafferty, *The Ozarks: Land and Life* (Fayetteville: University of Arkansas Press, 2001), 224.

7. Annie Gilbert Coleman, "Call of the Mild: Colorado Ski Resorts and the Politics of Rural Tourism," in *The Countryside in the Age of the Modern State: Political Histories of Rural America*, ed. Catherine McNicol Stock and Robert D. Johnston (Ithaca, NY: Cornell University Press, 2001), 281–303, esp. 298. See also, William Philpott, *Vacationland: Tourism and Environment in the Colorado High Country* (Seattle: University of Washington Press, 2013).

8. Oral History Interview with Harold L. Tomter, May 24, 1978, tape 4, side 2, WHS.

9. Wood, *Survival of Rural America*, 13; John Herbers, *The New Heartland: America's Flight Beyond the Suburbs and How It Is Changing Our Future* (New York: Times Books, 1986), 7–8; Healy and Short, "Changing Markets," in Macinko and Platt, *Beyond the Urban Fringe*, esp.127.

10. Harry Schwarzweller, "Migration and the Changing Rural Scene," *Rural Sociology* 44, no. 1 (Spring 1979): 11–12; Healy and Short, "Changing Markets," in Macinko and Platt, *Beyond the Urban Fringe*, 120, 122–24; Thomas Wolfe, *You Can't Go Home Again* (New York: Scribner, 2011), 95–96; Hubert B. Stroud, *The Promise of Paradise: Recreational and Retirement Communities in the United States Since 1950* (Baltimore: Johns Hopkins University Press, 1995), 9.

11. T. L. Smith was the first to study the rural-suburban fringe, in 1937, and the topic was well established in sociological circles by the late 1940s. Between 1970 and 2000, over a dozen articles about migration to rural areas appeared in journals like *Rural Sociology, American Sociological Review*, and *The Journal of the Community Development Society*. Books on the subject include Jon C. Teaford, *Post-Suburbia: Government and Politics in*

the Edge Cities (Baltimore: Johns Hopkins University Press, 1997); P. J. Boyle and Keith Halfacree, *Migration into Rural Areas: Theories and Issues* (Chicester, UK: Wiley, 1998); Sonya Salamon, *Newcomers to Old Towns: Suburbanization of the Heartland* (Chicago: Chicago University Press, 2003); and Joseph Goddard, *Being American on the Edge: Penurbia and the Metropolitan Mind, 1945–2010* (New York: Palgrave-Macmillan, 2012).

12. Henry Clay Tate, *Building a Better Home Town: A Program of Community Self-Analysis and Self-Help* (New York: Harper, 1954), 68; Grace Graham, *The Public School in the American Community* (New York: Harper & Row, 1963), 276, 283; William Mann Dobriner, *Class in Suburbia* (Englewood, NJ: Prentice-Hall, 1963), 127.

13. A. C. Spectorsky, *The Exurbanites* (Philadelphia: Lippencott Publishing, 1955), 21, 243–44.

14. Ibid., 101–3.

15. Stroud, *Promise of Paradise*, 55. For a concise discussion of education's effects on zoning, property taxes, and building in rural areas, see Tom Daniels, *When City and Country Collide: Managing Growth in the Metropolitan Fringe* (Washington, DC: Island Press, 1999), 140–43.

16. Herbert J. Gans, *The Levittowners: Ways of Life and Politics in a New Suburban Community* (New York: Pantheon, 1967), 90–95; "Committee on Policies and Programs for Rural Education," box 1881, folder 03, NEA Archives, GWU.

17. Dobriner, *Class in Suburbia*, 137–38; Catherine McNicol Stock, *Rural Radicals: Righteous Rage in the American Grain* (Ithaca, NY: Cornell University Press, 1996), 88–89; Andrew H. Malcolm, "Final Harvest: Grand Dreams Reap Tragedy," *Chicago Tribune*, March 23, 1986, B1; Bruce Weber and Robert Howell, *Coping With Rapid Growth in Rural Communities* (Boulder, CO: Westview Press, 1982), 118–19; Lapping and Furuseth, *Contested Countryside*, 2.

18. Albert Minor Adams, "Growing Pains in Raymond, New Hampshire" (PhD diss., Harvard University, 1984), 9, 33, 37.

19. Perrin, *Best Person Rural: Essays of a Sometime Farmer* (Boston: David R. Godine, 2006), 51–52.

20. Stuart Rosenfield, "Centralization versus Decentralization: A Case Study of Rural Education in Vermont," in *Education in Rural America: A Reassessment of Conventional Wisdom*, ed. Jonathan Sher (Boulder, CO: Westview Press, 1977), 205–70, esp. 208. See also, Winifred Margaret McCarthy, "The Migration of Cosmopolites to Rural Vermont" (PhD diss., New School for Social Research, 1986).

21. Rosenfield, "Centralization versus Decentralization," in Sher, *Education in Rural America*, 228, 240; "How to Wheedle Voters Into Consolidation," *Home Rule in Vermont Towns*, 1, no. 5 (June 1956): 1, UVM; James William Jordan, "The Summer People and the Natives: Some Effects of Tourism in a Vermont Vacation Village," *Annals of Tourism Research* 7, no. 1 (1980): 47–48.

22. Richard Krannich and Michael D. Smith, "Culture Clash Revisited: Newcomer and Longer-Term Residents' Attitudes Toward Land Use, Development, and Environmental Issues in Rural Communities in the Rocky Mountain West," *Rural Sociology* 65, no. 3 (2000): 396–421; Lapping and Furuseth, *Contested Countryside*, 2, 12; Stephen Essex, *Rural Change and Sustainability: Agriculture, the Environment, and Communities* (Wallingford, UK: CABI, 2005), 108.

23. Farm preservation legislation originated in Maryland in 1957 but spread in various forms to all fifty states over the next decade. Lapping and Furuseth, *Contested Countryside*, 19, 62–63; Jonathan King and Christopher Anderson, "Marginal Property Tax Effects of Conservation Easements: A Vermont Case Study," *American Journal of Agricultural Economics* 86, no. 4 (November.2004): 919–32; John C. Keene, "The Impact of Differential Assessment Programs on the Tax Base," *Property Tax Incentives for Preservation: Use-*

Values Assessment and the Preservation of Farmland, Open Space, and Historic Sites (Washington, DC: International Association of Assessing Officers, 1975), 40–61.

24. Kyle Mitchell Livie, "Wide Open Spaces: Rural Communities and the Making of Metropolitan California, 1870–1940" (PhD diss., UCLA, 2007), 435–36, 441.

25. Much has been written on suburbanization and the rise of environmental movements. In addition to Coleman, "Call of the Mild," see Gregory Summers, *Consuming Nature: Environmentalism in the Fox River Valley, 1850–1950*, (Lawrence: University Press of Kansas, 2006); Adam Rome, *The Bulldozer in the Countryside: Suburban Sprawl and the Rise of American Environmentalism* (New York: Cambridge University Press, 2001); Ellen Stroud, *Nature Next Door: Cities and Trees in the American Northeast* (Seattle: University of Washington Press, 2012); Peter Siskind, "Suburban Growth and Its Discontents: The Logic and Limits of Reform on the Postwar Northeast Corridor," in *The New Suburban History*, ed. Kevin M. Kruse and Thomas J. Sugrue (Chicago: University of Chicago Press, 2006), 161–82; and Louis A. Mozingo, *Pastoral Capitalism: A History of Suburban Corporate Landscapes* (Cambridge, MA: MIT Press, 2011). Also, it is important to note that not all newcomers opposed further development. See Paul Voss, "A Test of the 'Gangplank Syndrome' among Recent Migrants to the Upper Great Lakes Region," *Journal of the Community Development Society* 11, no. 1 (Spring 1980): 95–111.

26. Faith Dunne, "Choosing Smallness: An Examination of the Small School," in Sher, *Education in Rural America*, 84; Barnard Bicentennial Committee, *History of Barnard, Vermont, 1927–1975* (Taftsville, VT: Countryman Press, 1975), 25, 28–29; Garret Keizer, *No Place But Here: A Teacher's Vocation in a Rural Community* (New York: Penguin Books, 1988), 3, 22. E. B. White's quote is included in Tyack, *The One Best System: A History of American Urban Education* (Cambridge, MA: Harvard University Press, 1974), 26.

27. E. B. White, "Letter from the East," *The New Yorker*, March 27, 1971, 35–37. While most of Maine's one-room elementary schools had closed by the end of World War II, small-town high schools persisted through the 1970s. Susan K. Woodward, *The Evolution of School Consolidation in Maine* (Orono: University of Maine Press, 1997), 4.

28. American Association of School Administrators, *School District Organization* (Washington, DC: AASA, 1958), 279.

29. Calvin R. Ledbetter, "The Fight for School Consolidation in Arkansas, 1946–1948," *Arkansas Historical Quarterly* 65, no. 1 (Spring 2006): 45–57.

30. Brian Irby, "The Consolidation Battle of 1966 and the Creation of the Arkansas Rural Education Association," box 1, folder 24, 6–7, 26, 41, Arkansas Rural Education Association (AREA) Records, UCA; "Consolidation Foe Sees Need of Rural Schools for Suburbs," *Arkansas Gazette*, February 14, 1966, box 1, folder 13, AREA Records, UCA.

31. For a history of the region's schools, see J. Blake Perkins, "Mountain Stereotypes, Whiteness, and the Discourse of Early School Reform in the Arkansas Ozarks, 1910s–1920s," *History of Education Quarterly* 54, no. 2 (May 2014): 197–221.

32. Irby, "Consolidation Battle," 4, 20–21, 23, 30. "Baubus Cites Progress at Bridge Dedication," *Arkansas Democrat*, August 13, 1966, box 1, folder 13, AREA Records, UCA.

33. Jim Wecksler, "Orford Provided Political Springboard for Thomson," *Portsmouth (NH) Herald*, January 22, 1970, 2; Laura Barwicke DeLind, "Leisureville: A Developmental Study of Behavior and Social Organization within A Rural U.S. Community" (PhD diss., Michigan State University, 1978), 66–67, 75; Faith Dunne, "Good Government vs. Self-Government: Educational Control in Rural America," *Phi Delta Kappan* 65, no. 4 (December 1983): 253–54.

34. AASA, *School District Organization*, 276–77.

35. Ibid., 278. See also James Donaghue, *The Local Government System in Wisconsin* (Milwaukee: Wisconsin Blue Book, 1968), 58.

36. John Rury and Donna Gardner, "Suburban Opposition to District Reorganization: The 1968 Spainhower Commission and Metropolitan Kansas City and St. Louis," *Urban Review* 46 (2014): 125–45; John Rury, "Trouble in Suburbia: Localism, Schools and Conflict in Postwar Johnson County, Kansas," *History of Education Quarterly* 55, no. 2 (May 2015): 133–63.

37. Harry Bortin, "El Monte Group Hits Unruh Bill," *Long Beach (CA) Independent*, March 19, 1964, 6; Article on district reorganization [no title], *Pennsylvania Township News* 15, no. 6 (June 1962): 16; Terry Neal Bishop, *Small Schools: A History of the Texas Small Schools Association and the Texas Small Schools Project* (Austin: University of Texas Press, 1970), 43.

38. For material on housing and race, see notes to chapter 1, notes 5 and 25.

39. See Jack Dougherty, *More Than One Struggle: The Evolution of Black School Reform in Milwaukee* (Chapel Hill: University of North Carolina Press, 2004), 87.

40. See Adam R. Nelson, *The Elusive Ideal: Equal Educational Opportunity and the Federal Role in Boston's Public Schools, 1950–1985* (Chicago: Chicago University Press, 2005), 136–43; Matthew Lassiter, *The Silent Majority: Suburban Politics in the Sunbelt South* (Princeton, NJ: Princeton University Press, 2006), 132; James E. Ryan, *Five Miles Away, A World Apart: One City, Two Schools, and the Story of Educational Opportunity in Modern America* (New York: Oxford University Press, 2010), 81; Jeffrey Mirel, *The Rise and Fall of An Urban School System* (Ann Arbor: University of Michigan, 1999), 258–65.

41. The sentiment had been present in American jurisprudence since shortly after *Brown*. In 1957, for example, federal judge Irving Kaufman struck down segregated schools in New Rochelle, New York, writing, "the neighborhood school policy certainly is not sacrosanct. It is valid only insofar as it is operated within the confines established by the Constitution." Quoted in Thomas Sugrue, *Sweet Land of Liberty: The Forgotten Struggle for Civil Rights in the North* (New York: Random House, 2009), 197.

42. Swann v. Charlotte-Mecklenburg Board of Education, 402 U.S. 1 (1971). For more on busing, see James Patterson, *Brown v. Board of Education* (New York: Oxford University Press, 2001); Ronald Formisano, *Boston Against Busing: Race, Class, and Ethnicity in the 1960s and 1970s* (Chapel Hill: University of North Carolina Press, 1991); and Nelson, *The Elusive Ideal*, 61–150.

43. Sugrue, *Sweet Land of Liberty*, 482.

44. Mirel, *The Rise and Fall of An Urban School System*, 244–46.

45. The dissent in *Milliken* cites Attorney General ex rel. Kies v. Lowrey, 131 Mich. 639, 92 N.W. 289 (1902) and Imlay Township District v. State Board of Education, 359 Mich. 478, 102 N.W. 2d 720 (1960), as well as several other cases establishing state control of education. Milliken v. Bradley, 418 U.S. 717 (1974). Milliken was one of dozens of state and federal rulings to reaffirm local control in the 1970s, many of them decided on rural precedents but ultimately benefiting the suburbs. In addition to those discussed in later chapters, *Salyer Land Co. v. Tulare Lake Basin [CA] Water Storage District* 410 U.S. 719 (1973) overturned previous rulings on voting rights in special districts, making exceptions only for school board elections, as decided in *Kramer v. Union School District*, 395 U. S. 621 (1969). See Nancy Burns, *The Formation of American Local Governments: Private Values in Public Institutions* (New York: Oxford University Press, 1994), 12.

46. Congress eventually proposed a constitutional amendment against busing, an issue that helped both Richard Nixon and George Wallace in the 1972 election.

47. David Riddle, "Race and Racism in Warren, Michigan, 1971–1974: *Bradley v. Milliken* and the Cross-District Busing Controversy," *Michigan Historical Review* 26, no. 2 (Fall 2000): 3–4.

48. Quoted in Lassiter, *The Silent Majority*, 5.

49. Sugrue, *Sweet Land of Liberty*, 283.

50. Milliken v. Bradley.

51. The following examples, while representative, should not obscure the few liberal enclaves that welcomed interdistrict busing. See, for example, the participation of Weston, Massachusetts, in Boston's voluntary METCO busing program. Pamela W. Fox and Sarah B. Gilman, *Farm Town to Suburb: The History and Architecture of Weston, Massachusetts, 1830–1980* (Portsmouth, NH: Love Lane Press, 2002), 161–62.

52. Jeffrey St. John, "School Busing Issue Termed Child Cruelty," *Colorado Springs Gazette Telegraph*, November 17, 1971, B; "Busing Bill's Sponsor: Albert Harold Quie," *New York Times*, August 9, 1972, 75; "GOP Chairman Resigns, Charges Campaign Racism," *Waterloo Courier*, June 11, 1974, 5.

53. Minutes, 14 September 1957, WRSA Records; Verne Kaub to Pricilla Medler, September 7, 1960; Verne Kaub to Harold J. Olson, January 6, 1961; Verne Kaub To Harold J. Olson, January 10, 1961; Verne Kaub to Marie Cary Hartford, February 13, 1963, letters all in boxes 1-2, American Council of Christian Laymen (ACCL) Records (Part 2: Additions), WHS.

54. "Race Closer Than Expected," *Capital Times*, April 2, 1969, 2.

55. "Resolution," Atwater PTA, January 22, 1975, box 9, folder 5, Delmar DeLong Papers, WHS; "Resolution No. 2445," Common Council of the City of Brookfield, n.d. (1975), William R. Liska to George Klicka, September 30, 1975; H. P. Mueller to George Klicka, April 17, 1975, letters all in box 1, folder 21, George Klicka Papers, WHS.

56. Manuscript, n.d., box 3, folder 16, Kenneth Merkel Papers, WHS.

57. David Ross to Delmar DeLong, March 9, 1976, box 9, folder 5, Delmar DeLong Papers, WHS; James Poppe to George Klicka, June 11, 1979, box 1, folder 52, George Klicka Papers; Dottie Kellner to Kenneth Merkel, February 3, 1972; and Ray Scroggins to Kenneth Merkel, February 19, 1971, both in box 1, folder 48, Kenneth Merkel Papers, WHS.

4. THE STRUGGLE FOR STATUS

1. The foundational texts are Marjorie Murphy, *Blackboard Unions: The AFT & NEA, 1900–1980* (Ithaca, NY: Cornell University Press, 1990); and Wayne Urban, "Teacher Activism," in *American Teachers: Histories of a Profession at Work*, ed. Donald Warren (New York: MacMillan, 1989), 190–209. Also helpful, for this period, is Joseph A. McCartin, "Turnabout Years: Public Sector Unionism and the Fiscal Crisis," in *Rightward Bound: Making America Conservative in the 1970s*, ed. Bruce J. Schulman and Julian E. Zelizer (Cambridge, MA: Harvard University Press, 2008), 210–26.

2. See, for instance, Jerald E. Podair, *The Strike That Changed New York: Blacks, Whites, and the Ocean Hill-Brownsville Crisis* (New Haven, CT: Yale University Press, 2002); Steve Golin, *The Newark Teacher Strikes: Hopes on the Line* (New Brunswick, NJ: Rutgers University Press, 2002); Dorothy Shipps, *School Reform, Corporate Style: Chicago, 1880–2000* (Lawrence: University Press of Kansas, 2006); John F. Lyons, *Teachers and Reform: Chicago Public Education 1929–1970* (Champaign: University of Illinois Press, 2008); Christina Collins, *"Ethnically Qualified": Race, Merit, and the Selection of Urban Teachers, 1920–1980* (New York: Teachers College Press, 2011); and Jonna Perrillo, *Uncivil Rights: Teachers, Unions, and Race in the Battle for School Equity* (Chicago: University of Chicago Press, 2012).

3. The chapter defines a "small district" as one with fewer than two hundred faculty, a number inclusive both of remote, rural areas like Sequatchie County, Tennessee and inner-ring suburbs like Garfield, New Jersey, but (as will be clear from the examples provided) which were generally representative of consolidated rural districts and growing exurban areas, and clearly exclusive of even small cities. A full accounting of the incidents described is available at "Lists of Strikes," box 2975, folder 14; box 2984, folder 09, NEA Archives, GWU.

4. By 1930, there were 172,000 members of the NEA and 7,000 of the AFT. Murphy, *Blackboard Unions*, 277.

5. Historian Christine Ogren observes that most normal school students during this period were "from a small provincial town or village, experienced in the workforce as a teacher or a farmer, not well-off financially, and the first in the family to be educated beyond the common school." Christine A. Ogren, "'A Large Measure of Self-Control and Personal Power': Women Students at State Normal Schools during the Late-Nineteenth and Early-Twentieth Centuries," *Women's Studies Quarterly* 28, no. 3/4 (Fall–Winter 2000): 211–32. For a thorough description of the mixed effects of professionalization on rural pedagogy, see Larry Cuban, *How Teachers Taught: Constancy and Change in American Classrooms, 1890–1980* (New York: Longman Press, 1984), 113–40.

6. "Letter Says AEA Tries to 'Destroy' Smaller Schools," *Arkansas Gazette*, October 30, 1979, 4A. While union leadership almost always lobbied for consolidation, some smaller affiliates opposed measures that threatened their jobs. Alan J. DeYoung, *The Life and Death of a Rural American High School: Farewell, Little Kanawha* (New York: Garland, 1995), 196–97.

7. "Doubts Unruh School District Bill Will Pass," *San Mateo (CA) Times*, March 13, 1964, 3; "Report of the Committee on Tenure and Academic Freedom, 1950," box 2950, folder 6, NEA Archives, GWU.

8. "A Short History of the AFT," box 7, folder 2, American Federation of Teachers (AFT) Records, WHS.

9. See lists of locals in box 6, folder 1, as well as "Presidents of WFT Locals" and corresponding maps in box 7, folder 5, both in Wisconsin Federation of Teachers (WFT) Records, WHS. The dates at which WEAC affiliates incorporated are available in the *NEA Handbook, 1973–1974* (Washington, DC: National Education Association, 1974), 320–23.

10. Bethany Moreton documents a broad campaign by Wal-Mart and other companies to couple rural values with free-market, antiunion education programs. Bethany Moreton, *To Serve God and Wal-Mart: The Making of Christian Free Enterprise* (Cambridge, MA: Harvard University Press, 2009), 173–247. Frank Meinen to William Smeeth, April 18, 1963; Frank Meinen to William Smeeth, April 24, 1963; Robert N. Halmstad to Frank Meinen, February 20, 1964; Frank Meinen to Project Action, June 5, 1961, all in box 6, folder 32; Frank Meinen to Phyllis Schlafly, January 23 1962, box 6, folder 20, letters all in Frank Meinen Papers, WHS.

11. Oral History with Stanley Teacher, tape 45, side 2; Oral History with Bloomer Teacher, tape 41 side 1; Oral History with Ted Burns, tape 43, side 2, all in Wisconsin Education Association Council (WEAC) Records, WHS.

12. Charlie Cheng to Wilson Nickles, October 3, 1967; John O. Linstead, "Imlay Head Start Appeal Raises Broad Question," *Flint Journal*, February 3, 1967, both in box 10, folder 08, Michigan Federation of Teachers Records, Part III, Series 2, WSU.

13. "A Conflict between an Administrator and a Teachers' Organization," March 24, 1972, box 937, folder 06, NEA Archives, GWU; "Area's Population Continues to Rise," *Nashua (NH) Telegraph*, January 29, 1972, 58.

14. "Menominee Sanctions Investigation," September 17, 1967, box 928, folder 04, NEA Archives, GWU.

15. Rex Anderson, "A History of Millard Public Schools, 1946–1989: Forty-Four Years of Suburban Growth," (master's thesis, University of Nebraska, 1997), 17, 24, 33–34, 38, 50, 55, 79, 199.

16. For a typical case from upstate New York, see Arthur J. Vidich and Joseph Bensman, *Small Town in Mass Society: Class, Power, and Religion in a Rural Community* (Princeton, NJ: Princeton University Press, 1968), 174–75.

17. While one might speculate that rural voters would have supported the first measure and suburbanites the second, both passed with wide margins. "School Head in Manchester Asked to Quit," *Bennington Banner*, November 20, 1961, 1; "Manchester to Vote on Enlarging School Board," *Bennington* Banner, February 9, 1962, 7; Lee Harrison, "Solutions to Age-Old Mt. Anthony Problems Now Seem to Converge from All Directions," *Bennington Banner*, September 27, 1977, 16.

18. "Solon Sees Year of Revolution in Idaho Education Programs," box 893, folder 5; Elmer Crowley to Richard Kennan, January 10, 1964; Elmer Crowley to Owen Love, March 26, 1964; Elmer Crowley to Richard Kennan, April 30, 1964, all in box 893, folder 2, boxes all in NEA Archives, GWU; DeeAnn Grove, " 'Be Assured That You Do Not Stand Alone': Iowa's Only Teachers' Strike, Keokuk, Iowa, 1970," presented at the History of Education Society conference, 2009.

19. Jane A. Rahberg to Hugh Kahler, February 2, 1960, box 05, folder 08, Michigan Federation of Teachers Records, Part III, Series 2, WSU.

20. Murphy, *Blackboard Unions*, 227; Marshall O. Donley, *Power to the Teacher: How America's Educators Became Militant* (Bloomington: Indiana University Press, 1976), 80–86.

21. Oral History Interview with Reverend Ted Anderson, Nantucket Historical Society, tape 1, side B. Transcript available at http://www.nha.org/library/oralhistory/andersont .html.

22. *Nantucket's Public Schools: A Report of an Independent Study* (Nantucket, MA: Nantucket Town Board, 1957), 18.

23. Only two teachers had been approved for tenure since the 1940s. Most, unable to afford permanent housing because of inflated summer rents, had to live in cellars or rented rooms.

24. Gene Currivan, "N.E.A. Educators Have Warned of Extremist Efforts in Schools," *New York Times*, July 2, 1965, 10.

25. Charles Minnich, "It Can Happen in Your Town," box 851, folder 01, NEA Archives, GWU.

26. "Weak Schools Invite Extremists," *Bennington Banner*, February 13, 1965, 4; "Teacher Assn. Warns of Nantucket Boycott Action," *North Adams (MA) Transcript*, December 7, 1964, 3; "Kiernan Announces 'Our First Concern' Children in Nantucket Teacher Dispute," *North Adams (MA) Transcript*, February 4, 1966, 5; "Nantucket Fires Another School Superintendent," *Lowell (MA) Sun*, March 28, 1967, 3; "Teacher Claims Wedding a Black Got Her Fired," *Berkshire (MA) Eagle*, December 31, 1969, 3.

27. Murphy, *Blackboard Unions*, 229; Donley, *Power to the Teacher*, 80–95.

28. What might have been the first teachers' strike in American history took place in 1920, when seven one-room schoolteachers in Jasper County and Sioux County, Iowa, conspired to cancel classes. Coordinated work stoppages also occurred sporadically in the 1930s and 1940s, especially in rural areas with sympathetic coal miners or other unionized workers. "Educational Employees on Strike," 1947, box 2975, folder 14, NEA Records, GWU; Dan Golodner, "First Teacher Strike in U.S., 1920?", History of Education, H-NET listserv, posted 2 December 2011. Available through a word search for "Teacher Strike" at http://h-net.msu.edu.

29. "Portola Vote Defeats Bonds," *San Mateo Times*, June 15, 1960, 6; "Portola Valley School Advance," *San Mateo Times*, July 8, 1960, 17; "Teachers Go on 'Illness' At Portola," *San Mateo Times*, May 27, 1961, 2; "Portola to Permit Rose to Resign," *San Mateo Times*, May 13, 1961, 11; "Can Parents Sue School," *San Mateo Times*, June 16, 1961, 17; "Judge Rose Dismisses School Suit," *San Mateo Times*, March 28, 1962, 4; "Teacher Suit Filed Again," *San Mateo Times*, April 18, 1962, 35.

30. Board of Education, Borough of Union Beach v. New Jersey Education Association, 53 N.J. 29; 247 A.2d 867 (1968).

31. Phyllis Brown, "My First Ten Years—A Dream Deferred," *Action Bulletin* (March 1975), Greenburgh Teachers Federation (GTF) Records, WHS; Charles Hanley, "Battle-Weary Taylor Law Will Undergo Scrutiny by State," *The Oneonta (NY) Star*, October 10, 1973, 7; Mildred Zimmerman, "President's Message," *Action Bulletin* (February 1974), GTF Records, WHS.

32. Oral History Interview with Donald Dickinson, tape 14, side 1, WEAC Records, WHS; "Extended Hortonville School Day Likely Because of Space Shortages," *Appleton Post-Crescent*, March 16, 1974, 1; "Emotions as Well as Issues Led to Hortonville Impasse," *Capital Times*, April 29, 1974, 1.

33. With no unionization of small industry in the region, the Hortonville Education Association (HEA) was also the town's only organized workforce, adding another layer of tension to the situation. "Emotions as well as Issues Led to Hortonville Impasse," *Capital Times*, April 29, 1974, 1.

34. Darryl Holter, *Workers and Unions in Wisconsin: A Labor History Anthology* (Madison: State Historical Society of Wisconsin, 1999), 240–41; Oral History Interview with Morris Andrews, tape 8, side 1; Oral History Interview with Don Krahn, tape 4, side 1, oral history interviews in WEAC Records, WHS.

35. "Hortonville to Halt Classes for Hearings with Teachers," *Appleton Post-Crescent*, March 30, 1974, 1; Holter, *Workers and Unions*, 241–42.

36. Interview with Vigilantes, tape 56, side 1; Oral History Interview with Morris Andrews, tape 8, side 1, both in WEAC Records, WHS.

37. tape 51, side 1; Interview with Vigilantes, tape 56, side 1; Interview with Mill Owner's Family, tape 55, side 1, all in WEAC Records, WHS.

38. Oral History Interview with Jean Wall and Mike Wisnoski, tape 39, side 2, WEAC Records, WHS.

39. Interview with Vigilantes, tape 56, side 1, WEAC Records, WHS; Bill Knutson, "Lengthy Bargaining Talks on Strike Fail to Get Results," *Appleton Post-Crescent*, March 28, 1974, 1.

40. Bill Knutson, "School Delayed by Snow," *Appleton Post-Crescent*, March 25, 1974, 1; Oral History Interview with Two Unidentified Greenfield Teachers, tape 38, side 1, WEAC Records, WHS; Holter, *Workers and Unions*, 242.

41. Mike Dorgan, "The 'Sub,'" *Capital Times*, 29 April 1974, 1; Oral History Interview with Morris Andrews, tape 8, side 1; tape 50, side 1; Oral History Interview with Jean Wall and Mike Wisnoski, tape 39, side 2, oral history interviews all in WEAC Records, WHS.

42. Almost a third of the replacements did not hold teaching licenses, two of them had been convicted of crimes, and several others were parents or community members, yet at no point did Thompson cut off the town's funding, as required by state law. For more on the role of the DPI in the strike, see Richard Haws, "Mrs. Thompson against State Sympathy Strike," *Wisconsin State Journal*, April 24, 1974, 1; Holter, *Workers and Unions*, 242–43.

43. Holter, *Workers and Unions*, 242; Oral History Interview with Jean Wall and Mike Wisnoski, tape 39, side 2, WEAC Records, WHS.

44. "Judge Tells Hortonville to Give Strikers Jobs," *The Capital Times*, May 6, 1974, 1; Holter, *Workers and Unions*, 242–43.

45. Owen Coyle and Matt Pommer, "Lucey Opposes State Teacher Walkout," *Capital Times*, April 24, 1974, 1; Holter, *Workers and Unions*, 243.

46. David I. Bednarek, "Union's Survival is Last Strike Issue," *Milwaukee Journal*, April 26, 1974, 1. Oral History, Richland Center Counselor, tape 43, side 1, WEAC Records, WHS.

47. "No End in Sight to Teachers' Strike at Timberlane," *Nashua Telegraph*, September 3, 1974, 14.

48. Timberlane Regional School District v. Timberlane Regional Education Association, 114 N.H. 245 (1974); "New Hampshire Board Adopts Policy on Striking Teachers," *Nashua Telegraph*, January 23, 1975, 13; "Teachers in Timberlane Form Bargaining Units," *Nashua Telegraph*, December 23, 1974, 13.

49. Several legal analysts cite the Timberlane decision as the moment when the judicial system that had been "the primary vehicle for enforcing the strike proscription" commenced the "erosion of the legal sanctions against strikes." See, for example, Janice K. Rosenberg, "Teacher Strikes: A Proposed Solution," *Urban Law Annual* 16 (1979): 338.

50. School Dist. for Holland v. Holland Education Association, 380 Mich. 314, 321, 157 N.W.2d 206, 208 (1968); Rockwell v. Board of Education, 393 MI 314, 326, 157 N.W. 2d 206, 210 (1968); School Committee v. Westerly Teachers Association, 111 R.I. 96, 104, 299 A.2d 441, 446 (1973); *Public Sector Labor Law and Collective Bargaining* (Dearborn, MI: Institute of Continuing Legal Education, 1976), 204, 270–72. For subsequent references to the Timberlane case, see Joseph R. Grodin, June M. Weisberger, and Martin H. Malin, *Public Sector Employment: Cases and Materials* (St. Paul, MN: Labor Law Group, 2004), 296.

51. Danville Board of Directors v. Fifield, 132 VT 271, 276; 315 A.2d 473, 474 (1974); Rosenberg, "Teacher Strikes," 337; Grodin, Weisberger, and Malin, *Public Sector Employment*, 390.

52. Pickering v. Board of Education, 391 U.S. 563 (1968).

53. Grodin, Weisberger, and Malin, *Public Sector Employment*, 170.

54. Board of Education v. Associated Teachers of Huntington, 30 N.Y.2d 122 (1972); Acting Superintendent v. United Liverpool Faculty Association, 42 N.Y.2d 509 (1977); Grodin, Weisberger, and Malin, *Public Sector Employment*, 374–75.

55. Maryland v. Wirtz, 392 U.S. 183; 88 S.Ct. 2017; 20 L.Ed.2d 1020 (1968); National League of Cities v. Usery, 426 U.S. 833; 96 S.Ct. 2465 (1976); Garcia v. San Antonio Metropolitan Transit Authority, 469 U.S. 528 (1985). See also, McCartin, "Turnabout Years," 217.

56. One Milwaukee lawyer, after representing school boards in labor disputes, began sending his children to a conservative private school, "[knowing] I could not willingly let my children obtain their life's education at the knees of these collectivists [unionized teachers]—many actual revolutionaries." Walter Davis, "Brookfield Academy—The First Thirty Years," box 1, folder 11, Brookfield Academy Archives.

57. The most popular right-wing indictment of public unionization was Ralph de Toledano, *Let Our Cities Burn* (New Rochelle, NY: Arlington House Publishers, 1975). See also, McCartin, "Turnabout Years," 210.

58. For a list of states with right-to-work legislation, as well as the date of its adoption, see National Conference of State Legislatures, "Right-to-Work Laws," http://www.ncsl.org/issues-research/labor/right-to-work-laws-and-bills.aspx. On working-class culture and politics, see Jefferson Cowie, *Staying Alive: The 1970s and the Last Days of the Working Class* (New York: New Press, 2010).

5. THE FIGHT FOR FUNDING

1. Michael H. Ebner, *Creating Chicago's North Shore: A Suburban History* (Chicago: University of Chicago Press, 1988), 170. Similar disputes can be found in Mark Zaltman, *Suburban/Rural Conflicts in Late 19th Century Chicago* (San Francisco: International Scholars Publications, 1998).

2. Oral History Program Interview with Susan Eichhorn, tape 1, side 1, University of Wisconsin Archives; Leigh Atkinson, "Contest Legal Status of New School District," *Chicago Tribune*, August 4, 1949, N A1.

3. Richard John Hemme, "Cooperation vs. Consolidation of School District in Deerfield, Illinois" (PhD diss., Northern Illinois University, 1966); Thomas Sugrue, *Sweet Land of Liberty: The Forgotten Struggle for Civil Rights in the North* (New York: Random House, 2009), 237–38; Ernest Fuller, "Home Builder Will Donate 8 Schoolrooms," *Chicago Tribune*, October 22, 1955, B5; "Protest New Housing Area at Deerfield," *Chicago Tribune*, December 9, 1956, N5; and Jean Bond, "Zoning Clash Is Predicted in Deerfield," *Chicago Tribune*, October 20, 1960, N2.

4. The latter passed after speculation in canals in the 1830s and railroads in the 1870s sparked massive debt crises. See Tony A. Freyer, "Legal innovation and market capitalism, 1790–1920," in *The Cambridge History of Law in America*, ed. Michael Grossberg and Christopher Tomlins (New York: Cambridge University Press, 2008), 449–82.

5. Isaac Martin, *The Permanent Tax Revolt: How the Property Tax Transformed American Politics* (Stanford, CA: Stanford University Press, 2008), 6–7.

6. See Ethan Hutt, *Certain Standards: How Efforts to Establish and Enforce Minimum Education Standards Transformed American Schooling, 1870–1980* (Chicago: University of Chicago Press, forthcoming).

7. Ellwood P. Cubberley, *School Funds and Their Apportionment* (New York: Teachers College, 1905), 17, 25.

8. "School Funding Chart," League of Wisconsin Municipalities, Ephemera Collection (prints), WHS.

9. George D. Strayer and Robert M. Haig, *The Financing of Education in the State of New York*, (New York: MacMillan, 1923); Paul R. Mort. *State Support for Public Schools* (New York: Teachers College Press, 1926); Tracy Steffes, "Redefining State Responsibility in Education," in *School, Society, and State: A New Education to Govern America* (Chicago: University of Chicago Press, 2012), 83–118.

10. C. S. Benson, *The Cheerful Prospect: A Statement on the Future of Public Education* (Boston: Houghton-Mifflin, 1965), 51.

11. Rachel Tompkins, "Coping with Sparsity: A Review of Rural School Finance," in *Education in Rural America*, *Education in Rural America: A Reassessment of Conventional Wisdom*, ed. Jonathan Sher (Boulder, CO: Westview Press, 1977), 125–58, esp. 128.

12. Tompkins, "Coping with Sparsity," in Sher, *Education in Rural America*, 145; *Rutland Reorganization Study Criteria as Applied to Vermont* (Montpelier: Vermont Department of Education, 1973); "School's Out for Good in District 34: Rural Consolidation Continues," *Nebraska's New Land Review* 1, no. 3 (Summer 1975): 10.

13. The action attempted to complete a previous effort at statewide district consolidation, passed in 1959, which had stalled in court. "Assembly Passes Unruh School Bill," *Oakland Tribune*, April 23, 1964, 10E.

14. "Doubts Unruh School District Bill Will Pass," *San Mateo (CA) Times*, March 13, 1964, 3; Jerry Rankin, "Unruh School Reform Bill Sent to Governor," *Long Beach (CA) Independent*, May 21 1964, 1.

15. Robert Bendiner, *The Politics of Schools: A Crisis in Self-Government* (New York: Harper & Row, 1969), 197–98; "Rafferty Assails Unruh School Plan," *Oakland Tribune*, March 4, 1964, E9.

16. Robert Logormarsino, "The Unruh School Bill," *The Oxnard (CA) Press-Courier*, June 22, 1964, 8.

17. Arthur E. Wise, *Rich Schools, Poor Schools: The Promise of Equal Educational Opportunity* (Chicago: University of Chicago Press, 1968), 158.

18. Serrano v. Priest, 5 Cal. 3d 584 (1971).

19. The primary basis of this finding was Harper v. Virginia State Board of Elections 383 U.S. 663 (1966), a U.S. Supreme Court case invalidating poll taxes as an infringement of democratic rights.

20. The city's Baldwin Park district spent $577 with a $3,706 per pupil valuation, compared to $1,231 with $50,885 per pupil valuation in Beverly Hills.

21. Serrano v. Priest, 5 Cal. 3d 584 (1971).

22. John E. Coons, William H. Clune III, and Stephen D. Sugarman, *Private Wealth and Public Education* (Cambridge, MA: Harvard University Press, 1970), 33–35.

23. Ibid.

24. Rae Files Still, *The Gilmer-Aikin Bills: A Study in the Legislative Process* (Austin, TX: Steck Publishing, 1950).

25. *To Make Texas a National Leader in Education: The Challenge and the Chance* (Austin, TX: Governor's Committee on Public Education, 1968), 22, 29, 63.

26. Ibid., 23, 65.

27. See, for example, Karen Yates, "Residents Enthusiastic about School Proposals," *Denton Record-Chronicle*, February 16, 1975, 2; and Bill Gould, "Tye School May Combine With Abilene," *Abilene Reporter-News*, March 20, 1973, 1.

28. Texas had formally adopted tuition-based transfers in 1944. Terry Neal Bishop, *Small Schools: A History of the Texas Small Schools Association and the Texas Small Schools Project* (Austin: University of Texas Press, 1970), 40; "Statewide committee represents rural landowners, dwellers," *Seguin Gazette*, February 13, 1969, 11; H. M. Cherry, "State School Consolidation Side-Tracked, Says Speaker," *Victoria Advocate*, March 14, 1969, 7A.

29. United States v. State of Texas, 342 F.Supp. 24 (E.D., TX, 1971). This ruling drew both from Hobson v. Hansen (1967), which linked ability grouping and funding disparities to racial segregation in the Washington, DC schools, and Green v. New Kent County 391 U.S. 430 (1968), which struck down "freedom of choice" plans that perpetuated segregation in rural Virginia.

30. Paul Sracic, *San Antonio v. Rodriguez and the Pursuit of Equal Education: The Debate Over Discrimination and School Funding* (Lawrence: University Press of Kansas, 2006), 45–46.

31. The San Antonio district itself, released as a plaintiff, actually encouraged the court to find in favor of Rodriguez, confident that it too would benefit from the redistribution of property taxes. Don Politico, "Educational 'Wolf' at Area's Door," *San Antonio Light*, October 31, 1971, 12C; San Antonio Independent School District, "Brief for Amicus Curiae," no. 71-1332, August 24, 1972.

32. Wilson McKinney, "Moment of Truth Comes for School Equalization Suit," *San Antonio Express*, December 10, 1971, 1A; James E. Ryan, *Five Miles Away, A World Apart: One City, Two Schools, and the Story of Educational Opportunity in Modern America* (New York: Oxford University Press, 2010).

33. Sracic, *San Antonio*, 65–67; see also, 92–93, 96.

34. San Antonio Independent School District v. Rodriguez, 411 U.S. 1 (1973), note 38.

35. At this point one should note that legacies of rural school transportation served markedly different purposes in conservative arguments for local control during the 1970s. In *Rodriguez*, voluntary transfers represented a means of improving educational opportunity while preserving local governance and taxation, whereas a year later, in *Milliken*, forced busing was conflated with rural consolidation for the same dissolution of district boundaries. These were not entirely contradictory positions, but both made selective use of rural practices for the benefit of suburban autonomy. Sracic, *San Antonio*, 69–70.

36. *Rodriguez*, 411 U.S. at p. 54.

37. The court ordered the California legislature to institute tighter limits on wealthy districts' expenditures, and defined as legally suspect any interdistrict spending variations greater than one hundred dollars per pupil. Yet significant differences in funding persist, largely because wealthy districts are still allowed to keep excess tax revenue.

38. On the legacy of *Rodriguez*, see Joshua M. Dunn and Martin R. West, *From Schoolhouse to Courthouse: The Judiciary's Role in American Education* (Washington, DC: Brookings Institution Press, 2009), 97–101.

39. Tompkins, "Coping with Sparsity," in Sher, *Education in Rural America*, 133–34.

40. Christine Pawley, *Reading Places: Literacy, Democracy, and the Public Library in Cold War America* (Amherst: University of Massachusetts Press, 2010), 206, 237–40. For reactions to earlier consolidation attempts in Door County, see letters and newspaper clippings in box 3, folder 8, CESA No. 9 Records, WHS.

41. Sturgeon Bay Town Board to Angus Rothwell, June 18 1964, box 6, folder 4, CESA No. 9 Records, WHS.

42. For the interesting story of Washington Island education, see Sylvia Nelson and Goodwin Berquist, *Island Schools Then and Now* (Washington Island, WI: Jackson Harbor Press, 1998).

43. Sturgeon Bay Town Board to Angus Rothwell, June 18, 1964, box 6, folder 4, CESA No. 9 Records, WHS.

44. "Meeting of the Door County School Committee," June 30, 1964; "School Meeting at Gibraltar High School," March 15, 1965; Vote Tally, April 8, 1965, all in box 6, folder 4, CESA No. 9 Records, WHS.

45. For the committee's full records, see Series 2187, Wisconsin Governor's Task Force on Educational Financing and Property Tax Reform Records, WHS.

46. Rachel B. Tompkins, "Coping With Sparsity," in Sher, *Education in Rural America*, 134–36; Norman Gill to Archie Buchmiller, March 14, 1972, box 1, folder 6, Wisconsin Governor's Task Force, WHS; Nelson and Berquist, *Island Schools Then and Now*, 42.

47. Other towns included Twin Lakes, Eagle River, and Princeton, Wisconsin, all of which (not coincidentally) appear in subsequent chapters. Letter to Norman Gill, box 1, folder 7, Wisconsin Governor's Task Force, WHS.

48. "Green Lake Group to Fight School Negative Aid," *Oshkosh Daily Northwestern*, March 17, 1976, 1, box 9, folder 6, Delmar DeLong Papers, WHS.

49. Mrs. Helen Nencka to Grederick C. Schroeder, February 13, 1975, box 1, folder 21, George Klicka Papers, WHS.

50. John Wyngaard, " 'Home Rule' for Towns Long Procedure," *Appleton Post-Crescent*, March 19, 1974, 3; "Laws of 1975" in *Wisconsin Session Laws* (Madison, WI: Secretary of State, 1976), 51–314.

51. Glenn Buse was from the Nicolet Union High School District, comprising neighborhoods of West Allis, Wisconsin, a suburb of Milwaukee.

52. The basis of that finding was that negative aids, collected locally, comprised a local tax, and that although education was clearly a state prerogative, local taxes had to be expended on local services alone. Buse v. Smith, 247 N.W.2d 141 (1976), 24–25, 28–30. Critics have since questioned the basis of the Buse decision. Jack Stark, in a summary of Wisconsin's tax code, notes that "most of the cases that the court cited in its opinion were not about the uniformity clause, and in one that did relate to the clause an earlier court had found a similar law to be constitutional." He also points out that the court ignored precedents that held that the uniformity clause did not apply to the use of property tax revenue, and others that held that "in determining whether or not there is uniformity, the relevant geographical area is the unit of government that imposed the tax." Jack Stark, *A History of Property Tax and Property Tax Relief in Wisconsin* (Madison: Wisconsin Blue Book, 1992).

53. See "Case Comments: The Constitutional Restriction on School Finance Reform: *Buse v. Smith*," *Harvard Law Review*, (Cambridge, MA: Harvard University, 1976), 1528–39; Richard Briefault, "The Local School District in American Law," in *Besieged: School Boards and the Future of Education Politics*, ed. William Howell (Washington, DC: Brookings Institution, 2005), 24–55, esp. 49; and Linda Wilkins Rickman, "School Finance Reform Litigation: A Historical Review," *Peabody Journal of Education* 58, no. 4 (July 1981): 220–22.

54. "'Small Town' Deerfield Kisses and Tills," *Chicago Tribune*, May 9, 1982, N B1C; Ron Grossman, "'Exurbia: Harvard, Chicago's 'Last Suburb' Outside of the Urban Sprawl," *Chicago Tribune*, May 25, 1985, B1; Bruce R. Dold and Barbara Mahany, "Suburbanites Raise Voice Against Status Quo," *Chicago Tribune*, November 6, 1985, A3; George Papajohn, "Cities/Suburbs: Voters Get Chance to Be Advisers," *Chicago Tribune*, October 22, 1986, A8.

55. Allan D. Walker, "Consolidation Reform in Illinois," in *The Educational Reform Movement of the 1980s*, ed. Joseph Murphy (Berkeley, CA: McCutchan, 1990), 325–46, esp. 334–35. For examples of suburban opposition, see Tom Stites, "Foes Fight District Consolidation Plan," *Chicago Tribune*, June 28, 1984, section 2, 1; and Jean Latz Griffin, "Opposition to School Consolidation Gains among Lawmakers," *Chicago Tribune*, January 17, 1986, A2.

56. Jean Latz Griffin, "Casualties Reported on School Reform Front: No Change in Aid Rules on Horizon," *Chicago Tribune*, June 26, 1985, A1; Tim Franklin, "Stevenson Says He's Cool to School Consolidation," *Chicago Tribune*, January 9, 1986, A4; Walker, "Consolidation Reform in Illinois," in *The Educational Reform Movement of the 1980s*, 336–37.

57. Cronin v. Lindberg, 66 Ill.2d 47, 360 N.E.2d 360, (1976). The state's broadest ruling against equal financing came shortly after the consolidation controversy, in Committee for Educational Rights v. Edgar, 641 N.E.2d 602 (1994).

6. TAX REVOLTS

1. Albert Hirschman, who first proposed these categories, specifically used schools as a working example of "voice" and "exit." Albert Hirschman, *Exit, Voice, and Loyalty: Responses to Decline in Firms, Organizations, and States* (Cambridge, MA: Harvard University Press, 1970). David Labaree applies them to contemporary educational policy in David Labaree, "No Exit: Public Education as an Inescapably Public Good," in *Reconstructing the Common Good in Education: Coping with Intractable American Dilemmas*, ed. Larry Cuban and Dorothy Shipps (Stanford, CA: Stanford University Press, 2000), 110–29.

2. Thomas A. Downes, "An Examination of the Structure of Governance in California's School Districts before and after Proposition 13," *Public Choice* 86, no. 3/4 (1996): 286.

3. Becky Nicolaides, *My Blue Heaven: Life and Politics in the Working-Class Suburbs of Los Angeles, 1920–1965* (Chicago: Chicago University Press, 2002), 297–98, 302.

4. For other examples of racist resistance to school funding, see Jeffrey Mirel, "There Is Enough Blame for Everyone to Share," in *The Rise and Fall of An Urban School System: Detroit, 1907–1981* (Ann Arbor: University of Michigan, 1999), 293–398; and Joseph Crespino, "The Irony of School Desegregation," in *In Search of Another Country: Mississippi and the Conservative Counterrevolution* (Princeton, NJ: Princeton University Press, 2007), 173–204. Another description of events in California is Thomas Byrne Edsall and Mary D. Edsall, *Chain Reaction: The Impact of Race, Rights, and Taxes on American Politics* (New York: W. W. Norton, 1991), 130–31.

5. Nicolaides, *My Blue Heaven*, 298.

6. Fischel's argument speaks to a broader theoretical dispute in political science, between the Leviathan model, which characterizes government bureaucracy as self-serving and unresponsive to voters, and the median-voter model, which contends that it is responsive to the interests of the average voter. The latter median-voter model derives from rational choice theory, which (like Fischel) tries to reveal voter or consumer bias through an analysis of actual decisions rather than preference claims.

7. Robert O. Self, *American Babylon: Race and the Struggle for Postwar Oakland* (Princeton, NJ: Princeton University Press, 2003), 320.

8. Isaac Martin, "Does School Finance Litigation Cause Taxpayer Revolt? Serrano and Proposition 13," *Law & Society Review* 40, no. 3 (September 2006): 530.

9. Isaac Martin, *The Permanent Tax Revolt: How the Property Tax Transformed American Politics* (Stanford, CA: Stanford University Press, 2008), 5–7, 13, 38–41. On California reapportionment, see Stephen P. Teale and Don A. Allen, *One Man-One Vote and Senate Reapportionment, 1964–1966* (Berkeley: University of California, 1980).

10. Alvin Rabushka and Pauline Ryan, *The Tax Revolt* (Stanford, CA: Hoover Institution, 1982), 17, 22.

11. The following discussion focuses on school spending rather than assessment reform, but Martin's analysis of the latter comes to many of the same conclusions about conflict and compromise between rural and suburban interests. Because best-use formulas forced assessors to price farms in fringe areas as if they had already been subdivided, he observes, farmers were effectively penalized for suburban speculation and sprawl until the passage of "right to farm" exemptions and other types of preferential zoning during the mid-1970s. In regions of Appalachia, where much of the land was tax-exempt forest preserve, protesters likewise complained that rising assessments amounted to "a subsidy paid by poor rural people to affluent urbanites who used the forests for recreation." Protests also broke out in rural Ohio, New York, Tennessee, Michigan, and Pennsylvania as disempowered voters struggled to find new means to control rising property taxes and, to some degree, to find someone to blame for them. Martin, *Permanent Tax Revolt*, 13, 17, 54–56.

12. Thomas Goebel, *A Government by the People: Direct Democracy in America, 1890–1940* (Chapel Hill: University of North Carolina Press, 2002), 163–71, 186–91.

13. For an example of turn-of-the-century campaigns against corporate tax evasion, see the discussion of Chicago in Dorothy Shipps, "Shaping the Modern System: Vocationalism, Managerialism, and Efficiency," in *School Reform, Corporate Style: Chicago, 1880–2000* (Lawrence: University Press of Kansas, 2006), 16–49.

14. James S. Catterall and Emily Brizendine, "Proposition 13: Effects on High School Curricula, 1978–1983," *American Journal of Education* 93, no. 3 (May 1985): 331.

15. The earlier initiative in 1968 used a similar logic, pushing for county-wide equalization of school spending. Rabushka and Ryan, *Tax Revolt*, 112–16, 119. Martin notes that Jarvis rarely spoke about schools unless he had to. The topic did not come up even once in his memoir about the Proposition 13 campaign. Martin, "Does School Finance Litigation Cause Taxpayer Revolt," 531.

16. In 1971, a record sixty districts rejected increases in school taxes, thirty of which went bankrupt and required state loans to operate. Similar numbers continued thereafter. Joel S. Berke, *Answers to Inequity: An Analysis of the New School Finance* (Berkeley, CA: McCutchan Publishing, 1974), 9.

17. Gary Hoban, "The Untold Golden State Story: Aftermath of Proposition 13," *Phi Delta Kappan* 61, no. 1 (September 1979): 18–21.

18. Letter to the editor, *The Mountain Democrat (Placerville, CA)*, May 5, 1978, A-3; Elaine Snider, letter to the editor, *The Mountain Democrat (Placerville, CA)*, May 24, 1978, A-12.

19. Berke, *Answers to Inequity*, 9–10.

20. *Historical Statistics of the United States: Earliest Times to Present,* Vol. 2 (New York: Cambridge University Press, 2006), 480–84; LeRoy Peterson and Jean M. Flanigan, *Financing the Public Schools, 1960–1970* (Washington, DC: National Education Association, 1963), 12, 18–19, 22, 58.

21. Peterson and Flanigan, *Financing the Public Schools*, 57. See also *Financing Schools and Property Tax Relief: A State Responsibility* (Washington, DC: Advisory Commission on Intergovernmental Relations, 1973), 21–23.

22. Gordon Adams, *The Iron Triangle: The Politics of Defense Contracting* (New York: Council on Economic Priorities, 1981).

23. "Better Schools Question Leaves Taxing to Counties," *Charleston Gazette*, October 29, 1958, 15.

24. Rabushka and Ryan, *The Tax Revolt*, 188.

25. Timothy Weaver, "Class Conflict in Rural Education: A Case Study of Preston County, West Virginia," in *Education in Rural America: A Reassessment of Conventional Wisdom*, ed. Jonathan Sher (Boulder, CO: Westview Press, 1977), 159–204, esp. 162–63; Timothy Weaver, "Community Schools versus Consolidation for the 1980s," box 34, folder 2, PURE Records, ISU.

26. Lawrence Hennigh, "The Good Life and the Tax Revolt," *Rural Sociology* 43, no. 2 (1978): 178.

27. "South Umpqua Experimental Schools Project: The Basic Four Year Plan" (Washington, DC: National Institute of Education, 1973), 1–3. For a detailed discussion of property tax problems in another fast-growing Oregon town, see Bruce Weber and Robert Howell, *Coping With Rapid Growth in Rural Communities* (Boulder, CO: Westview Press, 1982), 109–10, 118–20.

28. Hennigh, "The Good Life," 182–83, 187–89.

29. Berke, *Answers to Inequity*, 27.

30. Rabushka and Ryan, *The Tax Revolt*, 188; Fred Thompson and Mark T. Green, "Vox Populi? Oregon Tax and Expenditure Limitation Initiatives," *Public Budgeting and Finance* 24, no. 4 (Winter 2004): 74–75; Alvin D. Sokolow, "The Changing Property Tax and State-Local Relations," *Publius* 28, no. 1 (Winter 1998): 165–87.

31. Passage of the law required an interesting evasion of the uniformity clause: The Wisconsin Supreme Court ruled that the measure was a matter of income rather than property and that it was a welfare program rather than a tax program per se. Jack Stark, *A History of Property Tax and Property Tax Relief in Wisconsin* (Madison: Wisconsin Blue Book, 1992), 36.

32. Carl W. Thompson, *Property Tax: Revolt, Reform, Relief* (Madison, WI: Government Printing Office, 1976), Pamphlet Collection, WHS.

33. George's single-tax program enjoyed bursts of popularity during most economic recessions, and was undergoing another reappraisal during the late 1960s. See Steven B. Cord, *Henry George: Dreamer or Realist?* (Philadelphia: University of Pennsylvania Press, 1965); Fred C. White, "State-Financed Property Tax Relief," *American Journal of Agricultural Economics* 61, no. 3 (August 1979): 409–19; and Jurgen G. Backhaus, "Henry George's Ingenious Tax: A Contemporary Restatement," *American Journal of Economics and Sociology* 56, no. 4 (October 1997): 453–74.

34. A short history of the WPOL is available online at http://www.cgocouncil.org /registry.php?cl=l&id=44.

35. A study found that lowering property taxes in small cities and rural areas would *not* result in capital gains for homeowners although it might for farmers. Melville McMillan and Richard Carlson, "The Effects of Property Taxes and Local Public Services

upon Residential Property Values in Small Wisconsin Cities," *American Journal of Agricultural Economics* 59, no. 1 (February 1977): 81–87.

36. Marian Piper, letter to the editor, June 10, 1972, box 1, folder 7, Wisconsin Governor's Task Force; "Newsletter," August–September–October, box 1, folder 1, Wisconsin Property Owners League (WPOL) Records, all located at WHS.

37. The group was especially strong in the southwest corner of the state and in the Fox River valley, which were also the areas of strongest opposition to school consolidation during the 1950s. Richard W. Jaeger, "Tax on Land Only Urged for Relief," *Wisconsin State Journal*, August 25, 1972, section 4, 1.

38. "CESA Coordinator Awaits Petition for School Change," *Appleton Post-Crescent*, November 11, 1972, B-1; "New London Board to Hire Attorney in District Issue," *Appleton Post-Crescent*, June 3, 1975, B-2.

39. "Town of Fox Lake Votes to Withhold Tax Payments from School District," *Fond du Lac Reporter*, February 7, 1972, 4.

40. Mrs. Peter J. Ruys to Mrs. Ruth Doyle, December 2, 1972, box 1, folder 9, Wisconsin Governor's Task Force, WHS.

41. Richard H. Davis to Richard Wisnewski, January 10, 1972, box 1, folder 5; Mrs. Ruth P. Doyle to Senator Raymond Heinzen, April 6, 1972, box 1, folder 6, both in Wisconsin Governor's Task Force, WHS.

42. Rachel B. Tompkins, "Coping with Sparsity," in Sher, *Education in Rural America*, 134–36; Thompson, "Property Tax: Revolt, Reform, Relief."

43. Tax and Expenditure Limitation, or TEL, was a common legislative strategy during the 1970s. For similar initiatives elsewhere, see Thompson and Green, "Vox Populi," 73–87; Edward Hill, *A Review of Tax Expenditure Limitations and their Impact on State and Local Government in Ohio* (Cleveland, OH: Cleveland State University, 2006); and Steven Deller and Judith I. Stallmann, "Tax and Expenditure Limitation and Economic Growth," *Marquette Law Review* 90 (2007): 497–553.

44. Robert B. Hawkins, "State Tax and Spending Limits, 1978," *Publius* 9, no. 1 (Winter 1979): 29.

45. Joseph E. Ryan to Kenneth Merkel, June 8, 1971, box 1, folder 48, Merkel Papers, WHS.

46. Wisconsin Education Association Council, "A Penny Saved is a Student Burned," box 1, folder 9, Wisconsin Governor Task Force, WHS. Similar arguments were made in other states that remained primarily reliant on property taxes for school funds. See Joyce Losure, "An Investigation of the Controlled Budget on Small Iowa School Districts," box 21, folder 34, PURE Records; and James Jess, "Revitalizing Rural Education and Small Schools in Iowa," box 34, folder 4, PURE Records, ISU.

47. These issues went largely unnoticed during Wisconsin's contentious 2011–12 debate over the collective bargaining rights of public workers, but they were integral to it. Governor Scott Walker justified the loss of collective bargaining as a means of flexibility for local governments, yet increasing state aid or loosening property tax rates, which also would have given much needed flexibility to rural districts, was never proposed.

48. Friedman's other categories included "natural monopolies," which resulted from bottlenecks or certain types of scarcity, leaving markets unable to sustain effective competition; "neighborhood effects," in which individuals' choices impinged on those of their neighbors and could not be remunerated, likewise impeding a fair exchange of services; and instances in which "paternalistic concern for children and other irresponsible individuals" outweighed the benefits of individual choice.

49. Milton Friedman, "The Role of Government in Education," in *Economics and the Public Interest*, ed. Robert A. Solo (New Brunswick, NJ: Rutgers University Press, 1955),

124–27. For more on Friedman's attempts to influence social reform, see Angus Burgin, "The Invention of Milton Friedman," in *The Great Persuasion: Reinventing Free Markets Since the Depression* (Cambridge, MA: Harvard University Press, 2012), 152–85.

50. Friedman, "Role of Government in Education," 129.

51. David K. Cohen and Eleanor Farrar, "Power to the Parents? The Story of Educational Vouchers," *The Public Interest* 48 (Summer 1977): 72–97.

52. By the mid-1960s the Supreme Court had struck down the use of vouchers to support "segregation academies" in the South—and Friedman himself denounced the practice—but it is worth noting that while cities could manipulate housing patterns and attendance zones, voters in the rural South saw vouchers as the only way to provide white parents with the "choice" of all-white schools. In a manner of speaking, they hoped that vouchers would *overcome* the dearth of schools. Friedman, "Role of the Government in Education," 130.

53. "GOP Candidate Suggests School Voucher Plan," *Stevens Point Daily Journal*, August 31, 1970, 19; Oscar B. Johansen, *Private Schools for All* (Roselle Park, NJ: Committee of One, 1959); Frank Meinen to William Smeeth, April 18, 1963, box 6, folder 20, Meinen Papers, WHS; "School Initiative," *Orange County Register*, April 23, 1978, G7.

54. Harold Grinnell, "Patterns of Expenditure among Rural New Hampshire School Districts," *Station Bulletin 491, Agricultural Experiment Station* (Durham: University of New Hampshire, 1967), 4–7, 16, 21, 29; "Statement of Aims, Public Schools Association," box 937, folder 5, NEA Archives, GWU.

55. Charles Stannard, *Problems of Project Direction and Coordination: North Country Supervisory Union, New Hampshire* (Cambridge, MA: ABT Associates, 1979), 53–54, 59, 83.

56. A good example was Salem, New Hampshire, which was having labor troubles at the same time. "New Supervisory School Union 57 Opens Office in Woodbury School," *Nashua Telegraph*, July 6, 1976, 6; "Board Members Question Hiring of Secretaries," *Nashua Telegraph*, July 16, 1976, 6.

57. "GOP Candidate Suggests School Voucher Plan," *Stevens Point Daily Journal*, August 31, 1971, 19.

58. Jim Carl, "Free Marketeers, Policy Wonks, and Yankee Democracy: School Vouchers in New Hampshire, 1973–1976," *Harvard Educational Review* 78, no. 4 (Winter 2008): 597; and Jim Carl, *Freedom of Choice: Vouchers in American Education* (New York: Praeger, 2011), 70.

59. Robert R. Mayer, *Social Science and Institutional Change* (New Brunswick, NJ: Transaction Books, 1982), 133.

60. Ibid.

61. Cohen and Farrar, "Power to the Parents," 76–78; *Education Vouchers: A Report on Financing Elementary Education by Grants to Parents* (Washington, DC: Center for the Study of Public Policy, 1970).

62. Cohen and Farrar, "Power to the Parents," 78–79; Carl, "Free Marketeers," 591.

63. Milwaukee and Cleveland have instituted the only large-scale voucher programs. South Dakota has experimented with statewide open enrollment.

64. One could say that New Hampshire remained more consistent in its commitment to local control. It was one of the only states that did not impose spending limits on its schools, and it has suffered through inordinately high property tax rates as a result.

65. Tompkins, "Coping With Sparsity," in Sher, *Education in Rural America*, 131.

66. Catterall and Brizendine, "Effects on High School Curricula," 332, 348; Rabushka and Ryan, *Tax Revolt*, 63–64.

67. William A. Fischel, "Did Serrano Cause Proposition 13," *National Tax Journal* 42, no. 4 (December 1989): 465–73, esp. 467.

68. Downes, "An Examination of the Structure of Governance," 301. See also, Perry Shapiro and Jon Sonstelie, "Representative Voter or Bureaucratic Manipulation: An Examination of Public Finances in California Before and After Proposition 13," *Public Choice* 39, no. 1 (1982): 113–42.

69. Margaret Weston, "Basic Aid School Districts," *Public Policy Institute of California* (September 2013): 14.

70. Jerry McCaffery and John H. Bowman, "Participatory Democracy and Budgeting: The Effects of Proposition 13," *Public Administration Review* 38, no. 6 (November/December 1978): 535.

71. See Shelly Tillery, "The Small School Districts' Association: A Historical Review," at the organization's website http://www.ssda.org/vnews/display.v/SEC/About%20SSDA| History.

7. THE BATTLE OF IDEAS

1. Mitchell Quelhurst, "Manchester's School Dispute," *Bennington Banner*, December 1, 1961, 4; "Vermont and County Both Seen Growing," *Bennington Banner*, July 28, 1976, 18. For the effects of exurban growth on education elsewhere in Vermont, see Winifred Margaret McCarthy, "The Migration of Cosmopolites to Rural Vermont" (PhD diss., New School for Social Research, 1986), 239; and "Couple Denies Failure to Obey State's Compulsory School Law," *Burlington Free Press,* January 31, 1974, 20.

2. Lawrence E. Harrington, "Problems of At-Large Voting," June 15, 1976, 4; Ray Murray, "Millstone Muckrakers," September 7, 1976, 4; "In Union, Strength," July 18, 1961, 4; Frederic O. Sargent, "Are Towns Obsolete?," November 3, 1966, 9; "MAU Dissolution Is the Topic Wednesday," August 9, 1976, 18; "Question of Seventh Graders Will Be on Sept. 8 Warning," August 10, 1976, 6; Rob Woolmington, "School-District Secession Moves Spread," December 1, 1976, 20; all in the *Bennington Banner.*

3. "The Good Men Do . . . ," September 18, 1976, 4; "Mt. Anthony's Too Big, Says Pelkie, Who Suggests District Be Dissolved," July 22, 1976, 1; "Eugene Smith Named MAU Principal," August 31, 1976, 1; "New Panel Named to Investigate 'Irregularities' in MAU Hiring," September 14, 1976, 1; "Principal Smith Resigns at MAU," March 16, 1977, 1; all in the *Bennington Banner.*

4. Rob Woolmington, "Threats and Harassments," *Bennington Banner,* July 16, 1976, 1, 16.

5. Nicolle Woodward, "Letter to the Editor," April 11, 1974, 5; Marie Legacy Tonihall, "Moral Atmosphere at MAU," June 4, 1976, 5; Rob Woolmington, "Curriculum Queries Go Unanswered," June 22, 1976, 1, 16; all in the *Bennington Banner.*

6. See Eli M. Oboler, *Censorship and Education* (New York: H. W. Wilson, 1981).

7. Stephen Provasnik, "Judicial Activism and the Origins of Parental Choice: The Court's Role in the Institutionalization of Compulsory Education in the United States," *History of Education Quarterly* 46, no. 3 (Fall, 2006): 312–13, 328, 344–46; Newton Edwards, *The Courts and the Public Schools: The Legal Basis of School Organization and Administration*, 3rd ed. (Chicago: University of Chicago Press, 1971), 592–97. On exceptions to the unitary view of curricular power, see State v. Webber, 8 N.E. 708 (Ind, 1886); Kidder v. Chellis, 59 N.H. 473 (NH 1879); Samuel Benedict Memorial School et al. v. Bradford, 36 SE 920 (GA, 1900). As Ethan Hutt has observed, the embrace of "compulsory education" also prompted courts to simplify their understanding of what constituted education at all. Whereas nineteenth-century courts had weighed educational outcomes, early twentieth-century courts "opted for formalistic, bright line tests of whether parents had complied with compulsory education laws," equating schools' facilities, term lengths, and other bureaucratic requirements with education. Ethan Hutt, "Formalism Over Function:

Compulsion, Courts, and the Rise of Educational Formalism in America, 1870–1930," *Teachers College Record* 114, no. 1 (January 2012): 1–27.

8. For a general discussion of curricular reform during the Progressive Era, see Herbert Kliebard, *The Struggle for the American Curriculum, 1893–1958* (New York: Routledge-Falmer, 2004).

9. Unfortunately, the new methods did not always hold student interest; they soon devolved into the dull "Dick and Jane" stories of the 1950s. See Arthur W. Foshay, "Textbooks and Curriculum during the Progressive Era: 1930–1950," in *Textbooks and Schooling in the United States*, ed. David L. Elliott and Arthur Woodward (Chicago: University of Chicago Press, 1990), 23–41, esp. 25; and Jeanne S. Chall, *Learning to Read: The Great Debate* (New York: McGraw Hill, 1983).

10. In the 1930s these issues were pointedly addressed by left-wing, "social reconstructionist" critics like George Counts, and reached their widest audience with the textbooks of Counts's colleague, Harold Rugg. See Kliebard, *Struggle for the American Curriculum*, 151–74. On conservative condemnations of Rugg's work, see *Whose America? Culture Wars in the Public Schools* (Cambridge, MA: Harvard University Press, 2002), 61–80; and Ronald Evans, *The Social Studies Wars: What Should We Teach the Children?* (New York: Teachers College Press, 2004), 39–83.

11. For the relationship between the two segments at midcentury, see relevant portions of Jonathan M. Schoenwald, *A Time for Choosing: The Rise of Modern American Conservatism* (New York: Oxford University Press, 2001); Rick Perlstein, *Before the Storm: Barry Goldwater and the Unmaking of American Consensus* (New York: Nation Books, 2009); and George Nash, *The Conservative Intellectual Movement in America Since 1945* (Wilmington, DE: International Scholastic Institute, 2008).

12. There were earlier curricular debates as well, but they usually dealt with religious sectarianism or the language of instruction. On the Scopes trial, see Adam Laats, *Fundamentalism and Education in the Scopes Era: God, Darwin, and the Roots of America's Culture Wars* (New York: Palgrave Macmillan, 2010); Charles A. Israel, *Before Scopes: Evangelicalism, Education, and Evolution in Tennessee, 1870–1925* (Athens: University of Georgia Press, 2004); Edward J. Larson, *Summer for the Gods: The Scopes Trial and America's Continuing Debate over Science and Religion* (Cambridge, MA: Harvard University Press, 1997); and Jeffrey P. Moran, *American Genesis: The Antievolution Controversies from Scopes to Creation Science* (New York: Oxford University Press, 2012). On science education reform after Sputnik, see John Rudolph, *Scientists in the Classroom: The Cold War Reconstruction of American Science Education* (New York: Palgrave, 2002). On the MACOS dispute, see Ronald W. Evans, *The Hope for American School Reform: The Cold War Pursuit of Inquiry Learning in Social Studies* (New York: Palgrave Macmillan, 2011), 153–66; and Peter B. Dow, *Schoolhouse Politics: Lessons from the Sputnik Era* (Cambridge, MA: Harvard University Press, 1991). On sex education, see Natalia Mehlman, "Sex Ed . . . and the Reds?: Reconsidering the Anaheim Battle over Sex Education, 1962–1969," *History of Education Quarterly* 47, no. 2 (May 2007): 203–32.

13. Bethany Moreton finds that by the 1970s, at least twenty-one states mandated instruction in free-market economics "that amounted to little more than industry propaganda." Bethany Moreton, *To Serve God and Wal-Mart: The Making of Christian Free Enterprise* (Cambridge, MA: Harvard University Press, 2009), 146. More examples can be found in Michelle Ann Abate, *Raising Your Kids Right: Children's Literature and American Political Conservatism* (New Brunswick, NJ: Rutgers University Press, 2011).

14. David Hulburd, *This Happened in Pasadena* (New York: Macmillan, 1951), 60–61, 86–90. For a right-wing interpretation of the Pasadena dispute, see Mary L. Allen, *Education or Indoctrination* (Caldwell, ID: Caxton Printers, 1955).

15. For a full list of incidents that Zoll inspired, see David L. Marden, "The Cold War and American Education," (PhD diss., University of Kansas, 1975), 93–112. A broader discussion of McCarthyism's effects on schools can be found in Ellen Schrecker, *Many Are the Crimes: McCarthyism in America* (Princeton, NJ: Princeton University Press, 1998); Stuart J. Foster, *Red Alert!: Educators Confront the Red Scare in American Public Schools, 1947–1954* (New York: Peter Lang, 2000); and Andrew Hartman, *Education and the Cold War: The Battle for the American School* (New York: Palgrave Macmillan, 2008).

16. Hartman, *Education and the Cold War*, 91–116.

17. Bernard Iddings Bell, *Crisis in Education: A Challenge to American Complacency* (New York: Whittlesey House, 1949); William F. Buckley Jr., *God and Man at Yale: The Superstitions of Academic Freedom* (Chicago: Regnery Publishing, 1951); Arthur Bestor, *Educational Wastelands: The Retreat From Learning in Our Public Schools* (Urbana: University of Illinois Press, 1953); Rudolf Flesch, *Why Johnny Can't Read: And What You Can Do About It* (New York: Harper & Row, 1955).

18. CBE to the William Volker Fund, March 20, 1956, box 1, book 1, Mortimer Smith Papers, UI.

19. Mortimer Smith to Arthur Bestor, February 16, 1956, box 2, Smith Papers, UI.

20. Mortimer Smith to Vernon G. Linderman, March 20, 1962, box 51, folder L; Mrs. Bruce V. Reagan to Mortimer Smith, May 29, 1961, box 46, folder Ra-Rh; Mortimer Smith to Mrs. Bruce V. Reagan, May 31, 1961, box 46, folder Ra-Rh, all in Council for Basic Education (CBE) Records, UI.

21. Mortimer Smith to Ralph E. Ellsworth, January 8, 1962, box 50, folder E; Mortimer Smith to Mrs. Charles ("Tess") Koch, July 30, 1962, box 51, folder K, both in CBE Records, UI.

22. Phyllis Schlafly to CBE, January 28, 1957, box 9, folder S-Sch; Phyllis Schlafly to CBE, December 5, 1959, box 30, folder Sc, both in CBE Records, UI.

23. Margaret Jefferson to CBE, December 27, 1961, box 51, folder IJ; Mortimer Smith to Ralph E. Ellsworth, January 8, 1962, box 50, folder E, both in CBE Records, UI.

24. Perlstein, *Before the Storm*, 172. "Educator Says Delinquency Shows Failure of Life Adjustment Classes," *Decatur Herald*, Feburary 28, 1961, box 46, folder Ra-Rh, CBE Records, UI.

25. Henrietta "Tess" Koch to Samuel Withers, June 5, 1962; Henrietta "Tess" Koch to Mortimer Smith, September 5, 1962, both in box 51, folder K, CBE Records, UI.

26. "Teachers' Boycott," *Time*, August 17, 1962.

27. Harold L. Clapp to Allen Zoll, February 3, 1951, box 11, folder XYZ, CBE Records, UI.

28. James D. Koerner to H. W. Luhnow, March 12, 1959, box 28, folder Lu-Ly, CBE Records, UI; Mary Anne Raywid, *The Ax-Grinders: Critics of Our Public Schools* (New York: MacMillan, 1962), 118. Other Volker Fund beneficiaries included the University of Chicago's economics department and the Foundation for Economic Education, which donated free conservative textbooks to underfunded school districts. Perlstein, *Before the Storm*, 114.

29. George Weber, "How One Citizens' Group Helped Improve the Public Schools: The East Greenbush Story," *Council for Basic Education: Occasional Papers Number Six* (Washington, DC: CBE, 1964), 1–3, 11–14.

30. James Coleman, *Community Conflict* (Glencoe, IL: Free Press, 1957), 17. While not quite rural enough to qualify as an exurb, the upper-crust community of Scarsdale, New York—only ten miles south of the towns that Spectorsky studied—experienced a vitriolic censorship campaign in 1948, led by the same sort of business ideologues that launched actions elsewhere. Robert Shaplen, "Scarsdale's Battle of the Books: How One Community Dealt with 'Subversive Literature,'" *Commentary*, December 1950, 530–40.

31. Verne Kaub to James Purcell, June 26, 1963, box 3, folder 10; Verne Kaub, type-script, n.d., box 8, folder 4, both in ACCL Records, WHS.

32. Verne Kaub to Conservative Information Service, November 23, 1962; Verne Kaub to Active Citizens' Opinion Poll, October 22, 1962; Verne Kaub to Mrs. Wilson K. Barnes, December 4, 1961, box 7, folder 42, all in ACCL Records, WHS.

33. When a UW-Milwaukee professor disparaged the film "Make Mine Freedom" as propaganda in 1959, Kaub and Grede worked together to orchestrate his reprimand. Verne Kaub to Harry Bradley, June 10, 1959, box 2, folder 10, ACCL Records, WHS; Verne Kaub to William Grede, July 3, 1959; William Grede to Verne Kaub, August 11, 1959, both in box 1, folder 4, William Grede Papers, WHS; Perlstein, *Before the Storm*, 151–52; "Professor at UW-M in Probe," *Capital Times*, August 1, 1959, 1.

34. "We, the People Meeting," *Free Enterprise*, February 15, 1955, box 7, folder 42, ACCL Records, WHS. In Florida, another Kaub contact, William Douglass, formed Let Freedom Ring in 1962. That organization was a key player in the John Birch Society's attempt to take over the Sarasota school board. Daniel R. Campbell, "Right-Wing Extremists and the Sarasota Schools, 1960–1966," *Tampa Bay History* 6, no. 1 (1984): 17, 21–23.

35. Greg Saucerman, *Summer Enchantment: The History of Twin Lakes* (Twin Lakes, WI: Western Kenosha County Historical Society, 1994), 11–16, 101–6; "McGuffey Reader Divides Town in Clash Between Old and New" (AP) *Nashville Banner*, November 6, 1961, 1.

36. Saucerman, *Summer Enchantment*, 91–98; Joyce Beula, interview by the author, January 16, 2008.

37. David Behrendt, "School's 1879 Reader Causes Wide Uproar," *Milwaukee Journal*, October 15, 1961, 1; Joyce Beula, interview by the author, January 16, 2008.

38. Mrs. William B. Smeeth to Mortimer Smith, June 19, 1961, box 47, folder Sk-Sp, CBE Records. For an excellent study of the range of "progressive" educational practice at midcentury, especially between urban, suburban, and rural schools, see Arthur Zilversmit, *Changing Schools: Progressive Education Theory and Practice, 1930–1960* (Chicago: University of Chicago Press, 1993), 1–89.

39. William Smeeth interview by author, January 17, 2008.

40. Smeeth had first written to Mortimer Smith in 1954, when he invited him to speak at a PTA meeting in Illinois. Mortimer Smith to William Smeeth, October 13, 1954, box 2, correspondence A-Z, Smith Papers, UI. A significant minority of the Freedom School's students were from Milwaukee, supported by Grede, Robert Baird, and C. W. Andersen. William Smeeth to Mortimer Smith and Tom Bledsoe, March 11, 1961, CBE Records; William Grede to Richard Cornuelle, January 27, 1958, box 7, folders 7–8; Richard Cornuelle to William Grede, February 4, 1958, box 33, folder 2, both in Grede Papers, WHS; Donald Janson, "Conservatives at Freedom School to Prepare a New Federal Constitution," *New York Times*, June 13, 1965, 66.

41. William Smeeth, interview by the author, January 17, 2008. Coffee parties and declarations of principles were a mainstay of grassroots conservatism, as demonstrated by Michelle Nickerson, "Moral Mothers and Goldwater Girls," in *The Conservative Sixties*, ed. David Farber and Jeff Roche (New York: Peter Lang, 2003), 51–62, esp. 51.

42. "Board Member Opposed McGuffey; Testifies He Was Told to 'Shut Up,'" *Racine Journal*, March 29, 1962; Behrendt, "School's 1879 Reader Causes Wide Uproar, " *Milwaukee Journal*, October 15, 1961, 1.

43. Gordon Brehm, "McGuffey Never Basic Reader, Beula Swears," *Milwaukee Sentinel*, December 20, 1961; Dan Smoot, "McGuffey's Readers," *The Dan Smoot Report*, February 22, 1960; box 2, folder 18, ACCL Records, WHS.

44. Margaret Gustafson to William Smeeth, October 12, 1961, box 1, DPI Correspondence; Richard Kienitz, "Start Defense of McGuffeys," *Milwaukee Journal*, March 29,

1962, 1; George Sovitzky, "Board Takes Stand in McGuffey Controversy," *Kenosha Evening News*, March 27, 1962, 1.

45. "McGuffey Hearing Underway," *Kenosha Evening News*, December 19, 1961, 1; Harold Persons to Warren Lucas, December 14, 1961; Margaret Gustafson to Angus Rothwell, October 23, 1962, all letters in box 1, DPI Correspondence, WHS; Behrendt, "School's 1879 Reader Causes Wide Uproar," *Milwaukee Journal*, October 15, 1961, 1.

46. *Education Forum*, a national journal, intoned, "The revival of the *McGuffey* readers by neoconservative elements in Twin Lakes, Wisconsin is indicative of a fundamental disagreement [about] . . . democracy itself." Donna Lee Younker, "The Moral Philosophy of William Holmes McGuffey," *Educational Forum* 28, no. 1 (November 1963): 71–78. See other clippings in DPI Correspondence, WHS.

47. Dennis Beula to Angus Rothwell, October 26, 1961; typescript, n.d., box 1, DPI Correspondence, WHS; Behrendt, "School's 1879 Reader Causes Wide Uproar," *Milwaukee Journal*, October 15, 1961, 1.

48. Augusta Owen to Angus Rothwell, October 30, 1961; Mrs. George Wagner to Angus Rothwell, October 31, 1961; Geraldine Trodono to Angus Rothwell, October 25, 1961, all in box 1, DPI Correspondence, WHS.

49. "McGuffey Reader for Reference Only, State Official Decrees," *Burlington Standard-Press*, October 26, 1961, 1; Behrendt, "School's 1879 Reader Causes Wide Uproar," *Milwaukee Journal*, October 15, 1961, 1; Donald Janson, "Eye 'Americanism' Plan After McGuffey Victory," *Des Moines Sunday Register*, November 5, 1961, box 1, DPI Correspondence, WHS.

50. Joyce Beula, interview by the author, January 16, 2008; William Smeeth, interview by the author, January 17, 2008.

51. Verne Kaub to Sidney DeLove, October 27, 1961, box 2, folder 18, ACCL Records, WHS.

52. Mrs. Ethelyn Korbel to Verne Kaub, October 21, 1961; John Chappel to Verne Kaub, November 3, 1961, both in box 2, folder 18, ACCL Records, WHS.

53. Claude J. Jasper, "Home Rule vs. Bureaucratic Thought Control," *Facts About Your Government*, October 21, 1961, box 1, DPI Correspondence, WHS.

54. "Patriotism New Issue at Twin Lakes," *Kenosha News*, November 2, 1961, 1; "Real Issue Comes to Light," *Racine Journal*, October 30, 1961, 1.

55. "McGuffey Charges Dismissed But Petition Not Malicious, Says Judge," *Burlington Standard-Press*, April 26, 1962, 1; "The Twin Lakes Decision," *Green Bay Press-Gazette*, April 27, 1962, 4; Walter Marlatt, "Are Teachers Fired, Or Not?" *Kenosha Evening News*, April 3, 1962, 1; Harlan Draeger, "McGuffey's Supporters Winners at Twin Lakes," *Kenosha News*, July 24, 1962, 1; Joyce Beula, interview by the author, January 16, 2008; Bernice Richter, interview by the author, January 16, 2008.

56. "McGuffey Dispute Used as Example in School Aids," *The Kenosha News*, April 19, 1965; Joyce Beula to Verne Kaub, March 13, 1963, box 3, folder 1; Verne Kaub to Robert DePugh, April 29, 1963, box 3, folder 4, letters in ACCL Records, WHS.

57. Two of the school's founders belonged to the JBS, as did a number of its key donors. Smeeth originally met these men through a study group at the First Congregationalist Church of Wauwatosa. Manuscript, n.d., box 56, folder 6, Grede Papers, WHS; Walter Davis, "Brookfield Academy—The First Thirty Years," Brookfield Academy Archives; William Smeeth, interview by the author, January 17, 2008; "School Stand is Postponed, Birch Link Charged," *Milwaukee Journal*, December 21, 1961, 3.

58. Verne P. Kaub to Mortimer Smith, October 20, 1961, box 60; "Reactionary Groups and Crackpots," CBE Records, UI.

59. William Smeeth to Mortimer Smith and Tom Bledsoe, March 11, 1961, box 47, folder Sk-Sp, CBE Records, UI.

60. William Smeeth to CBE, August 8, 1960, box 40, folder Si-Sm; Mrs. William Smeeth to Mortimer Smith, June 19, 1961, box 47, folder Sk-Sp; Samuel Withers to Mrs. William Smeeth, July 5, 1961, box 47, folder Sk-Sp, all in CBE Records, UI. Other anticonsolidation groups corresponded with the CBE as well. See, for example, letters from the Committee for Home Rule in Vermont Towns, in box 51, folder Ha, CBE Records, UI.

61. H. S. Tuttle to Council for Basic Education, January 14, 1963, box 60, "Reactionary Groups and Crackpots"; William Smeeth to Mortimer Smith, April 8, 1963, box 47, folder Sk-Sp, all in CBE Records, UI; "Academy of Basic Education Here to Sponsor California Educator," *Brookfield News*, October 24, 1963, 1; William B. Smeeth, ed., *Elementary Studies of the English Language: Grammar and Orthography* (Chicago: H. Regnery, 1962).

62. *Vilas County, Headwaters to Wisconsin: A Historical Reflection of the Towns in Vilas County, Wisconsin* (Eagle River, WI: Vilas County Chamber of Commerce, 1998).

63. Wisconsin Department of Public Instruction, "Annual Reports of High School Districts, 1939–1971," Department of Public Instruction Records, Series 674, WHS.

64. Dan Satran, "Federal Aid for High School Refused," *Vilas County News-Review*, July 20, 1961, 1.

65. Dan Satran, "Rap School Here for Talk Given by Pro-U. N. Speaker," *Vilas County News-Review*, October 19, 1961, 1; "Reading Teaching Methods Are Aired at Rotary Meeting," *Vilas County News-Review*, November 2, 1961, 1.

66. Robert Welch to H. S. Tuttle, March 21, 1961, box 1, H. S. Tuttle Papers, WHS.

67. Many of those who spoke out in Tuttle's defense during the school debate— specifically, Frank Carter, Tom Gaffney, and Herb Krueger—subscribed to McCarthy's newsletter in the late 1950s, although his rival, Everett Hoover, did as well. Joseph McCarthy to H. S. Tuttle, January 9, 1957; H. S. Tuttle to Joseph McCarthy, April 1, 1957, both in box 1, Tuttle Papers, WHS.

68. H. S. Tuttle to Theodore Sorenson, April 6, 1961, box 1, Tuttle Papers, WHS. While it is difficult to quantify membership or support for the JBS, rough estimates put its popularity in Wisconsin at twice the national average. Dan Satran, "Birchers Hit By Renk Here," *Vilas County News-Review*, August 30, 1962, 1; Dan Satran, "Oppose Sales Tax and J. B. Society but Favor U. N.," *Vilas County News-Review*, November 2, 1961, 1.

69. "Impressions on 'Operation Abolition,'" *Vilas County News-Review*, February 8, 1961, 6.

70. H. S. Tuttle to Verne Kaub, January 23, 1961, box 3, folder 11, ACCL Records, WHS; Mrs. William B. Smeeth to Ben Tuttle, August 9, 1962, Tuttle Papers, WHS; "We, the People Meeting," *Free Enterprise*, February 15, 1955.

71. Marian P. Welch to H. S. Tuttle, September 9, 1962, box 1, Tuttle Papers, WHS.

72. Hoover's accusations closely resembled "whisper campaigns" that the JBS used to take over school boards in California and New Jersey the same year. Joseph N. Bell, "I Fought Against Hatred among My Neighbors," *Good Housekeeping*, September 1965; Benjamin Epstein and Arnold Foster, *Report on the John Birch Society, 1966* (New York: Vintage, 1966), 47–48.

73. Everett Hoover, letter to the editor, *Vilas County News-Review*, July 19, 1962, 8; Verne P. Kaub, letter to the editor, *Vilas County News-Review*, August 2, 1962, 8; John Chapple, "Hit and Miss About Town," *Ashland Daily Press*, November 14, 1961, 4; Verne P. Kaub, typescript, n.d., box 8, folder 4, ACCL Records, WHS; Mrs. William B. Smeeth to H. S. Tuttle, August 9, 1962, box 1, Tuttle Papers, WHS.

74. Verne P. Kaub to Frank Carter, August 21, 1962, box 1; Everett Hoover, Report to the Eagle River School Board, December 27, 1962, box 1, Tuttle Papers, WHS; Dan Satran, "'Right' Literature Opinions Vary," *Vilas County News Review*, December 27, 1962, 1.

75. H. S. Tuttle to Verne Kaub, October 3, 1962; November 29, 1962; December 6, 1962, box 3, folder 11, ACCL Records, WHS; Frank W. Carter, Report to the Eagle River School Board, December 1, 1962, box 1, Tuttle Papers, WHS.

76. Dan Satran, "Legion Here Asks Library Censorship," *Vilas County News-Review,* March 14, 1963, 1. The censorship campaign drew attention across the state and nationally. See the letters to the editor, *Vilas County News-Review,* January 10, 1963, 6; and several letters in box 1, Tuttle Papers, WHS.

77. H. S. Tuttle to Verne Kaub, January 9, 1963, box 3, folder 11; Verne Kaub to Sherman A. Patterson, August 31, 1962, box 2, folder 18, ACCL Records, WHS.

78. "Judge Carter's Strange Attitude in Eagle River Literature Row," editorial, *The Capital Times,* January 7, 1963, 10; Dan Satran, editorial, *Vilas County News-Review,* January 10, 1963, 4; "Defense Bulletin," National Education Association (February, 1963), box 1, Tuttle Papers, WHS.

79. Dan Satran, "Teacher Challenges Glaeser to Debate Book Censorship," *Vilas County News-Review,* March 21, 1963, 1; "Eagle River School Board Director Resigns Post," *Rhinelander Daily News,* May 29, 1964, 1; Mark M. Gormley to Paul Bartolini, March 19, 1963; Leonard B. Archer to Paul Bartolini, April 30, 1963, letters in box 4, folder 5, Wisconsin Library Association (WLA) Records, WHS.

80. "Record Turnout of District Voters Provides Stormy Session at Annual School Meeting," July 26, 1962, 1; "Annual School Board Meeting," August 2, 1962, 1; "Classes Start Here With Record Enrollments," September 6, 1962, 1; "School Board President Reprimands Dr. Garro; Mevis Resigns, R.E. Calhoun Gets $1200 Raise," August 2, 1962, 1; "Local High School Board, Electors Told Story of Understaffed Faculty, Minimum Curriculum," February 28, 1963, 1, all in the *Princeton Times-Republic.*

81. "The Princeton Story," *Wisconsin School Board News* 15, no. 12 (March 1961): 6; "School Board President Reprimands Dr. Garro," 1.

82. "Edgerton to Offer More Classes in New High School," *Janesville Daily Gazette,* February 4, 1963, 1.

83. Mary A. Knauf, "Boy—Teacher—Parent—Book," *Edgerton Reporter,* January 31, 1963, 6; "Battle of Books Heard by 500 at Edgerton," *Janesville Daily Gazette,* January 23, 1963, 1; Elliott Maraniss, "Nasty, Dirty Business," *Capital Times,* February 27, 1963, 12.

84. "'Catcher in the Rye' Back on Edgerton Reading List," *Janesville Daily Gazette,* February 20, 1963, 1; "Parents Object to Material Used in Edgerton High English Course," *Edgerton Reporter,* January 21, 1963, 1.

85. H. Randall Spriggs, letter to the editor, *Edgerton Reporter,* February 21, 1963, 4; Elliott Maraniss, "Nasty, Dirty Business," *Capital Times,* February 27, 1963, 4; "School Policy Under Fire in Edgerton," *Janesville Daily Gazette,* January 21, 1963, 1.

86. "'Catcher in the Rye' Back on Edgerton Reading List," *Janesville Daily Gazette,* February 20, 1963, 1; "Schrader Out as Coach of Edgerton High," *Janesville Daily Gazette,* March 3, 1963, 1.

87. "Censorship in the Schools," 1967, box 66, folder 24, August Derleth Papers, WHS.

88. Department of Public Instruction, "Major advantages of the 'K–12' school district plan," April 22, 1963, Wisconsin Government Publications, WHS Library. In 1963 the Wisconsin Council of Teachers of English distributed questionnaires to over nine hundred school administrators and seven hundred English teachers statewide, asking about the effects of community censorship on their curriculum. Of the six hundred who responded, twenty-two percent of teachers and eighteen percent of administrators reported specific pressure to remove books or magazines from their classrooms, while another five percent suggested the same in marginal notes. Of the eighty books challenged, those that came under the most scrutiny were *The Catcher in the Rye,* George Orwell's *1984,* and *Animal Farm.* Lee A. Burress, Jr., *Special Bulletin No. 8—How Censorship Affects*

the School, (Madison: Wisconsin Council of Teachers of English, 1963); Armin C. Block, "Parents, Not CDL, Should Select Reading Material for Children," *Lakeland Times*, May 9, 1963, 1.

89. Among the disputed titles were D. C. Heath's *Communicating and Dynamics of Language*, McDougal-Littell's *Man*, Hougton Mifflin's *Interaction*, and Scott Foresman's *Man in Literature* and *Galaxy*.

90. *Kanawha County, West Virginia: A Textbook Study in Cultural Conflict* (Washington, DC: National Education Association, 1975), 2, 16–17. For more details of the Kanawha County controversy, see Joe Kincheloe, *Understanding the New Right and Its Impact on Education* (Bloomington, IN: Phi Delta Kappa, 1983); Daniel K. Williams, *God's Own Party: The Making of the Christian Right* (New York: Oxford University Press, 2010), 134–36; and Bill Bishop, *The Big Sort: Why the Clustering of Like-Minded America is Tearing Us Apart* (New York: Houghton-Mifflin, 2008), 105–28. Right-wing memoirs of the incident are now appearing as well. Karl Priest, *Protester Voices: The 1974 Textbook Tea Party* (Poca, WV: Praying Publishing, 2010).

91. Connaught Marshner, *Blackboard Tyranny* (New Rochelle, NY: Arlington House, 1978), 233.

92. NEA, *Textbook Study in Cultural Conflict*, 22.

93. See, for instance, NEA, *Textbook Study in Cultural Conflict*, 14; and Lester Faigley, "What Happened in Kanawha County," *The English Journal* 64, no. 5 (May 1975): 7–9.

94. Carol Mason, *Reading Appalachia from Left to Right: Conservatives and the 1974 Kanawha County Textbook Controversy* (Ithaca, NY: Cornell University Press, 2009), 24; Thomas Frank, *What's the Matter with Kansas?: How Conservatives Won the Heart of America* (New York: Metropolitan Books, 2004).

95. "Complaints and Petitions Won't Help; Only a Big Vote Will Do the Trick," *Charleston Daily Mail*, October 17, 1958, 6; "Better Schools Question Leaves Taxing to Counties," *Charleston Gazette*, October 29, 1958, 15.

96. During the 1930s, for example, a county superintendent embezzled thousands of dollars from the area, only to be acquitted by the board in a closed session. "State Board Drops Camp Ouster Case," *Charleston Daily Mail*, March 30, 1930, 1; "New Goals Set for Education," *Charleston Gazette*, June 16, 1959, 13.

97. While the county had over three hundred one-room schools in operation during the 1940s, only fifty were left in 1960. See, *West Virginia Blue Book* (Charleston: State of West Virginia, 1945–75); "One-Room Schools Still Get Things Done," *Charleston Daily Mail*, May 28, 1960, 11; "County's Last One-Room School at Laurel Fork," *Charleston Daily Mail*, September 23, 1965, 17; "Transportation Woes Beset Campbells Creek Students," *Charleston Daily Mail*, September 15, 1954, 14.

98. The rejection of property tax levies had a similar effect on neighboring counties. See "Many Reluctant to Pay More to Upgrade Education," *Charleston Daily Mail*, January 13, 1964, 13; and Berlin Basil Chapman, *Education in Central West Virginia, 1910–1975* (Charleston: West Virginia University Foundation, 1974), 625–45.

99. NEA, *Textbook Study in Cultural Conflict*, 8. Clippings and copies of the contested books are available at the West Virginia University archives.

100. Mason, *Reading Appalachia from Left to Right*, 31–32.

8. REDEFINING PARENTS' RIGHTS

1. *Concerned Citizens Newsletter* 3, no. 3 (May 1981); Phil Kerl to Gene Conrad, February 19, 1981, Gene Conrad Papers, WHS; "School Board Refuses to Ban Book," *Oshkosh Daily Northwestern*, February 10, 1981, 1; Karen Troxel, "Citizen Spokesman Responds to Rumor," *Portage Daily Register*, February 20, 1981, 1.

2. Edward B. Jenkinson, *Censors in the Classroom: The Mindbenders* (New York: Avon Books, 1979), 51–52; Richard V. Pierard and Robert G. Clouse, "What's New About the New Right," *Contemporary Education* 54, no. 3 (Spring 1983): 194–99.

3. Virginia Meves, "The American Textbook Scandal—How Homosexual Communities Are Created," *Wisconsin Report* 5, no. 19 (May 1980); Rev. John Sumwalt to Gene Conrad, n.d., box 1, folder 1, Conrad Papers, WHS.

4. Proceedings, tape 1, side 1, Wisconsin Interchange Records, WHS; Ruth Green to Gene Conrad, March 7, 1981; LuAnn Zieman to Carmen Stout, n.d., both letters in box 1, folder 1, Conrad Papers, WHS; "Library Check-Out Ruled Only for Students, Staff," *Oshkosh Daily Northwestern*, February 19, 1981, 1; Gene Conrad, "Tanner Sues Weiss for Slander," *Marquette County Tribune*, April 2, 1981, 1.

5. Jenkinson, *Censors in the Classroom*, 17–18. Anita Oliver responds to the same assumptions of outside manipulation in her analysis of a censorship controversy in California in 1990. "To say that either the district or [angry] parents were controlled by outside groups," she writes, "is seriously to underestimate local people, and to assume they could not deal with this controversy on their own." Anita Olive Oliver, "The Politics of Textbook Controversy: Parents Challenge the Implementation of a Reading Series," (PhD diss., University of Wisconsin, 1993).

6. "School District Electors Pass Referenda," *Wisconsin School Board News* 28, no. 6 (June 1974), 18; Anonymous to Gene Conrad, February 9, 1981, box 1, folder 1; Kris Mourn, "Parents, Not Vigilantes," *Oshkosh Northwestern*, n.d., box 1, folder 1, Conrad Papers, WHS.

7. Many of the most famous occurred in fast-growing towns like Montello, Wisconsin; Warsaw, Indiana; and Yucaipa, California. For those incidents, and a general overview of censorship in the 1980s, see George Beahm, ed., *War of Words: The Censorship Debate* (Kansas City, MO: Andrews and McMeel, 1993), 150–53; Eugene F. Provenzo, *Religious Fundamentalism and American Education: The Battle for the Public Schools* (Albany: State University of New York Press, 1990), 24.

8. Barbara Morris, *Change Agents in the Schools* (1979), quoted in Provenzo, *Religious Fundamentalism*, 49.

9. Stephen Arons produced the best contemporary work on evangelicals' shifting legal strategies. See Stephen Arons, "The Separation of School and State: *Pierce* Reconsidered," *Harvard Educational Review* 46 (1976): 76–104; *Compelling Belief: The Culture of American Schooling* (New York: McGraw Hill, 1983); and Stephen Arons and Charles Lawrence III, "The Manipulation of Consciousness: A First Amendment Critique of Schooling," *Harvard Civil Rights-Civil Liberties Law Review* 15 (1980): 309–61.

10. Engel v. Vitale, 370 U.S. 421 (1962); School District of Abington Township v. Schempp, 374 U.S. 203 (1963).

11. Burnside v. Byars, 363 F.2d 744 (1966), and Tinker v. Des Moines Independent Community School District, 393 U.S. 503 (1969), reinstated students who had been expelled for wearing black armbands to protest segregation and Vietnam, respectively. Kramer v. Union School District, 395 U.S. 621 (1969), enforced federal voting procedures, undercutting promises of rural overrepresentation on consolidated school boards. Lemon v. Kurtzman, 403 U.S. 602 (1971), established strict scrutiny for religious instruction in public schools.

12. Epperson v. Arkansas, 393 U.S. 97 (1968).

13. Meyer v. Nebraska, 262 U.S. 390 (1923). It was the court's ruling in Everson v. Board of Education (1947) that first extended the strictures of the Fourteenth Amendment to municipal institutions. The amendment had previously been confined to the federal government. James Fraser, *Between Church and State: Religion and Education in a Multicultural America* (New York: St. Martin's Press, 1999), 142–43.

14. West Virginia Board of Education v. Barnette, 319 U.S. 624 (1943).

15. Epperson, 393 U.S. at 107.

16. A typical case held that all aspects of "educational policy . . . [fell within] the exclusive managements provisions of the local board." Dunellen Board of Education v. Dunellen Education Association 64 N.J. 17, 311 A.2d 737 (1973).

17. Pico v. Island Trees School District, 474 F.Supp. 387 (1982). This case built on similar rulings from lower courts in the previous decade, including Todd v. Rochester Community Schools, 200 N.W.2d (1972); Minarcini v. Strongsville City School District, 541 F.2d 577 (1976); and Right to Read Defense Committee v. School Committee of Chelsea, 454 F.Supp. 703 (1978).

18. Keyishian v. Board of Regents, 385 U.S. 589 (1967); and Mt. Healthy City Board of Education v. Doyle, 429 U.S. 274 (1977). The basis in contract rights was not incidental: by 1980, more than a third of districts nationwide had contract clauses delineating teacher involvement in textbook selection and promoting a degree of academic freedom. Caroline Cody, "The Politics of Textbook Publishing," in *Textbooks and Schooling*, ed. David Elliott and Arthur Woodward, 127–45, esp. 142.

19. Right to Read Defense Committee v. School Committee, 454 F.Supp. 703, 715 (1978).

20. The case's dissent argued, with helpful overstatement, that the two basic propositions of the case were "first, whether local schools are to be administered by elected school boards, or by federal judges and teenage pupils; and second, whether the values of morality, good taste, and relevance to education are valid reasons for school board decisions concerning the contents of a school library." Even Hugo Black's concurring opinion found "no reason . . . why a State is without power to withdraw from its curriculum any subject deemed too emotional or controversial for its public schools." Pico v. Island Trees School District.

21. Jason Persinger, "The Harm to Student First Amendment Rights When School Boards Make Curricular Decision in Response to Political Pressure: A Critique of *Griswold v. Driscoll*," *University of Cincinnati Law Review* 80, no. 1 (May 2012): 291–316.

22. Jeffrey P. Moran, *American Genesis: The Evolution Controversies from Scopes to Creation Science* (New York: Oxford University Press, 2012), 91–123.

23. Daniel K. Williams, *God's Own Party: The Making of the Christian Right* (New York: Oxford University Press, 2010), 213–44.

24. Hand argued, "teaching that moral choices are purely personal and can only be based on some autonomous, as yet undiscovered and unfulfilled, inner self is a sweeping fundamental belief that must not be promoted by the public schools. . . . With these books, the State of Alabama has overstepped its mark, and must withdraw to perform its proper nonreligious functions.'" Smith v. Board of School Commissioners of Mobile County, 827 F2nd 684 (1987); Cody, "The Politics of Textbook Publishing," in *Textbooks and Schooling*, ed. David Elliott and Arthur Woodward, 128, 139–40.

25. A spate of lawsuits about "Intelligent Design" and other theistic explanations of human origins suggests that the issue remains both mutable and contentious. And while courts have never found in favor of creationist curriculum, critics have pointed out the drawbacks of having judges discern the meaning of "science" at all. In addition to the titles listed in chapter 8, note 16, see Amy Binder, *Contentious Curricula: Afrocentrism and Creationism in American Public Schools* (Princeton, NJ: Princeton University Press, 2002); and Benjamin Michael Superfine, "The Evolving Role of the Courts in Educational Policy: The Tension Between Judicial, Scientific, and Democratic Decision Making in *Kitzmiller v. Dover*," *American Educational Research Journal* 46, no. 4 (December 2009): 898–923.

26. John Andrew Hostetler, *Amish Society* (Baltimore: Johns Hopkins University Press, 1963), 198–99.

27. "Wisconsin vs. Amish on School Attendance," *Stevents Point Daily Journal*, April 2, 1971, 5; Hostetler, *Amish Society*, 199–207.

28. Robert Franzmann, "Amish Open a School: One-Room Building Near New Glarus," *Wisconsin State Journal*, September 20, 1968, 10.

29. Wisconsin v. Yoder, 406 U.S. 205 (1972). For more details on the case, see Shawn Frances Peters, *The Yoder Case: Religious Freedom, Education, and Parental Rights* (Lawrence: University Press of Kansas, 2003).

30. *Yoder* 406 U.S. at 206; William Law, "Brookfield Academy, Why?" box 1, folder 33, Brookfield Academy Archives.

31. *Yoder* 406 U.S. at 217. While many rural districts maintained religious exercises even after the school prayer decisions, it is also important to note that some had already banned bible reading in the nineteenth century. Indeed, the first district to do so was Edgerton, Wisconsin, in the 1880s. See Bruce J. Dierenfield, *The Battle Over School Prayer: How* Engel v. Vitale *Changed America* (Lawrence: University Press of Kansas, 2007), 34–35; and Benjamin Justice, *The War that Wasn't: Religious Conflict and Compromise in the Common Schools of New York State, 1865–1900* (Albany: State University of New York Press, 2005).

32. K. J. Glewen to Kenneth Merkel, March 6, 1967, box 1, folder 9, Merkel Papers, WHS.

33. Kenneth Merkel to Mrs. Byron Becker, July 10, 1972, box 1, folder 48; Robert Schneider to Members of the Wisconsin Assembly, February 21, 1967, box 1, folder 9, both in Merkel Papers, WHS.

34. In 1967, Assembly Bill 59A granted religious exemptions from physical education but was permanently tabled by the education committee. In 1971, Assembly Bill 1376, which repealed compulsory school attendance and truancy laws, and Assembly Bill 1248, which exempted students from school for religious reasons, both failed to pass. *Bulletin of the Proceedings of the Wisconsin Legislature: Assembly* (Madison: Wisconsin State Legislature, 1975).

35. Dottie Kellner to Kenneth Merkel, January 1972; Dottie Keller to Kenneth Merkel, February 3, 1972, both in box 1, folder 48, Merkel Papers, WHS. As noted below, private Christian schools in the state also cheered the *Yoder* decision. See Virginia Davis Nordin and William Lloyd Turner, "More than Segregation Academies: The Growing Protestant Fundamentalist Schools," *Phi Delta Kappan* 61, no. 6 (February 1980): 391–94.

36. "Unwanted Fame Forces Amish Leader to Move," *Capital Times*, October 2, 1973, 24.

37. Grove v. Mead School District No. 354, 753 F.2d 1528 (1985).

38. Mozert v. Hawkins County Board of Education, 827 F.2d 1058 (1987).

39. Ibid.

40. Susan Rose, *Keeping Them Out of the Hands of Satan: Evangelical Schooling in America* (New York: Routledge, 1988), 34. See also Alan Peshkin *God's Choice: The Total World of a Fundamentalist Christian School* (Chicago: University of Chicago Press, 1986); Melinda Bollar Wagner, *God's Schools: Choice and Compromise in American Society* (New Brunswick, NJ: Rutgers University Press, 1990); and Adam Laats, "Forging a Fundamentalist 'One Best System': Struggles over Curriculum and Educational Philosophy for Christian Day Schools, 1970–1989," *History of Education Quarterly* 50, no. 1 (February 2010): 55–83.

41. Christian academies were often the most explicitly racist in rural areas, which could not perpetuate the illusion of de facto segregation through gerrymandered attendance zones as larger towns could. Their appearance in rural communities could further depress public school enrollments, leading to more school closures. See David Nevin and Robert E. Bills, *The Schools That Fear Built: Segregationist Academies in the South* (Wash-

ington, DC: Acropolis Books, 1976). There were also instances, however, in which private academies stemmed the tide of school consolidation. For instance, when a consolidated board eliminated middle school grades in Tipton, Kansas, due to population loss, the town voted to build the Tipton Christian School, which kept the children in town and eventually secured public funding. Richard E. Wood, *Survival of Rural America: Small Victories and Bitter Harvests* (Lawrence: University Press of Kansas, 2008), 86–88. For a similar case in Bennington, Vermont, see Stephanie Banchero, "School's Twist on Going Private," *Wall Street Journal*, 15 January 2013, http://online.wsj.com/article/SB100014241 27887324595704578244131135328390.html.

42. Paul F. Parsons, *Inside America's Christian Schools* (Macon, GA: Mercer University Press, 1987), 115.

43. Proponents of Christian academies noted, with understandable frustration, that the guidelines exempted compliance of Jewish, Catholic, Muslim, and Amish schools. Crespino, "Civil Rights and the Religious Right," in *Rightward Bound: Making American Conservative in the 1970s,* ed. Bruce Schulman and Julian E. Zelizer (Cambridge, MA: Harvard University Press, 2008), 90–105, esp. 102. Although Congress passed resolutions remanding the IRS memo, and the Reagan administration made little effort to punish violators, within a few years most Christian schools enrolled at least some minority students. Milton Gaither challenges the notion that the prospect of desegregation led to an increase in homeschooling during the same period. The profusion of academies led to high turnover rates, he writes, and "many school closings were the consequence, not the cause, of the shift to homeschooling." Milton Gaither, *Homeschool: An American History* (New York: Palgrave Macmillan, 2008), 110–12.

44. Peter Skerry, "Christian Schools versus the I.R.S.," *Public Interest* 61 (Fall 1980): 30–31; Crespino, "Civil Rights and the Religious Right," in *Rightward Bound,* ed. Bruce Schulman and Julian E. Zelizer, 91, 101–3.

45. Robert N. Gross, "Public Regulation and the Transformation of Education in Modern America, 1870–1930" (PhD diss., University of Wisconsin, 2013).

46. Provenzo, *Religious Fundamentalism,* 83–84.

47. Pastor Tim LaHaye, author of the popular *Left Behind* book series, founded the Christian High School of San Diego in 1965 and within ten years had built a system encompassing more than 2,500 students, from preschool to college, and an institute to train its own teachers. Tim LaHaye, *The Battle for the Public Schools* (Old Tappan, NJ: Fleming H. Revell, 1983), 9.

48. Parsons, *Inside America's Christian Schools,* 40.

49. Nadine Brozen, "Swapping Strategies at Forum on Family," *New York Times,* August 2, 1982, n.p. Available online at http://www.nytimes.com/1982/08/02/style/swapping -strategies-at-forum-on-family.html.

50. In addition to Gaither, *Homeschool,* see Robert Kunzman, *Write These Laws on Your Children: Inside the World of Conservative Christian Homeschooling* (New York: Beacon Press, 2009); and Joel Spring, *The Primer Libertarian Education* (Montreal, QC: Black Rose Books, 1998). One can find early references to homeschooling in Vermont in Winifred Margaret McCarthy, "The Migration of Cosmopolites to Rural Vermont" (PhD diss., New School for Social Research, 1986), 28, 210; and "Couple Denies Failure to Obey State's Compulsory School Law," *Burlington Free Press,* January 31, 1974, 20.

51. Gaither, *Homeschool,* 113.

52. In the words of State v. Hoyt, 146 A. 170 (1929), a case out of New Hampshire, homeschooled children lacked "association with all classes of society."

53. State of Wisconsin v. Popanz, 112 Wis. 2d 166; 332 N.W.2d 750 (1983).

54. Although the issue did not come up during the hearings, Avoca subsequently appeared in an investigative report of unsafe, out-of-date school facilities. The elementary

school that the Popanz children attended was built in 1876. The failure of local bond proposals had prevented its renovation. Ron Seely, "Aging Schools Place Our Children in Peril," *Wisconsin State Journal*, June 5, 1988, 1; David I. Bednarek, "State Developing Legislation to Clear Up Laws on Private Schools," *Milwaukee Journal*, October 25, 1983, 11.

55. Relevant decisions include those in Illinois, Scoma v. Chicago Board of Education 391 F. Supp. 452 (1974); West Virginia, State v. Riddle 168 W.V. 429 (1981); North Carolina, Duro v. District Attorney 712 F.2d 96 (1983); Texas, Howell v. State 723 S.W.2d 755 (1986); Ohio, State v. Schmidt 29 Ohio St.3d 32 (1987); and North Dakota, State v. Patzer 382 N.W.2d 631 (1986). In one exception, State v. Nobel Nos. S-791-0114-A, S-791-0115-A (1980), the Michigan Supreme Court found "no compelling interest to infringe on the free exercise rights" of a fundamentalist family who held their children out of school. Nonetheless, in that case the mother was a certified teacher. Gaither, *Homeschool*, 178.

56. Edward B. Fiske, "Top Objectives Elude Reagan as Education Policy Evolves," *New York Times*, December 27, 1983; Edward B. Fiske, "Reagan Record in Education: Mixed Results," *New York Times*, November 14, 1982, n.p.

57. Terrell H. Bell, *The Thirteenth Man: A Reagan Cabinet Memoir* (New York: Free Press, 1988).

58. *A Nation at Risk: The Imperative for Educational Reform* (Washington, DC: U.S. Department of Education, 1983).

59. Brozen, "Swapping Strategies at Forum on Family."

60. Edward B. Fiske, "Top Objectives Elude Reagan as Education Policy Evolves," *New York Times*, December 27, 1983, n.p.

61. Fiske, "Top Objectives Elude Reagan as Education Policy Evolves."

62. Margaret Goertz, "Standards-Based Reform: Lessons from the Past, Directions for the Future," in *Clio at the Table: Using History to Inform and Improve Education Policy*, ed. Kenneth K. Wong and Robert Rothman (New York: Peter Lang, 2008), 201–20, esp. 204–5.

63. K. Forbis Jordan and Mary P. McKeown, "State Fiscal Policy and Education Reform," in *The Education Reform Movement of the 1980s*, ed. Joseph Murphy (Berkeley, CA: McCutchan Publishing, 1990), 97–120, esp.104.

64. Joseph Murphy, "The Educational Reform Movement of the 1980s: A Comprehensive Analysis," in *The Education Reform Movement of the 1980s*, Joseph Murphy, 3–56, esp. 19–21; Allan Odden and David Marsh, "Local Response to the 1980s State Education Reforms: New Patterns of Local and State Interaction," in *The Education Reform Movement of the 1980s*, Joseph Murphy, 167–87, esp. 169.

65. Margaret E. Goertz, *State Educational Standards in the 50 States: An Update* (Princeton, NJ: Educational Testing Service, 1988), 143–44. The Wisconsin Center for Education Research (WCER), based in Madison, received a number of large grants from the U.S. Department of Education and its subsidiaries to study effective administration and teaching. Worried that personnel at the DPI and increasingly large district offices "were not providing needed assistance to the schools," WCER launched a network of innovative schools and sketched new conceptual frameworks for effective secondary education. Herbert J. Klausmeier, *The Wisconsin Center for Education Research: Twenty-five Years of Knowledge Generation and Educational Improvement* (Madison, WI: WCER, 1990), 24–25, 58–75.

66. These tendencies were on full display at the Charlottesville Summit, in 1989. See Matthew McGuinn, *No Child Left Behind and the Transformation of Federal Education Policy, 1965–2005* (Lawrence: University Press of Kansas, 2006); Jesse H. Rhodes, *An Education in Politics: The Origin and Evolution of No Child Left Behind* (Ithaca, NY: Cornell University Press, 2012); and Maris Vinovskis, *From a Nation at Risk to No Child Left*

Behind: National Education Goals and Creation of Federal Education Policy (New York: Teachers College Press, 2009).

67. Neoconservative, in this context, refers to former liberals who had grown disillusioned with the Great Society or the divisive politics of the Left but, nevertheless, retained a faith in the state and federal role in education.

68. Right- and left-wing criticisms of Title I of the Elementary and Secondary Education Act overlapped as early as the 1960s, when the Coleman Report and subsequent studies showed little connection between federal spending and student outcomes. See David K. Cohen and Susan L. Moffitt, *The Ordeal of Equality: Did Federal Regulation Fix the Schools* (Cambridge, MA: Harvard University Press, 2009), 65–129.

69. On the ideological basis of the contemporary center-right educational coalition, see Michael Apple, *Educating the "Right" Way: Markets, Standards, God, and Inequality* (New York: Routledge, 2006).

70. Russell Kirk, "The End of Learning," *Intercollegiate Review* 24, no. 1 (Fall 1988): 23–24.

CONCLUSION. A PAST LOST

1. William Anderson, *The Nation and the States, Rivals or Partners?* (Minneapolis: University of Minnesota Press, 1955), 139–40, 216–17.

2. Daniel R. Davies, "Policies, Local Control, and Other Antiquities," *Updating School Board Policies* 19, no. 9 (October 1988): 1–3.

3. That approach has already yielded a preliminary ruling that challenges hiring and tenure practices in Vergara v. California (2014). Also see, Ethan Hutt and Aaron Tang, "The New Education Malpractice Litigation," *University of Virginia Law Review* 99, no. 3 (2013); Superfine, *The Courts and Standards-Based Education Reform* (New York: Oxford University Press, 2008), 177–80, 189–93; and Ryan, *Five Miles Away*, 300–303.

4. See Jeffrey Henig, "Reading the Future of Educational Policy," *Education Week*, 7 January 2013, http://www.edweek.org/ew/articles/2013/01/09/15henig_ep.h32.html.

5. See Gerald Grant, *Hope and Despair in the American City: Why There Are No Bad Schools in Raleigh* (Cambridge, MA: Harvard University Press, 2009); Stacey Teicher Khadaroo, "Busing to End in Wake County, N.C., Goodbye, School Diversity?" *Christian Science Monitor*, March 24, 2010, http://www.csmonitor.com/USA/Education/2010/0324/Busing-to-end-in-Wake-County-N.C.-Goodbye-school-diversity; and the Frontline documentary, "Separate and Unequal," *Frontline*, PBS, July 15, 2014, http://www.pbs.org/wgbh/pages/frontline/separate-and-unequal. On the fragmentation of districts elsewhere in the South, see Erica Frankenberg, "Splintering School Districts: Understanding the Link between Segregation and Fragmentation," *Law & Social Inquiry* 34, no. 4 (Fall 2009): 869–909.

6. See Jack Schneider, *Excellence for All: How a New Breed of Reformers Is Transforming America's Public Schools* (Nashville, TN: Vanderbilt University Press, 2011), 41–72; and Amy J. Binder, *Contentious Curricula: Afrocentrism and Creationism in American Public Schools* (Princeton, NJ: Princeton University Press, 2002), 1–135.

7. Katherine Cramer Walsh, "What the Hell is Going On in Madison?" Available at *The Monkey Cage*, http://themonkeycage.org/blog/2011/03/01/what_in_the_hell_is_going_on_i/. Appropriately, the loss of bargaining rights finally compelled Wisconsin's NEA and AFT chapters to merge, a rift that had lingered since the strikebreakers in Hortonville affiliated with the WFT in 2003. See Stephen Sawchuk, "More Mergers for NEA, AFT Affiliates," *Edweek*, February 19, 2013. Available online at http://www.edweek.org/ew/articles/2013/02/20/21merge.h32.html?tkn=TLYFNm5MDL9DjKmfqvAcgSNAh%2FuzPXPtx6PE&cmp=clp-edweek.

8. There was audible dissent from some rural Republicans, for whom Dale Schultz (R-Richland Center) became the de facto spokesman.

9. Fred Clark, "Time to Take a Stand for Rural Schools," *Capital Times*, June 11, 2014, 30.

10. Barry Adams, "Westfield, Montello School Districts Won't Consolidate," *Wisconsin State Journal*, November 3, 2010, http://host.madison.com/news/local/education/local _schools/westfield-montello-school-districts-won-t-consolidate-waunakee-elementary -expansion/article_fc083232-e70f-11df-b84f-001cc4c002e0.html.

Index

4–H clubs, 62

Abington v. Schempp, 25
academic freedom. *See* unions
Academy of Basic Education. *See* Brookfield Academy
Act 10 (Wisconsin), 186–88
African Americans, 9, 68, 70–71, 84, 134, 174
Age of Fracture, 26
The Age of Reform, 15–16, 18, 24
Alexander, Lamar, 178
Alinsky, Saul, 87
American Association of School Administrators, 44, 142
American Association of School Boards, 44
American Babylon, 120
American Civil Liberties Union, 131, 146, 163
American Council of Christian Laymen, 146, 150–54
American Federation of Teachers, 14, 78, 80, 82–83, 134. *See also* unions
American Legion, 26, 142, 146, 153–54
Amish, 73, 168–70
And Madly Teach, 143
annexation, 1–3, 20, 67, 81, 134, 169; opposition to, 21–23, 45, 48, 73, 81, 100, 111–12
Appalachia, 9, 59–60, 121n11, 157–61
arbitration. *See* unions
Arkansas, 59–60, 65–66, 68–69, 144
Arkansas Rural Education Association, 66
Asian Americans, 134
attendance zones, 8, 39–40, 132n52, 174–75, 182. *See also* transfers, interdistrict

baby boom, 29, 53, 95
Baker v. Carr, 20, 101, 167. *See also* legislative apportionment
Bath, Michigan, school massacre, 42
Bell, Daniel, 20
Bell, Terrell, 176–77
Bennington, Vermont, censorship controversy, 138–39
Bestor, Arthur, 143–44
Beula, Dennis, 147–51

bond issues. *See* referendums
Bradley Foundation, 146
Brennan, William, 167
Brookfield Academy, 151–52
Brown, Jerry, 136
Brown v. Board of Education, 9, 101–2, 181
Buckley, William F., 154
Burger, Warren, 14, 26, 71
Burke, Edmund, 24, 179
Buse v. Smith, 113
busing: and racial desegregation, 3, 67–73, 182, 185; in rural areas, 43, 53–54, 62; state subsidies for, 46

California: curricular debates, 142–44; district consolidation, 40, 60, 67–68; school funding debates, 99–103, 108–9, 117, 123, 134–37; unions, 84–85
California Small School Districts' Association, 137
Carnegie Corporation, 40–41
Catholics. *See* parochial schools
censorship, 13, 79, 81, 138–39; and conservatism, 142–45, 153–61, 162–64; legal grounds for, 165–67, 171–72
Charlottesville Summit, 178
charter schools, 7, 41, 185
Christian academies, 172–74
civil rights organizations, 6, 68–70, 131, 178, 184
Clapp, Harold, 144
class conflict: and conservatism, 9, 15–17, 33, 158; and municipal government, 19–20, 30–31, 94–95, 119; and school curriculum, 62–63, 141
Clinton, Bill, 178
Clune, William, 103
Coleman, James, 30, 145
collective bargaining. *See* unions
college attendance, 39, 124, 176; in rural areas, 62–63; for teachers, 77
Colorado, 59, 148
Committee for Home Rule in Vermont Towns, 51, 64
Common Core Standards, 5, 184